New Frontier
in
Evolutionary Algorithms

THEORY AND APPLICATIONS

New Frontier

in
Evolutionary
Algorithms

THEORY AND APPLICATIONS

Hitoshi Iba
Nasimul Noman
University of Tokyo, Japan

Imperial College Press

Published by

Imperial College Press
57 Shelton Street
Covent Garden
London WC2H 9HE

Distributed by

World Scientific Publishing Co. Pte. Ltd.
5 Toh Tuck Link, Singapore 596224
USA office: 27 Warren Street, Suite 401-402, Hackensack, NJ 07601
UK office: 57 Shelton Street, Covent Garden, London WC2H 9HE

British Library Cataloguing-in-Publication Data
A catalogue record for this book is available from the British Library.

NEW FRONTIER IN EVOLUTIONARY ALGORITHMS
Theory and Applications

ISBN-13 978-1-84816-681-3
ISBN-10 1-84816-681-8

Printed in Singapore.

Preface

This book delivers theoretical and practical knowledge on evolutionary algorithm (EA) and its extensions for real-world applications. It presents the methodology for EA-based search strategy with the integration of several Alife and AI techniques, such as memetic concepts, swarm intelligence and foraging strategies. To provide the reader with a better understanding of the working principles of these algorithms, the concepts are explained using several companion simulators. Some of these simulators are algorithm specific, while the others are problem specific. Experimenting with such tools may help the user obtain a better grasp of optimization methodologies when addressing complex tasks from the real world such as robotics, financial forecasting or biological data mining.

The book begins with the biological inspiration behind genetic algorithm (GA) explaining the connection between the theory of evolution and the basic principle of GA. Then a brief overview of the concepts of optimization using hill-climbing algorithms is presented with the help of MS Excel-based simulators. Thereafter, the components of GA, relating the biological notion and the computational counterpart, are presented. Different types of coding methods, selection schemes and GA operators are explained with appropriate examples. The method of explanation that makes use of the associated simulators provides the reader with hands-on experience in evolutionary algorithms. Then the book concentrates on solving practical problems using GA. Some carefully chosen real-life problems are used to show how the workable simulators can be used to solve practical problems for end-users. The following Excel-based simulators are used in this book:

- GA-2D simulator: allows optimization testing of one-dimensional functions using the hill-climbing method and GA
- GA-3D simulator: allows optimization testing of two-dimensional functions using the hill-climbing method and GA

- TSP simulator: uses GA to solve traveling salesman problems
- JSSP simulator: uses GA to solve job shop scheduling problems

The book also familiarizes the reader with different variants of real-valued GA, namely particle swarm optimization (PSO), BUGS and differential evolution (DE). These algorithms are comparatively newer developments in the field of EA. For each of these algorithms and real-valued GA the basic idea, algorithmic description, representation and operators are explained in detail. Further, two more simulators are associated to provide a closer look at PSO and BUGS, respectively. Empirical studies are also presented to judge the strengths and weaknesses of these algorithms.

Recent progress in the field of EA, like memetic algorithm (MA) and adaptive EA, are also covered in this book to meet the interest of advanced readers and researchers. What is the concept of local search? How can local improvement enhance the overall search performance? What is the memetic framework? Why is adaptation important in EAs? How can adaptive EAs be designed? Several such sub-topics are discussed.

The developments in this book aim to facilitate the research of extended EA frameworks with the fusion of other Alife and AI schemes. This book emphasizes on the application of EA to solve real-world problems, rather than merely presenting a treatise on theoretical aspects of EA. Tasks from the following practical application areas are studied:

- Trading rule optimization in foreign exchange (FX) and stock prices
- Economic load dispatch in power distribution system
- Exit/door placement for evacuation planning
- Gene regulatory network inference in bioinformatics

The empirical investigations demonstrate the effectiveness of EA-based approaches when solving such critical real-world tasks.

EA practitioners will find this book useful for studying evolutionary search, optimization techniques and GA. Undergraduate students will learn how to design and implement the basic mechanisms of a GA system, including the selection scheme, the crossover, and mutation learning operators. Researchers will learn advanced topics such as improving search control of EA systems and solving complex real-life problems using EAs.

H. Iba, N. Noman
Tokyo, Japan, September 2010

Acknowledgments

We hold a deep sense of gratitude toward many wonderful people, especially now that this book project has been completed. In particular, we acknowledge the pleasant research atmosphere created by colleagues and students from the research laboratory associated with Graduate School of Frontier Sciences and Graduate School of Engineering at the University of Tokyo. We owe a lot to Dr. Kohsuke Yanai for his help in formalizing the NFL proof. We are greatly indebted to Dhammika Suresh Hettiarachchi, Dr. Danushka Bollegala, Dr. Claus Aranha and Liu Shu for their comments on our manuscript.

The first author, Dr. Hitoshi Iba, is grateful to his previous group at Electro-Technical Laboratory (ETL), where he worked for ten years, and to his current colleagues at Graduate School of Engineering of the University of Tokyo. Particular thanks are due to Dr. Hirochika Inoue and Dr. Taisuke Sato for providing precious comments and advice on numerous occasions. And last, but not least, he would like to thank his wife Yumiko and his sons and daughter Kohki, Hirono and Hiroto, for their patience and assistance.

The second author, Dr. Nasimul Noman, gratefully acknowledges the support obtained from his colleagues and students in the Department of Computer Science and Engineering, University of Dhaka, Bangladesh. Special thanks go to his students Akhi Nasrin Khan and Sigma Ainul for their help in collecting and analyzing some experimental results. He is greatly indebted to his mother Selina, wife Nina and daughter Liyana for their sacrifice and understanding.

H. Iba, N. Noman
Tokyo, Japan, September 2010

Contents

Chapter 1

Introduction

1.1 Overview/motivation

What is "*evolution*"? When we hear the word "*evolution*", most of us probably think of Charles Darwin. Darwin is renowned for his theory of evolution, which, it is said, he developed from the observations he made during a stopover at the Galapagos Islands partway through a voyage on the H.M.S. Beagle. While there, Darwin is said to have observed that the shape of the beak of a finch, a bird living on the islands, differed slightly depending on the species. This story, however, is slightly exaggerated. Darwin never researched this particular bird in the area to any significant extent. In addition, his book *The Origin of Species* refers very little to data from the Galapagos Islands, and is primarily concerned with his theory of natural selection.

Still, there are still many unanswered questions about evolution. To cite just a few examples: "Why are the peacock's feathers so incredibly beautiful?", or "Why did the giraffe's neck become so long?", or "If a worker bee cannot have any offspring of its own, why does it work so hard to serve the queen bee?"

These and other biological phenomena are of interest to researchers even today. If we zero in on possible answers to these riddles, we see that biological organisms are solving certain types of optimization problems through the process of biological evolution. Achieving an effective computational system mimicking evolutionary phenomena is the aim of what is called the "evolutionary computation". This method is broadly applied to optimization problems, artificial intelligence learning, deduction, automated program synthesis and other fields; the aim being to solve problems taking inspiration from nature.

The evolutionary method is an engineering approach in which data structures are modified, synthesized, and selected by imitating the mechanisms of biological evolution. The goal of this method is to solve optimization problems and generate useful structures.

For example, consider the process involved in the design of an airplane. When building a new airplane or other aircraft, the most important objective is not necessarily to create something novel. Of course, creativity and gifted craftsmanship are needed, but in many cases, novel designs fail. What is more important is making minor changes to past designs, synthesizing the designs, and then selecting what works. This is exactly the type of process that the Wright brothers used when designing their airplane. Other examples from our everyday lives include horticultural hybridization as well as the breeding of livestock and dogs. It is widely known that dogs are bred over a number of generations to produce animals with the most desirable characteristics. These processes make implicit use of biological (genetic) mutation, crossover, and natural selection mechanisms. In other words, humans have been utilizing the biological evolutionary approach without even realizing it, and using it to create optimal solutions.

Realizing a computational system (evolutionary system) based on this reasoning is the aim of the evolutionary method. Typical examples of this are genetic algorithm (GA) and genetic programming (GP). There is also the field of artificial life (Alife) that uses the computational methods to model biological evolutionary mechanisms in order to study ecosystems. Research in these areas can be traced back to the 1970s.

1.2   What is evolutionary computation?

In order to answer this question, we must first examine what is necessary for evolution to take place. It may seem obvious, but evolution requires more than a single animal (person). In other words, evolution requires a group or a population. Furthermore, that population must have the following characteristics:

- The members must be capable of producing offspring (self-reproduction).
- The offspring must carry forward the characteristics of the parent(s), with some changes (variation).
- The offspring that have adapted to the environment must survive with a higher probability (survival of the fittest).

These properties do not necessarily mean that evolution will occur, but without them it would be difficult, if not impossible, for a population to evolve.

Developing a computational system (evolutionary system) based on this principle is the aim of the evolutionary method. The evolutionary method provides a mechanism for performing global and local search simultaneously [Nikolaev and Iba (2006)]. The main evolutionary paradigms are: genetic algorithm (GA) [Holland (1975); Goldberg (1989)]; genetic programming (GP) [Koza (1992, 1994); Banzhaf *et al.* (1998); Koza *et al.* (1999, 2003); Langdon and Poli (2002); Riolo and Worzel (2003); O'Reilly *et al.* (2005); Yu *et al.* (2006); Iba *et al.* (2009)]; evolution strategies (ES) [Schwefel (1995); Bäck (1996); Bäck *et al.* (2000); Eiben and Smith (2003)]; and evolutionary programming (EP) [Fogel *et al.* (1966); Fogel (1999)]. Each of the above methods conducts a population-based probabilistic search which is a powerful tool for broad exploration and local exploitation of the model space. The population-based strategy is an advantage over other global search algorithms such as simulated annealing [Kirkpatrick *et al.* (1983)] and tabu search [Glover (1989)], which work with only one hypothesis at a time, and over algorithms for local search [Atkeson *et al.* (1997)] that perform only narrow examination of the search space. Their stochastic character is an advantage over the heuristic AI [Nilsson (1980, 1998)] and machine-learning algorithms [Mitchell (1997); Smirnov (2001)] that also search with one hypothesis. In the following section, we will explain the fundamental principles of GA.

1.3   Basic principles of evolutionary computation

The fundamental data structures and operators of GA are based on genetic knowledge. Let's describe this simply. Gregor Mendel, a monk and natural scientist, focused on the seven traits of pea plants shown in Fig. 1.1(a).[1]

For instance, the trait of plant height was used to create the hybridization shown in Fig. 1.1(b) using characteristics of extreme tallness and extreme shortness. Mendel observed that in the F_2 generation, there were 787

---

[1]It was not until the early 20th century that the importance of his ideas was realized. Three botanists independently rediscovered Mendel's work in 1900. Mendel's experimental results have later been the object of considerable dispute. A renowned statistician, Ronald Fisher, analyzed the results of the F_2 ratio and found them to be implausibly close to the exact ratio of 3 to 1. However, it is often cited as an example of confirmation bias.

tall plants and 277 dwarf plants (in other words, a ratio of 2.84 : 1). He hypothesized two factors that determine these traits (today, these are called genes), and went on to call different genes that form pairs and that are present in the same individual or the same population "alleles". Mendel used uppercase letters to indicate alleles governing dominant traits, and

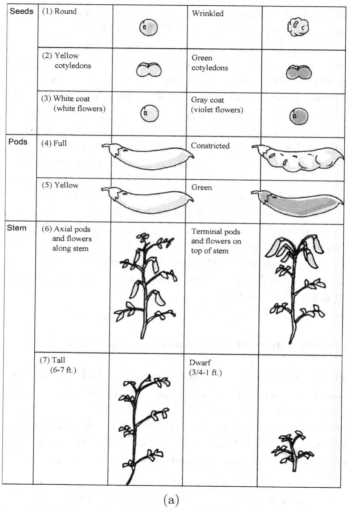

(a)

Fig. 1.1   Mendel's law of segregation (adapted from [Tamarin (2002)], pp. 22–24). (a) Seven characteristics that Mendel observed in peas. (b) First two offspring generations. (c) Assigning genotypes to the cross in (b).

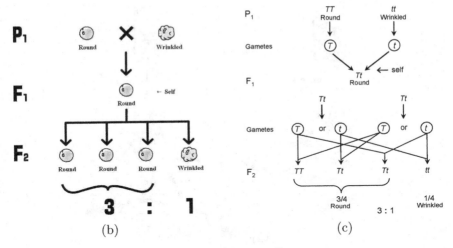

Fig. 1.1 (*Continued*)

lowercase letters to indicate recessive traits. Based on Mendel's law of segregation, as shown in Fig. 1.1(c), all of the plants in the F_1 generation will be tall, while in the F_2 generation, the proportion of tall plants to dwarf plants will be 3 : 1. The genotype of a biological organism is the collection of genes it has. In Fig. 1.1(c), the genotype for the tallness of both parents is expressed as TT, while the genotype of the F_1 generation is expressed as Tt. A phenotype is a biological characteristic that is visible. In the case of the above two genotypes, the phenotype of both TT and Tt is tallness. Gametes are mature reproductive cells that carry half of the genetic information of an organism. They unite during sexual reproduction.

Information handing in GA comprises a two-layer structure consisting of a PTYPE and a GTYPE. The GTYPE (also called the genetic code, which is equivalent to the chromosomes in the cells) is analogous to a genotype, and is an aggregate of low-level localized rules or regulations. This will be the operation target of the GA operators that we will be explaining in Section 2.2. The PTYPE is a phenotype. It generally indicates the expression of global actions and structures (e.g. produced proteins or biological functionalities) accompanying development within the GTYPE environment. The fitness value is determined from the PTYPE in response to the environment, and because of this, adaptive selection depends on the PTYPE (Fig. 1.2). For the time being, let us assume that the larger the fitness value, the better the fitness (in some other cases described in this

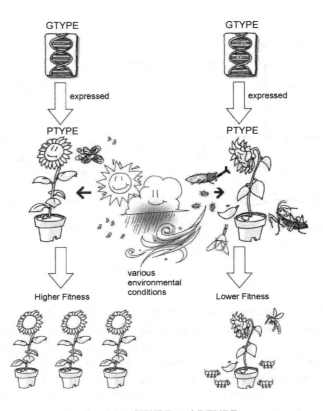

Fig. 1.2   GTYPE and PTYPE

book, however, we will assume that a smaller value is better). This would mean that if we had two individuals, one with a fitness value of 1.0 and the other with a fitness value of 0.3, the former one would adapt better to the environment and be more likely to survive.

Let's describe the fundamental mechanism of GA using the analogy of Fig. 1.3. Assume that we have a number of dogs that comprise a population. We will call these dogs "generation t". Each of these dogs has its own genetic code as a GTYPE, and the fitness value is determined in response to the PTYPE expressed by this GTYPE. In the figure, the fitness values are indicated as the numeric values in circles (remember that the larger the value, the better). These dogs reproduce and create the next generation of offspring, which is "generation $(t + 1)$". When they reproduce, the better (higher) the fitness value, the more offspring they are likely to have, while

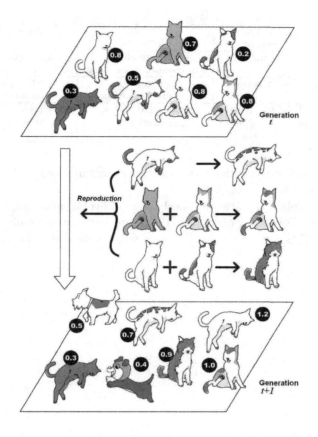

Fig. 1.3   A schematic illustration of GA

those with a poorer (smaller) fitness value are more likely to die out (in biological terminology, this is called "selection").

A schematic illustration of how the phenotype changes little by little in response to reproduction is shown in Fig. 1.3. As a result, we can expect that the fitness values of the individuals in the next generation (t + 1) will be better than those of the previous generation. Moreover, the fitness values of the population as a whole will likely be higher. Similarly, the dogs in the (t + 1) generation will then become parents, and will produce offspring that will be the (t + 2) generation. As this process continues to repeat, the fitness values for each successive generation will gradually improve for the population as a whole, in keeping with the basic GA mechanisms. The

Table 1.1   Analogy with biological organisms

	GTYPE Genotype	PTYPE Phenotype	Fitness value
Biology	Genes	Protein produced, expressed functionalities	Ease of survival, number of offspring
GP	Tree structure	Programs, conceptual structures	Performance measures
GA, ES EP	Character strings, numerical values, automata	Functional values, generated strings	Closeness to optimal solution

correspondence between the terminologies in actual biological organisms and EAs is shown in Table 1.1.

Here we explain the abstract mechanism of evolutionary algorithms on the background of theory of evolution. A more formal and detailed working principle of EAs with their applications will be presented in subsequent chapters.

Chapter 2

A Practical Guide to Genetic Algorithms Using Excel Simulators

2.1 Function optimization and hill-climbing methods

The objective of a genetic algorithm (GA) is to search for the solution to a problem. A number of ways to do this have been proposed in addition to GA. In this chapter, first we will look at what it means to search, and then we will look at what kinds of situations comprise problems.

Searching can be compared to climbing to the summit of a mountain range. The goal here is to reach the summit of the highest peak. For example, if we limit our search range to Japan, we could consider ourselves successful if we reach the top of Mount Fuji. Here, the top of Mount Fuji, the highest peak in Japan, is called the global optimum of our search range. If we reached the summit of another mountain, for example, Mount Tsukuba[1], we would have failed to locate the global optimum. But Mount Tsukuba is the highest point in its close neighborhood. Such a solution that is optimum within a neighboring set of solutions is called a local optimum (Fig. 2.1).

The analogy between climbing a hill or mountain and general search comes from the definition of a conditional search for a maximum value, such as the following:

Find the value of x in the equation $\max\{f(x)\}$ in $x \in X$ (2.1)

In other words, we are going to find the x that provides the maximum value of $f(x)$ in the field X. In the example just used, $X = Japan$ and

---

[1]Mount Fuji (3776 m) is the highest mountain in Japan and is well known as a symbol of Japan. It is located almost in the center of Japan. Mount Tsukuba (877 m) is one of the most famous mountains in Japan, particularly well known for its double peaks. It is located about 60 km north-east of Tokyo. On clear days Mount Fuji is visible from the top of Mount Tsukuba.

9

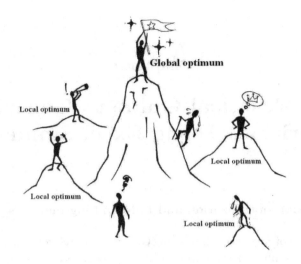

Fig. 2.1   A schematic illustration of searching

$f(x) = $ *the altitude of* x. Note that in some problems, the search is for the minimum value, and in that case the equation would be:

$$\min_{x}\{f(x)\} = \max_{x}\{-f(x)\} \qquad (2.2)$$

So a minimization problem can easily be converted to a maximization problem and vice versa. Therefore, the search problem can be reasonably thought of as a "hill-climbing" problem.

Let us use a Microsoft® Office Excel® (hereafter referred to as Excel) based simulator to look at the forms of various functions. We will be using the following Excel simulators (details about usage of these simulators is presented in Appendix A):

GA-2D simulator Allows optimization of one-dimensional functions.
GA-3D simulator Allows optimization of two-dimensional functions.

First, try running the GA-2D simulator. This should display an execution window like that shown in Fig. 2.2. Here, a graph is displayed in the upper-left area of the screen. This is the target function that has to be optimized. In other words, the problem is to search for the "summit" of this hill. The definition of the function is written in the box called "$F(x) =$", and changing this makes defining various functions possible. Also, "$0 \leq x < 17$" is displayed in the lower left of the function definition

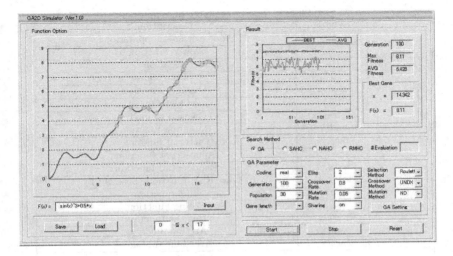

Fig. 2.2   GA-2D simulator

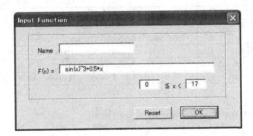

Fig. 2.3   Input Function window

field. In this example, the following function is indicated with a function definition field of "$0 \leq x < 17$":

$$F(x) = \sin^3(x) + 0.5 \cdot x \qquad (2.3)$$

Looking at the graph, we see that there are a number of mountains and hills. The line proceeds upward from left to right, but the progression of the line is fairly uneven in some places.

The function can be modified using the "Input" button. When this button is pressed, an input window like that shown in Fig. 2.3 is displayed. Functions that can be used in Excel can be written here, and the principal functions that can be used are listed in Table 2.1. These are single-variable functions, and the variable is x. The definition field (range of x: search space) can also be changed.

Table 2.1   List of available functions

	Symbol	Description
Operators	$+ \ - \ * \ /$	Four arithmetic operations
	$\wedge$	Power function
	$-$	Negation
	$!$	Factorial
Functions	abs(x)	Absolute function
	pi()	$\pi(3.14159...)$
	degrees(x)	Convert to angle
	round(x,0)	Rounding function
	fact(x)	Factorial function
	sqrt(x)	Square root function
	exp(x)	Exponential function
	log(x,y)	Logarithm function (base is y)
	sin(x)	Sine function
	cos(x)	Cosine Function
	tan(x)	Tangent function
	asin(x)	Arcsine function
	acos(x)	Arccosine function
	atan(x)	Arctangent function
	sinh(x)	Hyperbolic sine funcion
	cosh(x)	Hyperbolic cosine function
	tanh(x)	Hyperbolic tangent function
	rand()	Random number from 0 to 1
	Gauss(m,s)	Gaussian random number (mean=m, variance=s)
	Max(x,y)	A maximum value of x and y
	Min(x,y)	A minimum value of x and y
	if(bool,x,y)	Return x if bool is **true**, otherwise **false**

Now try inputting the following functions:

$F(x) = 10 - (x - 10) * (x - 10)$ (See Fig. 2.4)
$F(x) = \text{abs}(\sin(x))$ (See Fig. 2.5)
$F(x) = \text{abs}(\sin(x) * x)$ (See Fig. 2.6)
$F(x) = \text{rand}() * x$ (See Fig. 2.7)

For simplicity, leave the definition field as it is ($0 \leq x < 17$). If you make a mistake, press "Reset" to start over. When you have input the function, press "OK". This displays a schematic diagram of the function.

Looking at the forms of these functions, you will notice that the "hills" are of varying difficulty in terms of climbing. For example, $F(x) = 10 - (x-10) * (x-10)$ is a straightforward function with only one hill at $x = 10$ (see Fig. 2.4). Climbing this hill is extremely easy. Since there is only a single hill, you only have to move uphill to climb it. This type of function is called a single-peak (or unimodal) function.

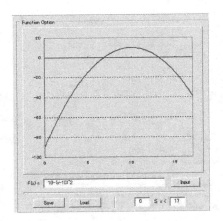

Fig. 2.4 $F(x) = 10 - (x - 10) * (x - 10)$

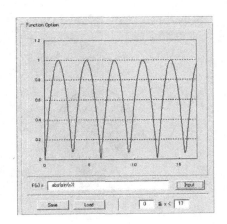

Fig. 2.5 $F(x) = \text{abs}(\sin(x))$

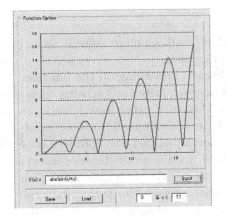

Fig. 2.6 $F(x) = \text{abs}(\sin(x) * x)$

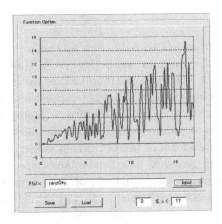

Fig. 2.7 $F(x) = \text{rand}() * x$

The functions $F(x) = \text{abs}(\sin(x))$ and $F(x) = \text{abs}(\sin(x) * x)$ (see Fig. 2.5 and 2.6, respectively), on the other hand, have more than one hill, making it hard to determine where to climb. These types of functions are called multi-peak (or multi-modal) functions. With $F(x) = \text{abs}(\sin(x) * x)$, in particular, the optimum hill is at the far right, but there are numerous hills to the left that are suboptimal. This kind of situation is difficult as there is a possibility of climbing the wrong hill.

$F(x) = \text{rand}() * x$ is a function using a random number (see Fig. 2.7). The form of this function is even more complex. Overall, it slants upward

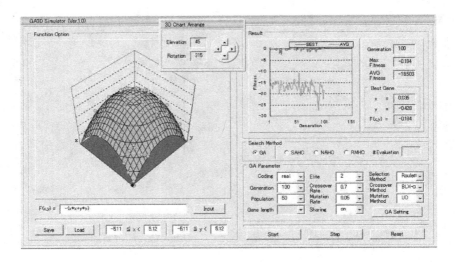

Fig. 2.8   GA-3D simulator

from left to right, but we can predict that it will be more difficult to find the optimum value (highest hill) of this function.

Clearly, searching can be easier or harder, depending on the function. One method of characterizing these functions quantitatively is using an approach known as the fitness landscape. These various objective functions that require optimization are known as fitness functions. This is a generalized form of the GA fitness value, and is developed from the approach used in genetics. The fitness landscape can be defined from the fitness function and the coordinate expression (genetic coding of the gene with GA, which will be explained in Section 2.2.1). In intuitive terms, this is the landscape of the search space. Considering the search for the maximum value (the location with the highest altitude) in this landscape, it is easy to imagine that differences in the landscape will affect the search.

In order to better understand the fitness landscape, try running the GA-3D simulator. This should produce an execution window like that shown in Fig. 2.8. As before, a graph is displayed in the upper-left area of the screen. This is the target function that should be optimized. The function definition is written in a box called "$F(x, y) =$". Note that this is a two-variable function, with x and y as the variables. The definition field, as displayed in the lower left, is $(-5.11 \leq x < 5.12, -5.11 \leq y < 5.12)$. In this example, the following function is displayed:

$$F(x) = -(x * x + y * y) \tag{2.4}$$

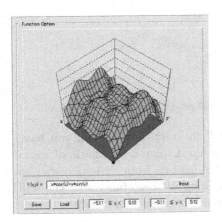

Fig. 2.9   Fitness landscape of $F(x) = x * \cos(x) + y * \sin(y)$

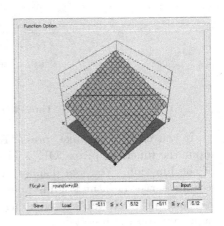

Fig. 2.10   Fitness landscape of $F(x) = \text{round}(x + y, 0)$

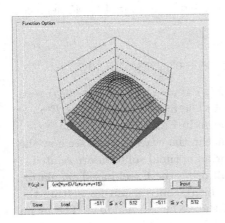

Fig. 2.11   Fitness landscape of $F(x) = (x + 2 * y + 5)/(x * x + y * y + 15)$

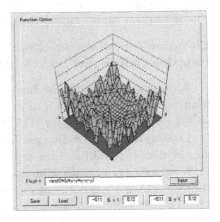

Fig. 2.12   Fitness landscape of $F(x) = \text{rand}() * (x * x + y * y - x - y)$

Looking at the graph, we can see that this is a single-peak (unimodal) function that consists of only one hill. Then, try inputting the following functions:

$$F(x) = x * \cos(x) + y * \sin(y) \qquad \text{(See Fig. 2.9)}$$
$$F(x) = \text{round}(x + y, 0) \qquad \text{(See Fig. 2.10)}$$
$$F(x) = (x + 2 * y + 5)/(x * x + y * y + 15) \qquad \text{(See Fig. 2.11)}$$
$$F(x) = \text{rand}() * (x * x + y * y - x - y) \qquad \text{(See Fig. 2.12)}$$

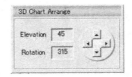

Fig. 2.13   Three-dimensional rotation panel

If you make a mistake, press "Reset" to start over. When you have input the function, press "OK". This should display a schematic diagram of the function. You can display target functions from various angles so as to observe the fitness landscapes. Looking at these functions, you will see that although you are climbing a hill, the degree of difficulty varies depending on the function.

To better visualize a function in a three-dimensional space, there is a set of buttons that rotate the graph vertically and horizontally (Fig. 2.13). Each time an arrow button is pressed, the figure is rotated by 45 degrees. The movement options are as follows:

Elevation (up/down) : $-45°, 0°, 45°$
Rotation (left/right) : $0°, 45°, 90°, 135°, 180°, 225°, 270°, 315°$

An overview showing the function $F(x) = x * \cos(x) + y * \sin(y)$ seen from various angles is shown in Fig. 2.14. The fitness landscape of $F(x) = (x + 2 * y + 5)/(x * x + y * y + 15)$ is shown in Fig. 2.15.

Looking at the three-dimensional space in this way, you can see how the idea of climbing a hill and the search for an optimal solution are related.

Now, let's try actually climbing a hill using the Excel-based simulator. Run the GA-2D simulator again. This brings up a menu for setting the "Search Method" in the center-right of the execution window. The menu options are as follows(Fig. 2.16):

- GA: Genetic Algorithms
- SAHC: Steepest-ascent hill-climbing
- NAHC: Next-ascent hill-climbing
- RHC: Random-mutation hill-climbing
- #Evaluation: Iteration count (specified when using hill-climbing)

The first option, GA, the main focus of this book, will be explained in detail in the next subsection and in subsequent chapters. The next three options are variants of hill-climbing. The classic hill-climbing is a simple local search method that starts with a random or potentially poor solu-

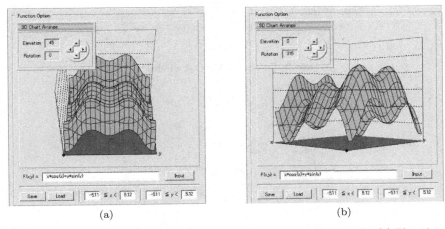

Fig. 2.14 Overview of $F(x) = x * \cos(x) + y * \sin(y)$ from different angles (a) Elevation 45°, rotation 0° (b) Elevation 0°, rotation 315°

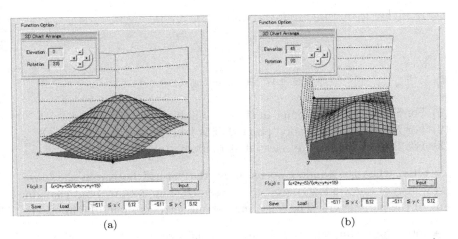

Fig. 2.15 Overview of $F(x) = (x + 2 * y + 5)/(x * x + y * y + 15)$ from different angles (a) Elevation 0°, rotation 315° (b) Elevation 45°, rotation 90°

tion (search point), and progresses by making small changes to the solution (choose a nearby search point) iteratively, each time improving it a little. The algorithm stops when any further improvement is not possible. The algorithmic description of the basic hill-climbing method is presented in Section 5.2.2. The hill-climbing search method has different variants in terms of how search points in the surrounding area are selected. More specifically:

Fig. 2.16   Search Method window

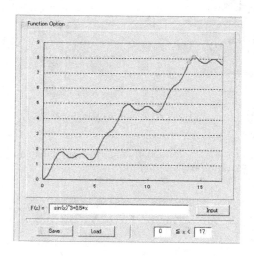

Fig. 2.17   Hill-climbing search

(1) For SAHC, the best point in the surrounding area is selected.
(2) For NAHC, the first good point that is found is selected.
(3) For RMHC, points are selected at random.

First, when the window opens, press the "Start" button in the lower-right area of the window to execute the search (Fig. 2.2), without changing any of the parameters. The following default settings should be in effect:

- Function definition: $F(x) = \sin^3(x) + 0.5 * x$
- Function field: $0 \le x < 17$
- Search method: SAHC
- Iteration count: 200

When this is executed, a green[2] dot moves on the function display window, indicating that hill-climbing has begun (Fig. 2.17). The movement of the dot is actually the visualization of how SAHC updates the search point. Execution stops after a few moments, but as you will see, you can make

---

[2] Use the simulator for confirming the color description hereafter.

Fig. 2.18   Data window for the best individual

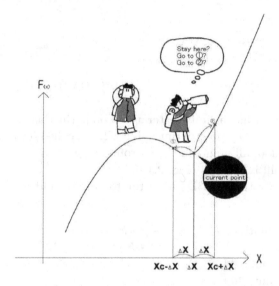

Fig. 2.19   Fitness evaluation by SAHC

the dot climb the hill again by pressing "Start". Choose a starting point at random and start climbing the hill. When the summit (the highest point of all) is reached, another starting point is selected to start climbing the hill. The highest point found so far is displayed in orange. The coordinates of this optimum value (the orange dot) are displayed in the "Best Gene" box when the execution is finished (Fig. 2.18). In this case, the coordinates will probably be around $x = 14.277$, $F(x) = 8.11$. However, since random numbers are being used, this will not necessarily be the same. The execution result will probably be different in different runs.

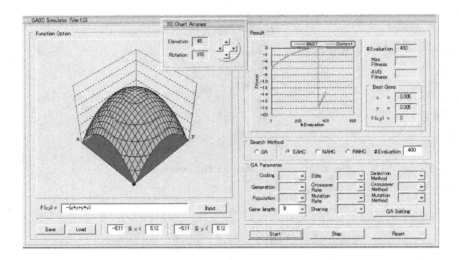

Fig. 2.20   Hill-climbing search using the GA-3D simulator

Each execution has a limited iteration count (in this case, 200). The iteration count is the number of times that $F(x)$ is called (evaluated). With the SAHC method, all points in the surrounding area have to be evaluated each time the hill is climbed (Fig. 2.19).

Next, let's use the GA-3D simulator to climb a hill. Set the default settings as follows:

- Function definition: $F(x, y) = -(x * x + y * y)$
- Function field: $-5.11 \leq x < 5.12, -5.11 \leq y < 5.12$
- Search method: SAHC
- Iteration count: 400

Then select the SAHC, NAHC and RMHC search methods, climb the hill, and compare the results. This is a straightforward single-peak landscape, and is a problem that allows the summit to be reached right away using SAHC. When you run it, you will see that the green dot behaves differently depending on the search method. If the iteration count is set at around 30, you will be able to observe the degree of evaluation needed in order to climb the hill (for the orange line to ascend. See Fig. 2.20).

The characteristics of the three methods are summarized below:

(1) SAHC: The entire surrounding area is carefully surveyed, so success is guaranteed, but evaluation is carried out for more than the necessary number of times.

(2) NAHC: This falls somewhere between SAHC and RMHC, and uses a heuristic approach in which the ascent continues largely in the same direction.
(3) RMHC: Only one point is chosen at random. Thus, if all goes well, fewer evaluations are needed, but there are likely to be more failures.

The success of these three methods depends on the shape of the landscape, so it is impossible to say which method is the best. For example, let's try comparing the three methods using the examples from earlier (see Fig. 2.9–2.12):

$$F(x) = x * \cos(x) + y * \sin(y)$$
$$F(x) = \text{round}(x + y, 0)$$
$$F(x) = (x + 2 * y + 5)/(x * x + y * y + 15)$$
$$F(x) = \text{rand}() * (x * x + y * y - x - y)$$

The hill-climbing method is simple, but there are numerous problems. First, the hill-climbing method is successful to some extent, but it frequently ends up producing localized solutions. You may arrive at an optimal solution eventually by executing the process repeatedly, but it is not a very efficient approach.

Another problem is caused by something called the "curse of dimensions". In the examples seen up to this point, we've used one-variable (one-dimensional) and two-variable (two-dimensional) functions. In practical applications, however, you will need to solve problems with larger numbers of dimensions (variables). For example, the optimization of gene regulatory network problems involves $2N(N + 1)$ parameters where N is the number of genes (see Section 6.5 and [Noman and Iba (2005b)] for more detail). This means that even for a five gene network, the problem involves $2 \times 5 \times (5 + 1) = 60$ dimensions. As we saw earlier, using SAHC in an n-dimensional space, the evaluation of a neighborhood of size 2^n has to be done each time the hill is climbed. This means that with 60 dimensions, function evaluation (comparison) has to be done the following number of times at every step of movement:

$$2^{60} \approx 10^8$$

This exceeds what ordinary computers can handle.

Thus, as the number of dimensions increases, the problem becomes exponentially more complex, something we call the "curse of dimensions". One effective way around this difficulty is using GA, which will be discussed next.

2.2 Basic mechanisms of genetic algorithms

This section will explain GA in greater detail. GA became popular through the work of John Holland in the early 1970s, and particularly his book *Adaptation in Natural and Artificial Systems* [Holland (1975)]. First, let's briefly review the principles of GA that were introduced in Section 1.3.

2.2.1 *Let's try using genetic algorithms*

Information handled using GA comprises a two-layer structure consisting of GTYPE and PTYPE. The PTYPE results from the expression of the GTYPE. The operators of genetic algorithms (GA operators) act on the GTYPE, and the fitness value is determined from the PTYPE, based on the environment. For the time being, let's assume that the larger the fitness value, the better. At the moment, let's also use the target function values $F(x)$ and $F(x, y)$ that we explained in the previous section for the fitness value. The fact that a larger fitness value is better means that, with respect to the landscape, the taller the hill, the more preferable it is for climbing.

To better understand how GA works, let's try running a simple example. Execute the GA-3D simulator, and change the initial settings as follows (Fig. 2.21):

- Function definition: $x * \cos(x) + y * \sin(y)$
- Function field: $-5.11 \leq x < 5.12, -5.11 \leq y < 5.12$
- Search method: GA

Other parameters may be left as they are. Press the "Start" button at the lower right to execute the simulator. You should be able to see numerous green dots moving around within a defined space. Each of these green dots represents an individual of GA. In this particular case, we are running GA that involves a 50-individual population and a maximum of 100 generations. As the algorithm proceeds, the green dots move slowly along the fitness landscape, and an orange dot appears to climb up the hill. Here, the orange dot represents the maximum value seen up to the current point in time, and the green dots are the current points being searched. The green dots move around to various points, but the orange dot should arrive immediately at the highest hill. When execution finishes, the positions of the various individuals in the final generation will be displayed as green dots. By now, you can see the mean fitness value for each generation (the mean fitness values for the population) and the best fitness value displayed

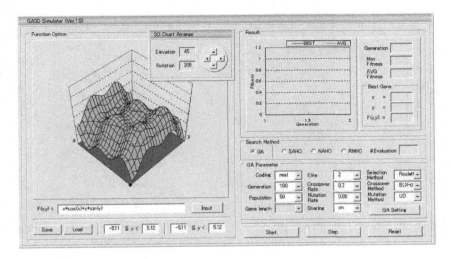

Fig. 2.21   GA-3D simulator (GA execution)

in the upper right of the screen. The trends of both are displayed on the graph (Fig. 2.22). You can see that the search advances (the fitness value increases) as it proceeds through successive generations. There is also a box in the upper right of the screen that displays the results (Fig. 2.23). These results consist of the following items:

- Generation: Maximum number of generations
- Max Fitness: Best fitness value
- AVG Fitness: Mean fitness value
- Best Gene: The (x, y) coordinates of the best individual found at the end of the search and the function values $F(x, y)$ are displayed

When the execution of the simulator has finished, you can start the GA search again by pressing the "Start" button. The results should be different each time because the initial generation is generated randomly. Try inputting various functions and executing the GA. You should see that the populations of green dots come closer together and move farther apart as they move to the top of the hill. You will also see that some of the green dots descend instead of ascend, as if wandering around. The orange dot, however, should rapidly arrive at the top of the hill.

For the time being, we will think of a one-dimensional bit string (a string of 0s and 1s) as the GTYPE of GA, and take the result of the binary conversion of this string as the PTYPE (this conversion will be explained in

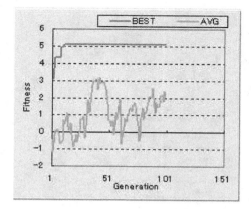

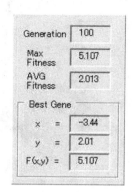

Fig. 2.22   Fitness transition with generations

Fig. 2.23   Result display (generation, fitness value, gene code)

the next section). The location of the gene on the chromosome is called the "locus" in biology. With GA, as well, we use the word "locus" to specify the location of the GTYPE. For example, for GTYPE 010, the genes would be as follows:

- Gene of the 1st locus → 0
- Gene of the 2nd locus → 1
- Gene of the 3rd locus → 0

Before going any further, let's take a brief look at the process of selection. With GA, selection takes place in such a way that the larger the fitness value of an organism, the higher the probability for it to reproduce. On the other hand, the organisms with smaller fitness values are more likely to die out. The simplest way of achieving this is to create a roulette wheel of all individuals. Each individual gets a surface area in the roulette proportional to its fitness value, hence it is called a "weighted roulette". Selection is performed by rotating this roulette wheel andchoosing the individual in the place where the roulette wheel stops. This is called the "fitness-proportionate strategy" (as will be described in detail in the next section).

When reproduction occurs, the operators shown in Fig. 2.24 are applied to the selected GTYPE to generate new GTYPE for the subsequent generation. These operators are called GA operators. To keep the explanation simple, we express the GTYPE as a one-dimensional array here. Each operator is analogous to the recombination or mutation of a gene in a biological

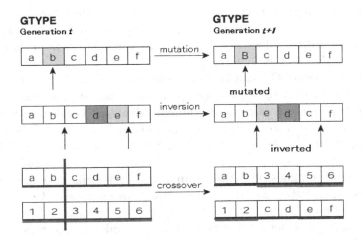

Fig. 2.24   GA operators

organism (Fig. 2.25). Generally, the frequency with which these operators are applied, as well as the sites at which they are applied, are determined randomly. In more precise terms, the crossover shown in Fig. 2.24 has one crossover point, so it is called a one-point crossover. Following are some methods for performing the crossover operation:

(1) One-point crossover (hereafter abbreviated as 1X)
(2) Multi-point crossover (n-point crossover, hereafter abbreviated as nX)
(3) Uniform crossover (hereafter abbreviated as UX)

We have already explained the one-point crossover operation (Fig. 2.26 (a)). The n-point crossover operation has n crossover points, so if $n = 1$, this is equivalent to the one-point crossover operation. With this crossover method, genes are carried over from one parent alternately between crossover points. A case in which $n = 3$ is shown in Fig. 2.26 (b). Two-point crossovers, in which $n = 2$, are often used. Uniform crossovers are a crossover method in which any desired number of crossover points can be identified, so these are realized using a mask for a bit string consisting of $0, 1$. First, let's randomly generate a character string of 0s and 1s for this mask. The crossover is carried out as follows. Suppose the two selected parents are designated as Parent A and Parent B, and the offspring to be created are designated as Child A and Child B. At this point, the genes for offspring Child A are carried over from Parent A when the corresponding mask is 1, and are carried over from Parent B when the mask is 0. Conversely, the genes for offspring Child B are carried over from Parent A when the corresponding mask is 0, and are carried over from Parent B when the mask is 1 (Fig. 2.26 (c)).

The basic flow of GA can be summarized as follows (Fig. 2.27). Let's say that the GTYPE $\{g_t(i)\}$ is a group of individuals at generation t. For the phenotype $p_t(i)$ of each $g_t(i)$, a fitness value $f_t(i)$ is calculated in the environment. The GA operators are generally applied to GTYPEs with a larger fitness value, and the newly bred GTYPE is substituted for a GTYPE with a smaller fitness value. Based on the above, selection is carried out based on fitness values, and the group $\{g_{t+1}(i)\}$ for the next generation $(t + 1)$ is generated. The process described above is repeated generation after generation.

To confirm this, let's try executing GA in order to optimize a one-variable function. Try executing the GA-2D simulator. After inputting the following initial conditions, press the "Start" button:

- Function definition: $F(x) = \sin^3(x) + 0.5 * x$
- Function field: $0 \leq x < 17$
- Search method: GA

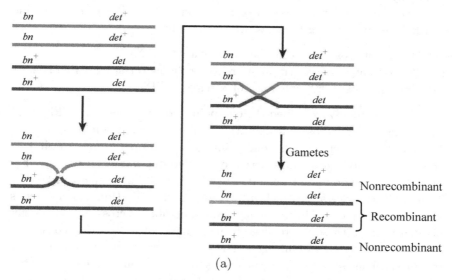

(a)

Fig. 2.25   Gene crossover and mutation in biology (adapted from [Tamarin (2002)], pp. 183–184) (a) Crossover of homologues during meiosis. (b) Consequence of a crossover in the loop region.

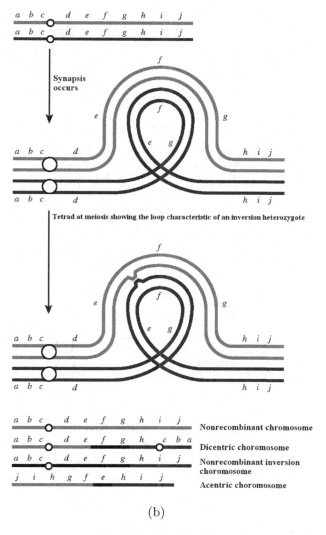

Tetrad at meiosis showing the loop characteristic of an inversion heterozygote

Nonrecombinant chromosome

Dicentric choromosome

Nonrecombinant inversion choromosome

Acentric choromosome

(b)

Fig. 2.25 (*Continued*)

When you execute the simulator, you will see that the population of green dots on the function display window at the left-hand side of the screen moves and begins to climb the hill (Fig. 2.28). The highest peak found up to this point is indicated by an orange dot. After execution finishes, the

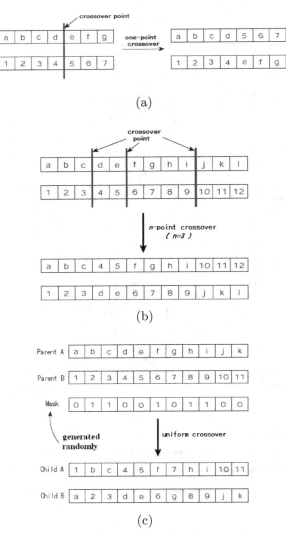

Fig. 2.26　GA crossovers: (a) one-point crossover, (b) n-point crossover, (c) uniform crossover

coordinates of the best value (the orange dot) are displayed in the "Best Gene" box. Be aware of the following points here:

(1) At the beginning of the GA simulation, there are nearly 50 green dots. These are the individuals of the first generation (Fig. 2.29).

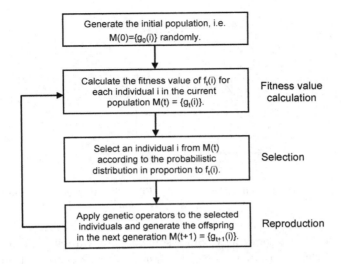

Fig. 2.27   Flow chart of GA

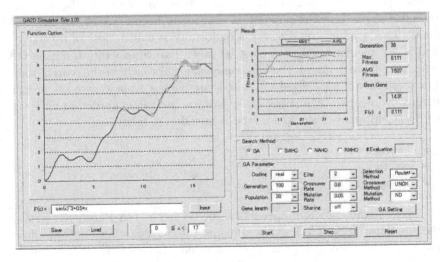

Fig. 2.28   GA-2D simulator for $F(x) = \sin^3(x) + 0.5 * x$

(2) When GA execution is completed, fewer green dots will be displayed (Fig. 2.30).

The fewer number of green dots does not mean that the number of individuals in the final generation has decreased, rather that some individuals

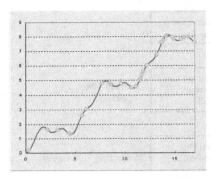

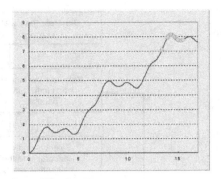

Fig. 2.29   Population at the initial generation

Fig. 2.30   Population at the final generation

have the identical x coordinate. Since some dots overlap, it looks as if there are fewer of them. In other words, the first generation is created randomly, so it has many individuals that differ from each other. As the search proceeds, however, superior parents produce larger numbers of offspring that resemble them, and the population eventually becomes more or less uniform. This gradual trend towards uniformity is called "loss of diversity", and is one phenomenon that must be taken into consideration during GA searches. In particular, if this phenomenon occurs early in the search, there is a possibility of a localized solution occurring, an event known as "premature convergence". A number of devices are used in conjunction with GA to boost efficiency. Principal methods include the following:

- Coding
- Selection
- GA operators

These parameters and options can be set in the GA Parameter part of the simulator (Fig. 2.31). Also, pressing the "GA Setting" button allows for a more detailed adjustment of these parameters (Fig. 2.32). In the subsequent sections, we will describe typical GA techniques based on this simulator. Unless otherwise specified, the following assumptions will apply regarding the fitness value:

(1) The fitness value is a positive number.
(2) The larger the fitness value, the better.

Fig. 2.31 GA parameters setting panel   Fig. 2.32 GA parameters setting box

Table 2.2 Conversion from GTYPE to PTYPE

GTYPE	PTYPE
000	1.0
100	1.5
010	2.0
110	2.5
001	3.0
101	3.5
011	4.0
111	4.5

2.2.2 *Genotype and phenotype encoding*

Let's consider the optimization of one-dimensional functions, with x as the variable. The genotype (GTYPE) of the GA will indicate a real number x (PTYPE). The method of expressing a genotype for GA is called "coding" (or "encoding"). This is a mapping from a coordinate of the space being searched (in this case, x) to the genotype. This reverse mapping is called "decoding". The form of expression most commonly used with GA is binary expression. In binary expression, a correspondence is created between an ordinary binary number and an area x. For example, if the definition field is $1 \leq x < 5$ and the gene length is 3, the conversion from the GTYPE to the PTYPE (decoding) will be as shown in Table 2.2.

In other words, conversion is carried out in such a way that each time there is an increase of 1 bit, the PTYPE increases by only $\Delta x = (5.0 - 1.0)/2^3 = 0.5$.

The gene length is specified using the "Gene Length" parameter in the "GA Parameter" box (Fig. 2.33). Be aware that with this simulator, the most significant bit (MSB) of the bit string is at the right. In other words, the bit farthest to the left is the least significant digit, and the bit farthest to the right is the most significant digit.

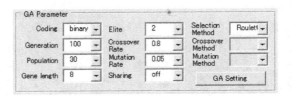

Fig. 2.33   Setting the gene length parameter

When "binary" is specified in the GA Parameter box, GA is executed based on a genotype (binary expression) like that shown above. If "gray" is specified, the genotype is created by means of "gray coding". Gray coding is a coding method in which neighboring codes are only different by one bit. This means that the Hamming distance is 1. For example, the codes for 0 to 15 are as shown in Table 2.3. Note that binary expressions $(b_1 b_2 \cdots b_{t-2} b_{t-1})$ and gray expressions $(g_1 g_2 \cdots g_{t-2} g_{t-1})$ are generally converted as follows:

- Binary expression ⇒ gray expression

$$g_k = \begin{cases} b_{t-1} & \text{When } k = t - 1, \\ b_{k+1} \oplus b_k & \text{When } k \leq t - 2, \end{cases} \qquad (2.5)$$

- Gray expression ⇒ binary expression

$$b_k = \sum_{i=k}^{t-1} g_i (mod\ 2) \quad k = 0, 1, \cdots, t - 1 \qquad (2.6)$$

where $\oplus$ represents the exclusive OR (XOR) operation.

Let's try GA searches using both coding methods, binary expressions and gray expressions, for various functions. The executions of GA using a binary expression and a gray expression, respectively, for the same function are shown in Fig. 2.34 and Fig. 2.35. Compare the outcomes of these two methods. Which outcome would you say is better? Why is it better?

Generally, the outcome of gray expressions is better than that of binary expressions. The reason is as follows: With binary coding, there can be instances in which the Hamming distances corresponding to adjacent values may not produce 1 in decimal notation. For example, 3 is 011, 4 is 100. Here, let's assume that the fitness value of a function is maximum at $x = 3$, while $x = 4$ also gives a fairly good value. Assumptions such as this are probably appropriate when considering the smoothness of the fitness value function. Also, let's assume that during the GA search, the individuals in the population have converged at $x = 4$. In other words, the search is going

Table 2.3　Binary expression and gray expression

Decimal expression	Binary expression ($b_1b_2b_3b_4$)	Gray Expression ($g_1g_2g_3g_4$)
0	0000	0000
1	1000	1000
2	0100	1100
3	1100	0100
4	0010	0110
5	1010	1110
6	0110	1010
7	1110	0010
8	0001	0011
9	1001	1011
10	0101	1111
11	1101	0111
12	0011	0101
13	1011	1101
14	0111	1001
15	1111	0001

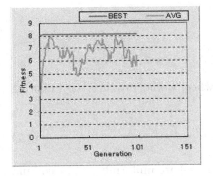

Fig. 2.34　GA execution with binary coding

Fig. 2.35　GA execution with gray coding

fairly well, and we have found a fairly good outcome as far as $x = 4$. At this point, it will be difficult to find an optimal point (e.g. 3) by mutations of individuals at $x = 4$ using binary coding. This is because mutations should occur simultaneously in three locations. This phenomenon is called a "Hamming cliff".

With gray expressions, however, neighboring numbers are different by only one bit, making it easier to find nearby values using mutations. In other words, using gray expression makes it possible, to some extent, to have the mutation serve the role of a localized search.

2.2.3 Selection method

There are many selection strategies in GA. Basically, candidates must be selected for reproduction in such a way that the larger (better) the fitness value, the more offspring the parent will be able to reproduce. There are a number of ways to do this and the following two are the most commonly used.

1. Fitness-proportionate strategy (roulette wheel)

With this method, candidates are selected at a percentage proportional to the fitness value. The simplest way of doing this is to use a weighted roulette wheel. A roulette wheel that has fields that are proportional to individuals' fitness values is rotated, and the individuals in the field in which the roulette ball lands are selected. For example, let's consider a case with the following values:

$$f_1 \quad 1.0$$
$$f_2 \quad 2.0$$
$$f_3 \quad 0.5$$
$$f_4 \quad 3.0$$
$$f_5 \quad 3.5$$

Selection using a weighted roulette wheel would produce the following outcome:

$$f_1 + f_2 + \cdots + f_5 = 10.0 \qquad (2.7)$$

As a result, random numbers from 0.0 to 10.0 are uniformly produced, and selection takes place in accordance with the following rules:

If the value of the random number is between 0.0 and 1.0, individuals with f_1 will be selected.

If the value of the random number is between 1.0 and 3.0, individuals with f_2 will be selected.

If the value of the random number is between 3.0 and 3.5, individuals with f_3 will be selected.

If the value of the random number is between 3.5 and 6.5, individuals with f_4 will be selected.

If the value of the random number is between 6.5 and 10.0, individuals with f_5 will be selected.

For example, if the random numbers resulting are as follows:

$$1.3 \quad 5.5 \quad 8.5 \quad 4.5 \quad 7.5 \tag{2.8}$$

the following individuals will be selected:

$$f_2 \quad f_4 \quad f_5 \quad f_4 \quad f_5 \tag{2.9}$$

The fitness-proportionate strategy selects n individuals in this manner.

Let's describe the fitness-proportionate strategy formally:

$$f_1 \quad f_2 \cdots f_n \tag{2.10}$$

When n individuals and each of their fitness values are provided, the probability p_i of the i-th individual being selected is as follows:

$$p_i = f_i / \sum f_i \tag{2.11}$$

Consequently, the expected value for the number of offspring produced by the i-th individual will be:

$$np_i = \frac{n f_i}{\sum f_i} = \frac{f_i}{\frac{\sum f_i}{n}} = \frac{f_i}{f_{avg}} \tag{2.12}$$

where f_{avg} is the average fitness value $f_{avg} = \sum f_i / n$. In particular, the number of individuals having the average fitness will be as follows:

$$n \times p_{avg} = \frac{f_{avg}}{f_{avg}} = 1 \tag{2.13}$$

Thus a single individual will be reproduced in the next generation if it has the average fitness value.

2. Tournament strategy

This is a strategy in which a certain number (say S_t) of individuals are randomly selected from a population, and the best of these individuals is finally chosen. This process is repeated until the size of the population is reached. Let's use the same values as in the fitness-proportionate strategy example:

$$
\begin{array}{ll}
f_1 & 1.0 \\
f_2 & 2.0 \\
f_3 & 0.5 \\
f_4 & 3.0 \\
f_5 & 3.5
\end{array}
$$

We will use 3 for S_t. At this point, let's assume that the individuals selected in five tournaments resulted in the following scenarios:

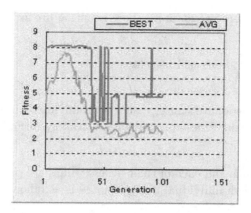

Fig. 2.36   GA execution without elite strategy

1st tournament:	f_1, f_2, f_3
2nd tournament:	f_3, f_4, f_1
3rd tournament:	f_1, f_5, f_2
4th tournament:	f_2, f_4, f_1
5th tournament:	f_5, f_2, f_4

Let's assume that the winners of the above tournaments at this point are f_2, f_4, f_5, f_4 and f_5, and these individuals are selected. With this method, a number of different values are made available for the tournament size (S_t).

Another strategy where the parent candidates are selected completely randomly (random selection) and irrespective of their fitness values is also applied for comparison purposes. With the above selection methods, the parent candidates are always selected on a probabilistic basis, so the best individual will not necessarily remain in the next generation. Even if they survive the selection process as parent candidates, mutations and crossovers could occur in those candidates. As a result, the outcome will not necessarily improve over successive generations. There is another method, however, by which the best individual (or several individuals with the highest scores) will definitely be carried over to the next generation. This is called the "elite strategy". In the elite strategy, genes are simply copied, without crossovers or mutations being applied. Consequently, as long as the fitness value functions are the same, the outcome of the current generation is minimally guaranteed at the next generation. Simulators are designed so that a percentage of individuals with the highest scores that have to be carried

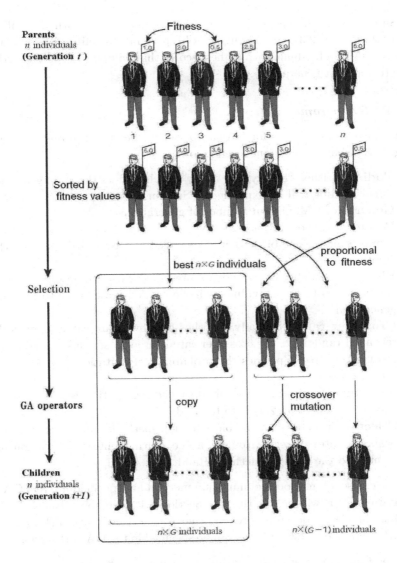

Fig. 2.37   Alteration of generation by GA

over to the next generation can be specified. If zero is specified, the elite strategy is not carried out. At this point we should check to make sure that the best individuals at each generation do not increase monotonically (Fig. 2.36).

Summarizing the above, the alteration of generations with GA will be as shown in Fig. 2.37. In this figure, G represents the elite ratio (i.e. the percentage of individuals with highest scores that will be copied and carried over to the next generation).

2.2.4   *GA parameters*

The principal parameters for GA can be set in the "GA Parameter" panel (Fig. 2.31). These are summarized below:

- **Coding**: Either "binary" or "gray" is selected as the coding method ("real" coding will be explained in Section 3.1)
- **Generation**: Maximum number of generations
- **Population**: Population size
- **Gene length**: The bit length to be coded is determined based on this length
- **Elite**: The number of individuals preserved with the elite strategy; if this is set to 0, no individuals will be carried intact over to the next generation
- **Crossover rate**: Normally, whether crossovers are carried out is determined randomly: the crossover rate is used to set this probability
- **Mutation rate**: Specifies the probability of mutation for the bits in the chromosome
- **Sharing**: This is turned on if the niche segregation function (to be explained in Section 2.4) is to be used
- **Selection method**: Available selection methods include the fitness-proportionate strategy (Roulette), the tournament strategy (Tournament) and the random method (Random)

The crossover method and mutation method are specified if a real GA is being used. This will be described in Section 3.1. The above items can be specified in greater detail by pressing the "GA Setting" button (Fig. 2.32). In particular, the following items can be specified in the GA Setting window:

- The tournament size used with the tournament strategy.
- The σ_{share} of the assignment function used in the sharing method.

2.2.5   *GA simulator details*

The above completes our basic discussion of GA. We will now move to a more detailed look at how GA operates, while at the same time incorpo-

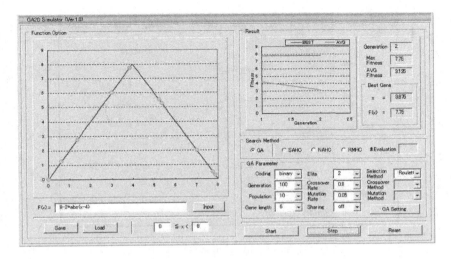

Fig. 2.38 GA-2D simulator for $F(x) = 8 - 2 * \text{abs}(x - 4)$

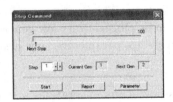

Fig. 2.39 Step Command window

rating a review of what we've learned up to now. To do this, we will use the "Step" and "Report" commands.

For instance, try executing the GA-2D simulator. Set the initial settings as follows (Fig. 2.38):

- Function definition: $F(x) = 8 - 2 * \text{abs}(x - 4)$
- Definition field: $0 \leq x < 8$
- Search method: GA
- Gene length: 6
- Population: 10
- Coding: binary
- Elite: 2
- Sharing: off

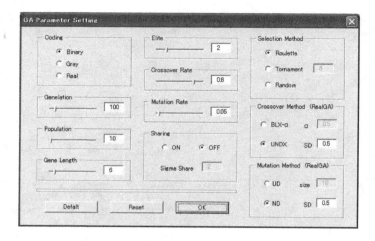

Fig. 2.40   GA parameters setting

These settings allow us to closely observe the behavior of GA. At this point, press the "Step" button. This opens the "Step Command" window (Fig. 2.39). Execution can be paused every few generations to view detailed information as well as to change parameters. The items in this window have the following meanings:

- Step: This specifies how many generations are to be processed before execution is paused.
- Current Gen: This is the number of the current generation.
- Next Gen: This specifies the number of the next generation after which execution is to pause; and Next Gen = Current Gen + Step.

Set appropriate values for these items and press the "Start"/"Continue" button. When the generation specified for the "Next Gen" is reached, execution should pause. Holding down this button executes the simulator for the specified number of generations. Pressing the "Parameter" button when execution is paused, displays the "GA Parameter Setting" window (Fig. 2.40). Parameters can be confirmed and changed in this window.

After execution is complete, press the "Report" button. At this point, a window like that shown in Fig. 2.41 opens, providing detailed information about the population. The genes of the parents and offspring generations are displayed here, along with the maximum fitness value and average fitness value. The gene information comprises the following items:

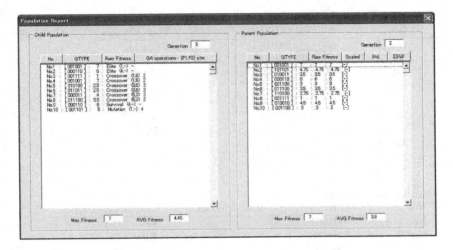

Fig. 2.41   Population Report window

- No.: Gene number
- GTYPE: Genotype
- Raw Fitness: Fitness value calculated from $F(x)$
- GA operations: How the offspring genes were generated
  - Elite: The genes were copied exactly as they were, as elite individuals (the number of the parent is displayed)
  - Crossover: The genes were generated by means of one-point crossover (the two parent individuals and crossover point are displayed)
  - Mutation: The genes were generated as a result of mutation (the individual number of the parent and the mutation point are displayed)
  - Survival: The genes are not elite, but were copied just as they were, without applying either crossover or mutation (the number of the parent is displayed)

For example, we would have the following result after the above command is executed:

Parent population:

No.	:	GTYPE	:	Raw Fitness
No. 1	:	[001001]	:	7
No. 2	:	[101101]	:	4.75
No. 3	:	[010011]	:	3.5
No. 4	:	[000110]	:	6
No. 5	:	[001100]	:	3
No. 6	:	[011100]	:	3.5
No. 7	:	[110100]	:	2.75
No. 8	:	[001111]	:	1
No. 9	:	[010010]	:	4.5
No. 10	:	[001100]	:	3

Offspring population:

No.	:	GTYPE	:	Raw Fitness	:	GA Operations	
No. 1	:	[001001]	:	7	:	Elite (1,-)	-
No. 2	:	[000110]	:	6	:	Elite (4,-)	-
No. 3	:	[001111]	:	1	:	Crossover (1,8)	2
No. 4	:	[001001]	:	7	:	Crossover (1,8)	2
No. 5	:	[010100]	:	2.5	:	Crossover (3,6)	3
No. 6	:	[011011]	:	2.5	:	Crossover (3,6)	3
No. 7	:	[000011]	:	4	:	Crossover (5,3)	2
No. 8	:	[011100]	:	3.5	:	Crossover (5,3)	2
No. 9	:	[000110]	:	6	:	Survival (4,-)	-
No. 10	:	[001101]	:	5	:	Mutation (1,-)	4

In this case, we assume that the GTYPE is a six-bit binary expression and the definition field is $0 \leq x < 8$. In other words, conversion is carried out in such a way that each time the bit is increased by 1, the PTYPE is increased by only $\Delta x = (8.0 - 0.0)/2^6 = 0.125$. For example, if the No. 1 GTYPE of the offspring is 001001, this PTYPE will be as follows:

$$0.0 + \Delta x \times (2^2 + 2^5) = 4.5 \tag{2.14}$$

Remember that the bit on the right end is the MSB. Based on this, the fitness value will be as follows:

$$F(4.5) = 8 - 2 * \text{abs}(4.5 - 4) = 7.0 \tag{2.15}$$

The No. 1 and No. 2 genes of the offspring are copies of the No. 1 and No. 4 genes of the parent.

The No. 5 and No. 6 genes of the offspring were generated by means of crossovers of No. 3 and No. 6 genes of the parent. The third loci is selected as the crossover point:

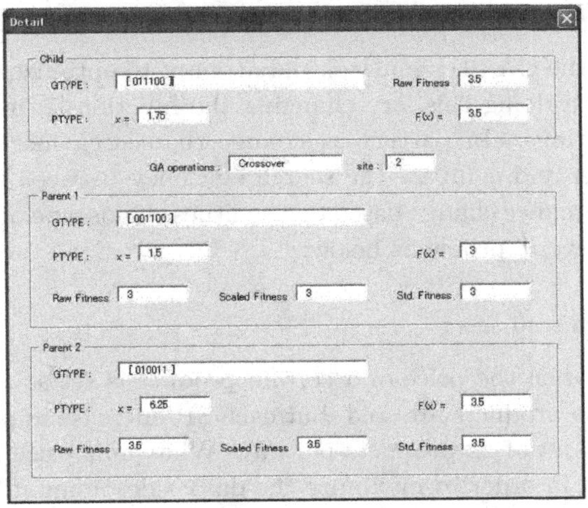

Fig. 2.42   Detailed information of gene codes

No. 3   :   010 011
No. 6   :   011 100
        ↓ **Crossover**
No. 5   :   010 100
No. 6   :   011 011

Here, a blank is inserted for the crossover point. Also, the No. 10 gene of the offspring indicates that a mutation occurred in the fourth locus of the No. 1 gene of the parent:

No. 6   :   001001
            ^

        ↓ **Mutation**
No. 10   :   001101
             ^

where a ^ symbol is inserted below the mutation point. Be aware that a mutation can also occur after a crossover in some cases. Additionally, the No. 9 gene of the offspring is a copy of the No. 4 gene of the parent. The gene was copied as it was, without any crossovers or mutations being applied to the individual. Clicking on a gene of the offspring under "Population Report" displays a window showing detailed information regarding this type of behavior (Fig. 2.42). Take a look at the behavior of GA in various functions.

2.2.6   *How to solve a problem using GA*

Now, let's use the GA-2D simulator and attempt to optimize a one-variable function. When doing this, try changing the function (fitness landscape) and initial settings. In particular, change the search method from hill-climbing to GA and compare the search efficiency between the two. How does the performance change based on the fitness landscape of the function? Let's look at several problems below.

2.2.6.1   *Maximizing sales*

Suppose that when the price of a certain product is set at a unit price of $120, 500 of the products are sold, but each $10 increase in price results in a decrease in sales of 22 products per day. What unit price should we set for the product in order to maximize the daily sales amount?

This problem is an example of the simplest kind of optimization. Let's try solving it using GA.

The daily sales amount $f(x)$ when the price is increased by $10 \times$ dollars would be as follows:

$$f(x) = (120 + 10x) \times (500 - 22x) \qquad (2.16)$$

Let's try optimizing this function with a range of $0 \leq x < 10$ using GA simulation (Fig. 2.43). If you repeat execution several times, you will see that at a value of around $x = 5.35$, the maximum sale amount will be around $66,300$. Naturally, x is an integer, so $x = 5$ will be optimum, and the sales price will be $170.

For someone who is good at mathematics, it might not be necessary to use GA to solve this problem. In actuality, because we have the following:

$$f(x) = 20\{-11(x - \frac{59}{11})^2 + 3000 + \frac{59^2}{11}\} \qquad (2.17)$$

the maximum value of x applied as $59/11$, and because x is an integer value, $x = 5$ will be optimum. With GA, however, the algorithm can be executed immediately as long as the form of the target function is known, so that we can obtain an answer.

Let's consider the next problem, which is more realistic:

Approximately 500 of a certain product are sold when the unit price is $120, but each time this is increased by $10, the sales volume drops by around 22 products per day. What unit price do we need to set in order to achieve the maximum daily sales volume?

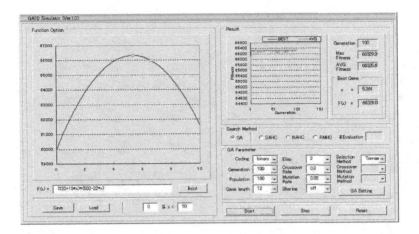

Fig. 2.43   Solving the maximizing sales problem 1 by GA

In other words, here we are not sure of the exact quantity. By acquiring data repeatedly, we know that the dispersion of the quantity sold is two at the highest, in accordance with the normal distribution. This makes it possible to execute GA as follows:

$$f(x) = (120 + 10x) \cdot \text{Gauss}(500 - 22x, 2) \tag{2.18}$$

Try optimizing this function in a range of $0 \leq x < 10$, using GA simulation. If you repeat the execution several times, you will see that a value of around $x = 5$ is optimum (Fig. 2.44). This shows that GA enables robust searching for complex problems where differentiation is not possible.

In this case, the graph of the best fitness values will not increase monotonically even if the elite strategy is used. This is because random numbers are included in the fitness-value function. Each time the target function (fitness-value function) is evaluated at various points, the value of the function differs because of the random number. Consequently, elite members of the previous generation will not necessarily be superior at the next generation. The graph of functions (fitness landscape) actually displays the values obtained at the point when the initial evaluation was done. Since the evaluation values for each generation differ because of the use of random numbers, be aware that the evaluation points (the green dots) will not necessarily always be on the graph.

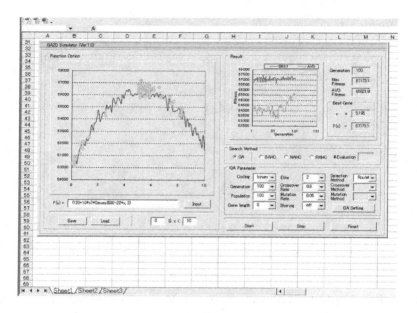

Fig. 2.44   Solving the maximizing sales problem 2 by GA

2.2.6.2 *A slightly more complicated problem*

Next, let's consider a design problem. If we were going to create a conical funnel that has a uniform cubic capacity (for example, 300 cm³), how should it be made so that the material would be used most economically? Here, we need to look at the ratio between the side height and the radius of the funnel mouth (Fig. 2.45).

Assuming a mouth radius r, a depth h, a generating line length (side height) l, a side surface area S and a cubic volume $V = 300$ (uniform), with the center angle of the expanded fan shape as θ, we would have the following formula:

$$2\pi r = \theta l \tag{2.19}$$

$$l^2 = h^2 + r^2 \tag{2.20}$$

$$V = \frac{1}{3}\pi r^2 h = 300 \tag{2.21}$$

Additionally, taking cost into consideration, S, given as follows, needs to be minimized:

$$S = \frac{1}{2}l^2\theta = \pi r l \tag{2.22}$$

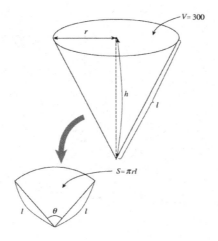

Fig. 2.45   Funnel design task

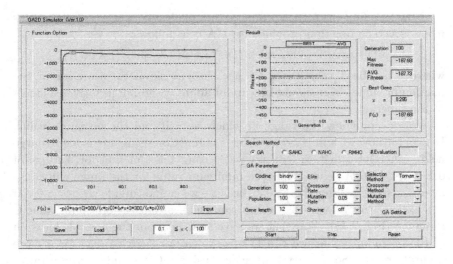

Fig. 2.46   Funnel design task solved by GA (1)

Taking l and r out of the above formula we have:

$$S = \pi \sqrt{\frac{3V}{\pi h} \cdot (h^2 + \frac{3V}{\pi h})} \tag{2.23}$$

$$= \pi \sqrt{\frac{3 \cdot 300}{h \cdot \pi} \cdot (h^2 + \frac{3 \cdot 300}{h \cdot \pi})} \tag{2.24}$$

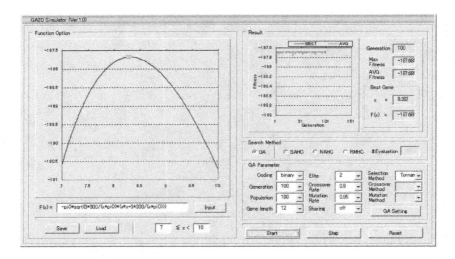

Fig. 2.47   Funnel design task solved by GA (2)

Now let's find the h that produces the smallest S. Let's try solving this using GA. The function provided for GA is as follows:

$$-pi() * sqrt(3 * 300/(x * pi())) * (x * x + 3 * 300/(x * pi())))$$

where x has been substituted for h. The GA simulator searches for the maximum value. You should be careful about assigning negative elements to the function.

We do not know the range in which we will find the optimum value. Hence, for now we will try optimizing the function using a reasonably large field. Therefore, first we will try optimizing this function for a range of $0.1 \leq x < 100$. Assigning 0 as the minimum value for the range will cause an error, so we will set this to 0.1 (because we cannot divide with $x = 0$). If you execute this a number of times, you will see that the optimum value is around 8 (Fig. 2.46). Now that we have an idea about the possible location of the optimum value, we can narrow down our search range for a more accurate result. So, let's try optimizing using a GA simulation in a range of $7 \leq x < 10$. This shows that the optimum value is around 8.3 (Fig. 2.47).

We see that the condition for providing the optimum value for this function is as follows:

$$\frac{l}{r} = \sqrt{3} \tag{2.25}$$

By repeatedly executing this using GA, we have obtained the optimum value that empirically satisfies this condition.

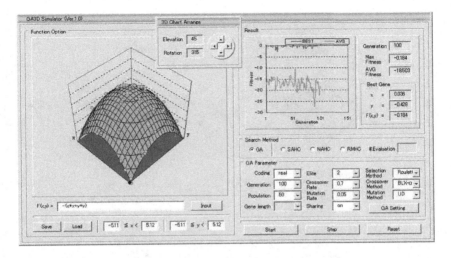

Fig. 2.48   GA-3D simulator

2.3   Two-dimensional landscape and its genotype

In this section, we will attempt to optimize two-variable functions. Try executing the GA-3D simulator (see Fig. 2.48). This simulator is operated in much the same way as the GA-2D simulator that we described in the previous sections. In the case of the GA-3D simulator, the search results are displayed in a three-dimensional space, making it easier to visually understand the optimization process. As we explained earlier, the window of the search space (fitness landscape) can be observed from various viewpoints. The process by which the GA individual traverses the landscape is shown in Fig. 2.49. In this example, the GA search is carried out without changing any parameters with respect to the following landscape:

$$F(x, y) = \frac{1}{5x^2 + 5y^2 + 0.7} \tag{2.26}$$

Fig. 2.49 shows individuals from (a) the initial generation (randomly generated), (b) the 2nd generation, (c) the 12th generation, (d) the 18th generation, and (e) the 50th generation.   We can see that with the progress of the search more and more individuals are approaching the peak. Fig. 2.49(f) shows the changes in fitness values (displayed for each generation) with the search progress, i.e. the fitness transition with generations.

With the GA-3D simulator, functions defined by the user can also be used for optimization. In addition, De Jong's standard functions are also

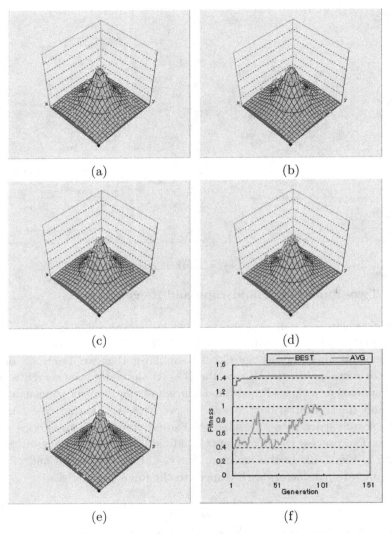

Fig. 2.49   GA search results (a) Initial generation (b) 2nd generation (c) 12th generation (d) 18th generation (e) 50th generation (f) Fitness transition with generations

defined for this simulator. Press the "Load" button. This should open a window like that shown in Fig. 2.50. Pre-defined functions can be loaded here.

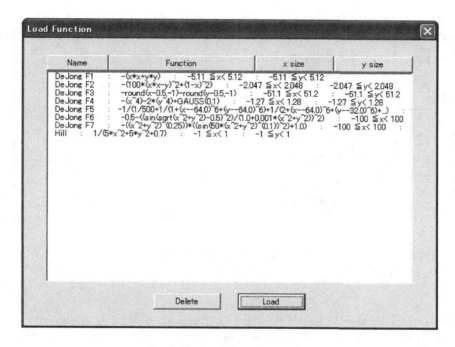

Fig. 2.50   Load Function window

De Jong's standard functions are benchmark tests for GAs, and are used for determining the minimum value. The definitions of these functions, along with the definition fields and optimum values, are shown in Table 2.4. The form of the functions and plots projected on the $x_1 - x_2$ plane are shown in Fig. 2.51. Benchmark functions $F4$ and $F5$ seem to be more difficult than the others. The $+\text{GAUSS}(0, 1)$ of $F4$ shows the addition of values from the normal distribution with average 0 and dispersion 1. In other words, noise is included in the various points in $F4$. With $F5$, there is a series of 5×5 valleys lined up in a grid alignment, but the valleys do not have a uniform depth. The trough of the valley at the lowermost left is the minimum value (≈ 1), while the local minimum values of the remaining troughs increase sequentially from left to right and from bottom to top, as 2, 3, etc. Once a dot leaves these troughs, it rapidly approaches the maximum value of 500. Note that the coordinates of a_{ij} are as follows:

```
int a[2][25] = {
    {-32, -16, 0, 16, 32, -32, -16, 0, 16, 32, -32, -16, 0, 16, 32,
     -32, -16, 0, 16, 32, -32, -16, 0 16, 32},
```

Table 2.4   De Jong's standard functions

Function Name	Definition	Domain	Optimum Value
$F1$	$\sum_{i=1}^{3} x_i^2$ Paraboloidal surface	$-5.11 \leq x_i < 5.12$	0
$F2$	$100(x_1^2 - x_2)^2 + (1 - x_1)^2$ Rosenbrock's saddle	$-2.047 \leq x_i < 2.048$	0
$F3$	$\sum_{i=1}^{5} \lfloor x_i \rfloor$ Step function	$-5.11 \leq x_i < 5.12$	30
$F4$	$\sum_{i=1}^{30} i x_i^4 + \text{GAUSS}(0, 1)$ Quartic function with noise	$-1.27 \leq x_i < 1.28$	0
$F5$	$\left[\frac{1}{500} + \sum_{j=1}^{25} \frac{1}{j + \sum_{i=1}^{2}(x_i - a_{ij})^6} \right]^{-1}$ Shekel's foxholes	$-65.535 \leq x_i < 65.536$	1

{-32, -32, -32, -32, -32, -16, -16, -16, -16, -16, 0, 0, 0, 0,
   0, 16, 16, 16, 16, 16, 32, 32, 32, 32, 32}
};

Originally the De Jong's standard functions are defined as minimization problems. In the GA-3D simulator, however, the sign is reversed and the functions are defined as maximization problems. Also, $F1$, $F2$ and $F3$ can have generalized definition with three or more variables (see Chapter 3), but here we reduced the number of dimensions in the functions to make those two-variable problems that are much simpler to work with.

With GTYPEs in binary coding, binary expressions will be used for x_1 and x_2, and these will be juxtaposed. Let's consider a case in which the gene length for the $F5$ function is 34. Be aware that the definition field of $F5$ is $-65.535 \leq x_i < 65.536$. We are using 17 bits for each variable, so the width of 1 bit will be $\delta x = (65.536 - (-65.536))/2^{17} = 0.001$. As a result, the following is -65.535:

00000000000000000

and conversion will be carried out in such a way that each 1-bit increase causes the PTYPE to increase by $\delta x = 0.001$.

Now, let's convert a GTYPE such as the following:

11011001111111011001111100111110011

to a PTYPE and determine the fitness value. To do this, first we have to make x_2 a decimal value. As a binary expression, x_2 is as follows:

00111100111110011

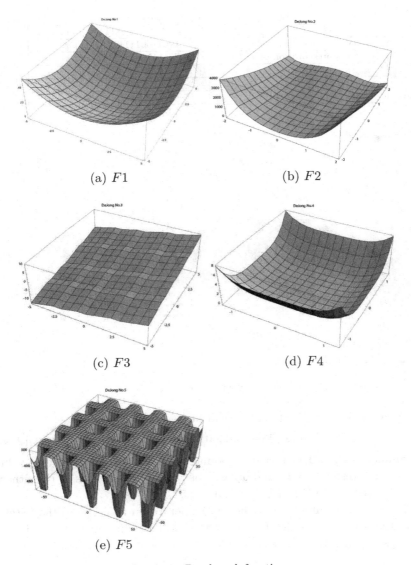

(a) $F1$

(b) $F2$

(c) $F3$

(d) $F4$

(e) $F5$

Fig. 2.51 Benchmark functions

The rightmost bit is the MSB. Thus, when this is converted to a decimal expression, it will be as follows:

$$2^{16} + 2^{15} + 2^{12} + 2^{11} + 2^{10} + 2^9 + 2^8 + 2^5 + 2^4 + 2^3 + 2^2$$
$$= 106300 \qquad (2.27)$$

Table 2.5 GTYPEs and PTYPEs

GTYPE	11011001111111011001111100111110011
Binary representation of x_1	11011001111111011
Binary representation of x_2	00111100111110011
PTYPE(x_1)	49.052
PTYPE (x_2)	40.765
Function value on $F5$	49.9715

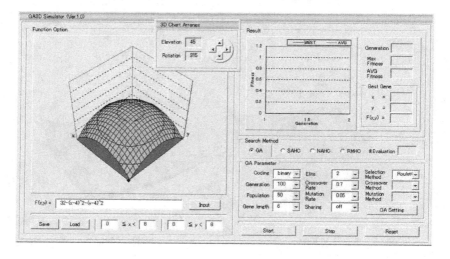

Fig. 2.52   GA-3D simulator for $F(x) = 32 - (x-4)^2 - (y-4)^2$

As a result, the PTYPE of x_2 will be:

$$-65.535 + 106300 \times \Delta x_i = 40.765 \qquad (2.28)$$

Similarly, the PTYPE of x_1 is found to be 49.052. The function value of $F5$ with respect to x_1 and x_2 will be 499.9715, and this is the fitness value for the above GTYPE (see Table 2.5).

Let's examine more closely how GA operates in response to the "Step" and "Report" commands. Execute the GA-3D simulator, with the initial settings as indicated below (Fig. 2.52):

- Function definition: $F(x) = 32 - (x-4)^2 - (y-4)^2$
- Definition field: $0 \le x < 8$, $0 \le y < 8$
- Search method: GA
- Population: 10
- Gene length: 6
- Coding: binary

- Elite: 2
- Sharing: off

Pressing the "Step" button opens the "Step Command" window in the 3D-simulator. Set the number of steps to any value and press "Start"/"Continue" to interrupt the operation. Next, press the "Report" button. This opens a window like that shown in Fig. 2.53, where you can see detailed information regarding the population. The genes of the parent and offspring generations are displayed, along with the maximum fitness values and average fitness values. For example, the display shown in Fig. 2.53 would be as follows:

Parent population:

No.	:	GTYPE	:	Raw Fitness
No. 1	:	[000110001001]	:	30.75
No. 2	:	[011010110110]	:	30.047
No. 3	:	[111000001100]	:	15.984
No. 4	:	[001011001011]	:	19.5
No. 5	:	[000011100111]	:	18.234
No. 6	:	[101000100000]	:	5.594
No. 7	:	[101000100111]	:	10.844
No. 8	:	[000011100000]	:	12.984
No. 9	:	[011011001000]	:	12.188
No. 10	:	[100110110110]	:	30.844

Offspring population:

No.	:	GTYPE	:	Raw Fitness	:	GA Operations	
No. 1	:	[100110110110]	:	30.844	:	Elite (10,-)	-
No. 2	:	[000110001001]	:	30.75	:	Elite (1,-)	-
No. 3	:	[111000001100]	:	15.984	:	Survival (3,-)	-
No. 4	:	[000011100000]	:	12.984	:	Survival (8,-)	-
No. 5	:	[111000001100]	:	15.984	:	Crossover (3,8)	11
No. 6	:	[000011100000]	:	12.984	:	Crossover (3,8)	11
No. 7	:	[000011100111]	:	18.234	:	Survival (5,-)	-
No. 8	:	[001011001011]	:	19.5	:	Survival (4,-)	-
No. 9	:	[011011100000]	:	9.422	:	Crossover (2,8)	4
No. 10	:	[000010110010]	:	25.359	:	Crossover & Mutation (2,8)	4 & 10

Remember that GTYPE was a 6-bit binary expression and the definition field was $0 \leq x < 8$ and also $0 \leq y < 8$. In other words, conversion will be carried out in such a way that each 1-bit increase in both the x and y coordinates causes the PTYPE to increase by $\Delta x = \Delta y = (8.0 - 0.0)/2^6 = 0.125$. For example, since the GTYPE of the No. 1 offspring is 000110001001, the GTYPE for x is the first six bits (000110) and the

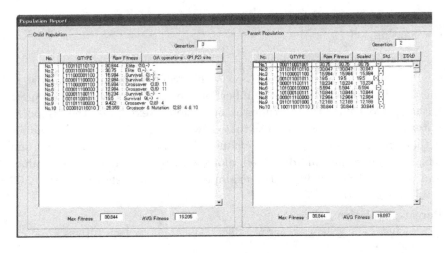

Fig. 2.53   Population Report window

GTYPE for y is the second six bits (001001). As a result, their PTYPE will be as follows, with the rightmost bit being the MSB:

$$x = 0.0 + \Delta_x \times (2^3 + 2^4) = 3.0 \tag{2.29}$$

$$y = 0.0 + \Delta_y \times (2^2 + 2^5) = 4.5 \tag{2.30}$$

Because of this, the fitness value will be as follows:

$$F(3.0, 4.5) = 30.75 \tag{2.31}$$

The No. 1 and No. 2 genes of the offspring are copies of the No. 10 and No. 1 genes of the parents.

Let's look at individuals generated by means of crossovers. For example, the No. 9 and No. 10 genes of the offspring are generated by crossovers of the No. 2 and No. 8 genes of the parents. The fourth loci is selected as the crossover point. Additionally, the results indicate that a mutation occurred at the tenth locus of the No. 10 gene of the offspring following the crossover:

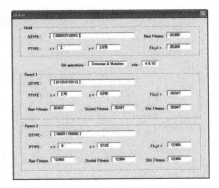

Fig. 2.54 Detailed information of gene codes

Fig. 2.55 Save Function window

No. 2 : 0110 10110110
No. 8 : 0000 11100000
↓ **Crossover** (crossover points: 4)
No. 9 : 0110 11100000
No. 10 : 0000 10110110
^

↓ **Mutation** (tenth locus)
No. 9 : 0110 11100000
No. 10 : 0000 10110010
^

where we entered a blank to indicate a crossover point, and a ^ to indicate a mutation point.

Also, the No. 3 gene of the offspring is a copy of the No. 3 gene of the parent. In this individual, the gene has been copied just as it is, without applying crossover or mutation.

Clicking on the gene of an offspring under "Population Report" displays a window showing detailed related information (Fig. 2.54).

Try observing the behavior of GA using various functions.

A "Save" option is available with the GA simulator. Pressing the "Save" button opens the window shown in Fig. 2.55. If a name is assigned at this point and the function definition is saved, then the function can be used afterwards using the "Load" command. Be aware that data such as the parameters of GA are not saved.

Fig. 2.56   Mayfly and its larva

2.4   Niche segregation

In biological ecology, there is a basic approach called "niche segregation" that involves the compartmentalization and segregation of species. In Japan, Kinji Imanishi, a prominent Japanese ecologist and anthropologist, advocated the theory of evolution based on this niche segregation approach, and is renowned for having had a significant impact on society. Imanishi collected mayflies (Fig. 2.56) around the Kamo River in Kyoto and noticed that they immediately segregated into different habitats in response to the flow velocity of the river (see [Imanishi and Asquith (2002)] for more detail).

This thinking led to the "sharing method", by which selection pressure is applied to the individuals in GA to segregate them. The expansion of this technique maintains the diversity of a population and makes the search of multi-peak functions not only possible, but effective as well.

Let's look at what advantages there are in terms of promoting species formation.

Take a look again at the following two functions, which we saw earlier:

$$F(x) = abs(sin(x)) \qquad \text{(See Fig. 2.5)}$$
$$F(x) = abs(sin(x) * x) \qquad \text{(See Fig. 2.6)}$$

Suppose we are executing a multi-peak fitness landscape defined by these two formulae. When doing this, if the first generation of individuals is uniformly random, we can expect that they will be distributed evenly over the definition field of the function. In other words, there will be about the same number of individuals near any of the hills. As the generations progress, the populations will climb these hills. Eventually, most of the individuals will collect near the top of one of the hills. This is called "loss of diversity".

However, there could also feasibly be a necessity for individuals to collect, to some extent, at each of the hills and form local populations. For

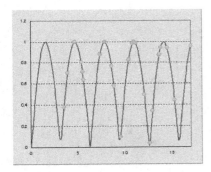
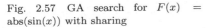

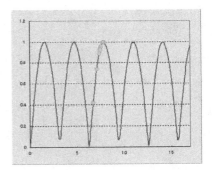

Fig. 2.57 GA search for $F(x) =$ abs(sin(x)) with sharing

Fig. 2.58 GA search for $F(x) =$ abs(sin(x)) without sharing

example, suppose that the hills are of different heights. With ordinary GAs, individuals will end up gathering on the highest hill. On the other hand, we might expect to assign local populations in proportion to the hill height; in other words, higher numbers of individuals would be assigned to higher hills, while a small number of individuals would still be assigned to lower hills.

In a case like this, species formation and sharing are effective approaches. In order to see the efficacy of the sharing function, let's activate it and run a GA search using the fitness value of a multi-peak function. First, when we execute GA with $F(x) =$ abs(sin(x)), we get a distribution after a few generations in which we have more or less the same number of individuals at each hill (Fig. 2.57). If we search using GA with the sharing function turned off, we find a larger number of cases in which the diversity has been lost and populations have collected at only one hill (Fig. 2.58). In a different example, let's try using $F(x) =$ abs(sin(x) × x) as the landscape. With a genetic algorithm that uses sharing, we will see local populations in which individuals are distributed according to the height of the hill (Fig. 2.59). With a genetic algorithm that does not use sharing, however, individuals will converge at the highest hill (Fig. 2.60).

Now we explain how sharing works. In this scheme, a penalty is imposed on the fitness function to prevent the occurrence of too many very similar genotypes. The sharing function has been proposed as a way of doing this. With this function, neighborhoods and the degree of sharing that will divide the fitness values among the individuals in a population are decided. A simple sharing function is shown in Fig. 2.61. In this figure, the horizontal axis shows the distance (proximity) between individuals, and the

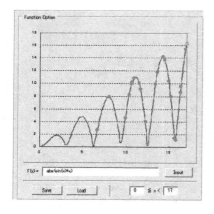

Fig. 2.59 GA search for $F(x) =$ abs$(\sin(x) * x)$ with sharing

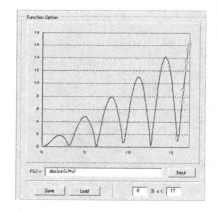

Fig. 2.60 GA search for $F(x) =$ abs$(\sin(x) * x)$ without sharing

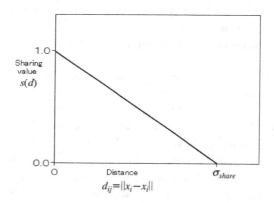

Fig. 2.61 Sharing function

vertical axis shows the sharing determined by the proximity. With a bit string, the distance between individuals is measured using the Hamming distance, while with real GA, the distance is measured using the Euclidean distance. The degree of sharing for any individual is decided by the sum of the sharing function values for all other individuals in the population. In other words, individuals who are close to (similar to) a certain individual require a large amount of sharing (close to 1), while those farther away (not similar) will require less (close to 0). The individual is extremely close to itself, so that the sharing function value will be 1. Once the total of the

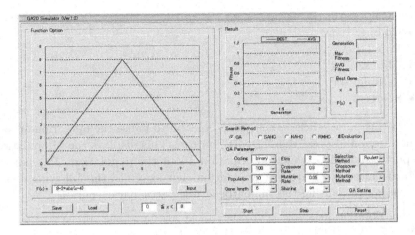

Fig. 2.62   GA-2D simulator with $F(x) = 8 - 2 * \text{abs}(x - 4)$

sharing functions required by all of the individuals has been determined this way, the fitness values ($f(x_i)$) of the individuals (i) are divided based on sharing. Here, the following formula will apply:

$$f_s(x_i) = \frac{f(x_i)}{\sum_{j=1}^{n} s(d(x_i, x_j))} \tag{2.32}$$

where $f_s(x_i)$ is the fitness value after sharing. The number of individuals is n, while s is the sharing function shown in the previous figure and $d(x_i, x_j)$ is the distance between x_i and x_j. Be aware that because $d(x_i, x_i)$ is 1, the denominator ($\sum_{j=1}^{n} s(d(x_i, x_j))$) will always be 1 or more. The smaller the denominator (the closer to 1), the less x_i will resemble another individual.

Based on what is described above, when a large number of individuals are in the same neighborhood, the total number of times that sharing takes place increases and the fitness value decreases. As a result, promotion of only certain species in the population will be discouraged.

Clicking "On" in the "Sharing" box (in window of Fig. 2.40) activates this function and corrects the fitness function. Note that the value of the x fragment (σ_{share}) of the sharing function is set for the SigmaShare parameter. This can be set by pressing the "GA Setting" button and setting the parameter in the "Sharing" panel of the displayed window.

Let's use the sharing function with the GA-2D simulator. We will use the following settings again (Fig. 2.62):

- Function definition: $F(x) = 8 - 2 * \text{abs}(x - 4)$
- Search Method: GA

- Gene length: 6
- Coding: binary
- Population: 10
- Elite: 2
- Sharing: on
- Share: 3

At this point, click on the "Step" button to pause the operation at any generation, and press the "Report" button. This displays the "Population Report", showing detailed information about the population. Pay particular attention to the parent population. For example, the following result was obtained pausing the simulator at one particular execution:

Parent population:

No.	:	GTYPE	:	Raw Fitness	:	Std.	$\sum S(d)$
No. 1	:	[111110]	:	7.75	:	2.325	[3.333]
No. 2	:	[111110]	:	7.75	:	2.325	[3.333]
No. 3	:	[111101]	:	4.25	:	1.159	[3.667]
No. 4	:	[111001]	:	6.25	:	1.442	[4.333]
No. 5	:	[010001]	:	7.5	:	3.214	[2.333]
No. 6	:	[111010]	:	5.75	:	1.568	[3.667]
No. 7	:	[010010]	:	4.5	:	1.929	[2.333]
No. 8	:	[010110]	:	6.5	:	2.786	[2.333]
No. 9	:	[111001]	:	6.25	:	1.442	[4.333]
No. 10	:	[111001]	:	6.25	:	1.442	[4.333]

The numeric values for these would be indicated as follows:

- Raw Fitness: The raw fitness value calculated from $F(x)$
- $\sum S(d)$: The sum of the sharing functions $\sum_{j=1}^{n} s(d(x_i, x_j))$
- Std.: The final fitness value, i.e. the Raw Fitness value divided by $\sum S(d)$

For example, the following would result for the No. 1 individual:

$$Std. = \frac{7.75}{3.333} = 2.325 \qquad (2.33)$$

The denominator of 3.333 would be calculated as follows. First, since $\sigma_{share} = 3$ when d is the Hamming distance, the sharing function would be as follows:

$$f(d) = \begin{cases} -\frac{1}{3}d + 1 & \text{; When } 0 \le d \le 3, \\ 0 & \text{; When otherwise} \end{cases} \qquad (2.34)$$

Thus, calculating the sharing function for the No. 1 individual would give us the result shown in Table 2.6. Consequently, the total would be 3.333.

Table 2.6 Sharing function values for the individual No. 1.

Individual No	GTYPE	Hamming distance	Sharing function value
No. 1	111110	0	1
No. 2	111110	0	1
No. 3	111101	2	$\frac{1}{3}$
No. 4	111001	3	0
No. 5	010001	5	0
No. 6	111010	1	$\frac{2}{3}$
No. 7	010010	3	0
No. 8	010110	2	$\frac{1}{3}$
No. 9	111001	3	0
No. 10	111001	3	0
Total			3.333

Comparing the "Std." and "Raw Fitness" values, we see that conversion is carried out in such a way that a larger number of similar individuals will produce a smaller fitness value. No. 1 and No. 2 were the best in terms of "Raw Fitness", but because both are effectively the same individual, the fitness value is subtracted following conversion. The best sharing results are produced for No. 5, which has a relatively good "Raw Fitness" and has only a small number of individuals that are similar to it.

The fitness values following the conversion for sharing scheme are used in the selection process and elite strategies. Because of this, the graph of the best fitness values (Best) will not increase monotonically even if the elite strategy is used. This is because the graph displays the "Raw Fitness" values.

2.5   Scaling

In the explanations up to now, we have been assuming that the fitness function returns a positive value. Although it is not likely with biological organisms, there are times when the fitness function may return negative values. In such cases, the fitness-proportionate strategy and sharing function cause problems. Given that, we can convert the fitness value to an appropriate positive value; a process known as "scaling".

In the simplest scaling method, the minimum value for the fitness function is subtracted from the "Raw Fitness" value. We can see that this will absolutely produce a positive fitness value following conversion. This technique is used in both GA-2D and GA-3D simulators.

The "Scaled" value of the parent population displayed in the "Population Report" shows fitness values that have undergone scaling (Fig. 2.63). Consequently, scaled values are used as the fitness values to which the sharing method described in the previous section has been applied.

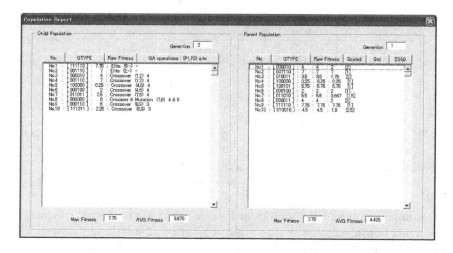

Fig. 2.63   Population Report window

More specifically, the minimum value of the fitness function must be known in advance with this method. For information on the scaling method please refer to [Goldberg (1989)].

2.6   How to solve a practical problem with GA

Let's try applying the GA-3D simulator to a real-life problem. Imagine a complex gear such as that shown in Fig. 2.64, consisting of a drive mechanism, a shaft, and a driven pulley. There are 12 teeth on the drive mechanism and 12 gear teeth in contact with the driven pulley. The objective is to determine the number of teeth on the two gears to meet the following conditions:

(1) The target gear ratio should be as close as possible to $1/6.931$.
(2) The size of the overall mechanism should be minimized.
(3) The minimum number of teeth on each of the gears should be 12, and the maximum number 60.

If the number of teeth on the two gears are x and y, respectively, as shown in the figure, these conditions can be written as follows:

(1) $f_1(x, y) = \{1/6.931 - 12 \times 12/x \times y\}^2 \rightarrow$ Minimize
(2) $f_2(x, y) \rightarrow$ Minimize

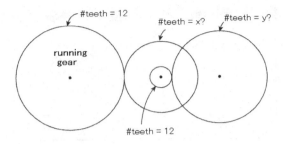

Fig. 2.64   Gear-system design task

(3) $12 \leq x, y < 60$

where $f_2(x, y)$ is a function that calculates the total number of teeth on the outer side, as indicated below:

$$f_2(x, y) = \begin{cases} 12 + x + y & 12 \leq x, \\ 12 + 12 + y & 12 > x, \end{cases} \tag{2.35}$$

where two target functions have been produced. Optimization for problems in which multiple target functions are optimized simultaneously is called "multi-objective optimization". A detailed description of the problem can be found in [Deb (2001)]. The simplest method of applying GA to problems like this is to use the weighted sum of multiple target functions in the fitness function. In this case, we may use the following:

$$\text{Fitness value} = -f_1(x, y) - r f_2(x, y) \tag{2.36}$$

To convert these minimization problems into a maximization problem, we negate both f_1 and f_2. r is the weight of f_2 (in relation to f_1). This makes it possible to search for an individual that would optimize f_1 and f_2 simultaneously, using GA.

Input the following using the "Input" menu and run the GA-3D simulator (see Fig. 2.65).

$$-((1/6.931 - 12 * 12/(x * y))^2) - \text{If}(12 > x, 12 + 12 + y, 12 + x + y) * 0.0001$$

An "If" statement is used here to judge the conditions. Also, r is set to 0.0001.

Executing this returns the following solution: $x = 29.625$, $y = 31.5$, and $F(x) = -0.007$ (see Fig. 2.66). Considering, however, that x and y are integer values, we see that the following provides the solution:

$$f_1(30, 31) = 1.13 \times 10^{-4} \tag{2.37}$$

$$f_2(30, 31) = 73 \tag{2.38}$$

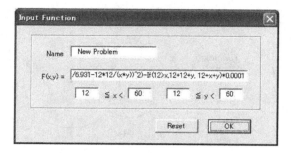

Fig. 2.65   Input Function window

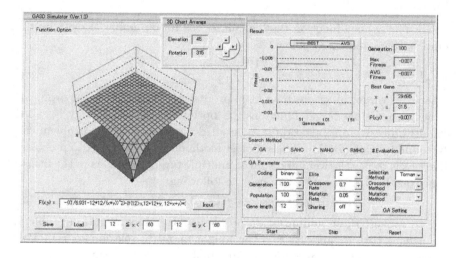

Fig. 2.66   GA search result for gear-system design task

In other words, the number of teeth on the two gears will be 30 and 31, respectively (i.e. $x = 31$ and $y = 30$).

Various researches have been conducted with respect to multi-objective optimization. Setting the weight (r value) appropriately is difficult, and recently, optimizing multiple target function values simultaneously as vectors (Pareto optimization) is considered particularly effective. For more information, see other reference documents e.g. [Deb (2001); Coello *et al.* (2007); Abraham *et al.* (2005)].

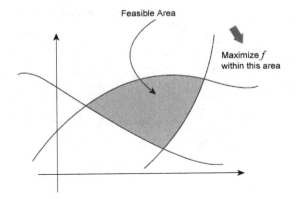

Fig. 2.67   Constraint problem

2.7   How to solve a constraint problem with GA

With optimization, there are numerous problems that involve restricting conditions, or constraints (see Fig. 2.67). In general, constraint problems can be written as follows:

$$f(x) \rightarrow \text{Maximize} \tag{2.39}$$

where x must satisfy the following constraints:

$$g_j(x) \leq 0 \quad (j = 1, \cdots, m) \tag{2.40}$$

$$h_k(x) = 0 \quad (k = 1, \cdots, l) \tag{2.41}$$

$$a \leq x < b \tag{2.42}$$

$f(x)$ is the target function, and $g_j(x)$ and $h_k(x)$ are the functions that impose the constraints.

When applying GA to problems like this, a fitness value like that shown below is determined in order to apply a penalty to genes that do not satisfy the constraints:

$$\text{Fitness value} = f(x) - r_1 \sum_{j=1}^{m} P_1(g_j(x))) - r_2 \sum_{k=1}^{l} P_2(h_k(x))) \tag{2.43}$$

where P_1 and P_2 will have a value of 0 if they fulfill the constraint, and otherwise, the degree to which the constraint is not met (a positive value) will be returned. Moreover, r_1 and r_2 are the weights (positive values) of the penalties. This reduces the fitness values of genes that do not satisfy the constraints. Eventually, individuals that satisfy the constraints will have

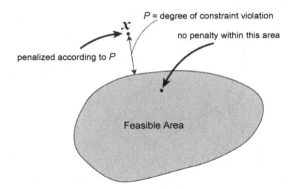

Fig. 2.68   Constraint and penalty

better fitness values and will be promoted to evolve. Naturally, the larger the fitness value, the better (see Fig. 2.68).

As an example, let's try solving the following minimization problem:

$$f(x) = max\{\sin(2x), \cos(x)\} + \frac{3}{10} \implies \text{Minimize} \qquad (2.44)$$

where x satisfies the following constraints:

$$g_1(x) = |\sin^3(2x) + \cos^3(x)| - \frac{2}{5} \leq 0 \qquad (2.45)$$

$$0 \leq x < 2\pi \qquad (2.46)$$

In this case, we will enter a fitness function like the one shown below in the "Input Function" window (see Fig. 2.69):

$$-\text{Max}(\sin(2*x), \cos(x)) - 3/10 + 10*\text{Min}(0, (2/5, -\text{abs}(\sin^3(2*x) + \cos^3(x))))$$

Because this is a minimization problem, we will make the fitness value function negative. Also, in the second term we calculate a penalty that will be 0 if $g_1(x) \leq 0$ and if not, will be $-g_1(x)$. The weight r_1 of the penalty is set as 10.

Input this formula and execute the GA-2D simulator (see Fig. 2.70). The solution obtained will be $x = 1.949$, $F(x) = 0.07$. Checking the constraints for x results in the following, which certainly satisfies the condition:

$$g_1(x) = |-0.37362| - \frac{2}{5} = -0.026383 \leq 0 \qquad (2.47)$$

Additionally, the following is obtained as the value of the target function:

$$f(x) = -0.07 \qquad (2.48)$$

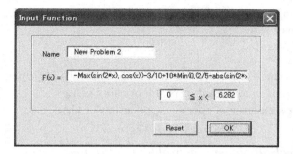

Fig. 2.69 Input Function window

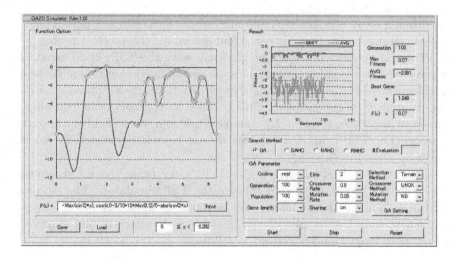

Fig. 2.70 Search result for a constraint problem

2.8 How to solve a combinatorial problem with GA

GAs are a general problem-solving tool, so they can be applied to a wide variety of problems. However, when applying GA, the user must decide the following items:

- What type of expression will be used for GTYPE and PTYPE, and how will they be converted?
- How will fitness values be calculated?
- How will the various types of parameters be set? For instance:
  - Number of populations

- Maximum number of generations
- Crossover rate
- Mutation rate

As long as these items are designed appropriately, in principle, it should be possible to solve any kind of problem using GA.

Below, let's examine a specific application of GA.

2.8.1 *Traveling salesman problem (TSP)*

In TSP (traveling salesman problem), there are a number of cities located in different places on a map, and the aim is to look at all of the paths that go through every city exactly once and return to the starting point (this is called a Hamiltonian cycle or path) and determine the shortest route.

There is no efficient algorithm that will solve the TSP; in all cases, an exhaustive investigation is required in order to find the optimum solution. Consequently, as the number (N) of cities grows, we see a dramatic leap in the complexity of the problem. This is called a "combinatorial explosion", and is an important issue (an NP-complete problem) in the field of computer science. The TSP is applied in areas such as commodity distribution cost and LSI pattern technology.

To better understand this problem, let's try using the Excel simulator (Fig. 2.71). Go ahead and execute the TSP simulator. The detailed information about this simulator can be found in Appendix A.3.

When using GA to solve the TSP, the fitness value will be the inverse of the path length, and is defined as follows:

$$Fitness(\text{PTYPE}) = \frac{1}{Length(\text{PTYPE})} \qquad (2.49)$$

Length (PTYPE) is the length of the PTYPE path. As a result, this will be a positive number, and the larger the number, the better.

Now consider how we can solve the TSP using GA. To do this, we will design a GTYPE/PTYPE for this particular problem. If the path is defined as the GTYPE just as it is, we will end up producing points other than the path as a result of crossovers. For example, suppose that we have a route that includes five cities: *a*, *b*, *c*, *d* and *e*. We will assign numbers to these, calling them 1, 2, 3, 4 and 5. Let's pick out the following two paths and examine them.

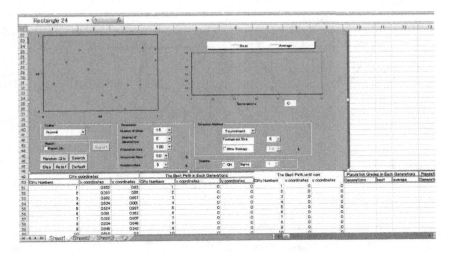

Fig. 2.71   TSP simulator

Name	GTYPE	PTYPE
P1	13542	$a \to c \to e \to d \to b \to a$
P2	12354	$a \to b \to c \to e \to d \to a$

Suppose that a crossover occurs between the second and the third cities. This will produce the following:

Name	GTYPE	PTYPE
C1	12542	$a \to b \to e \to d \to b \to a$
C2	13354	$a \to c \to c \to e \to d \to a$

This does not solve the TSP, i.e. these GTYPEs are not even feasible candidates, because C_1 and C_2 both visit the same city ($2 = b$ and $3 = c$) more than once. This type of GTYPE (genetic codes) is called a "lethal gene". To do an effective search, we need to suppress the occurrence of these lethal genes.

The following shows one way to design a GTYPE for a TSP. First, we assign a sequence $1, 2, 3, 4, 5$ to the cities to be visited, which are a, b, c, d, e. This is a relative sequence in the following sense. Here, the GTYPE of the path called *acedb* (PTYPE) is configured as follows: City "a" is the first city in the above sequence, so we write this as "1". Then we delete "a" from this sequence, leaving *bcde* in the sequence of 1234. In this new

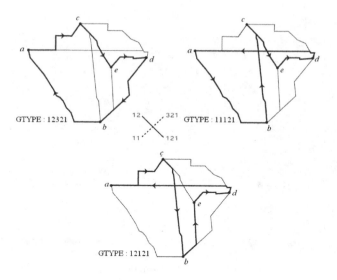

Fig. 2.72   TSP crossover example

sequence, "c" is the second city after "a", so we write "2". We continue in the same way until the GTYPE for *acedb* is found to be 12321.

City	Sequence	Genetic code
a	$abcde \to 12345$	1
c	$bcde \to 1234$	2
e	$bde \to 123$	3
d	$bd \to 12$	2
b	$b \to 1$	1

Using the same method, the GTYPE for the path *abced* will be 11121. Reversing the procedure makes it easy to determine the path from one city to another (PTYPE) from the GTYPE expression. What is important about this GTYPE expression is that the GTYPE obtained as a result of normal crossovers indicates the path from one city to the next (Hamiltonian path), i.e. it never becomes a lethal gene. For example, let's consider the crossover we saw earlier (Fig. 2.72):

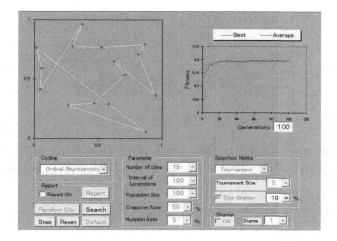

Fig. 2.73   Results of TSP simulation

Name	GTYPE	PTYPE
P1	12321	$a \to c \to e \to d \to b \to a$
P2	11121	$a \to b \to c \to e \to d \to a$
C1	12121	$a \to c \to b \to e \to d \to a$
C2	11321	$a \to b \to e \to d \to c \to a$

Thus, the GTYPE resulting from the crossover now expresses the path from one city to the next as well. This GTYPE expression is called an "ordinal representation".

Mutations and crossovers are used as GA operators for an ordinal representation. These are basically the same as the operators explained in Section 2.2. However, since the GTYPE is expressed as an ordinary character string, rather than a binary expression (a string comprising 0s and 1s), we need to select the gene that will mutate from an appropriate character set. For example, let's consider the GTYPE of the above P1 (12321). Generally, with ordinal representations, characters possible for the i-th gene, when the number of cities is N, will be $1, 2, 3, \cdots N-i+1$. As a result, if the first gene (1) mutates in the above GTYPE, possible characters following the mutation will be 2, 3, 4 and 5. With the No. 2 gene (2), they will be 1, 3 and 4. Fig. 2.73 shows the experimental result of the TSP simulator for 15 cities. See Appendix A.3 for more detail.

Fig. 2.74   GA parameters setting

Let's examine the operation of GA in greater detail using the "Report" command of the TSP simulator. Use the following initial settings (Fig. 2.74):

- Number of Cities: 10
- Report ON: Check this
- Interval of Generations: 5
- Coding: Ordinal Representation
- Sharing: Clear this

These settings enable better observation of how GA behaves. If the number of cities was changed, execute the "Random City" command.

At this point, press the "Search" button. This executes processing of five generations and then stops. Next, press the "Report" button. This opens the "Population Report" window (Fig. 2.75), showing detailed information about the populations. The genes of the parent and offspring generations are displayed, along with the maximum fitness values and average fitness values. The genetic information is as follows:

- No.: Gene number
- GTYPE: Genotype
- Fitness: Fitness value
- GA operations: How the offspring genes were generated (for offspring genes)
    - Elite: The genes were copied exactly as they were, as elite individuals (the number of the parent is displayed)
    - X (Crossover): The genes were generated by means of one-point crossover (the number of two parent individuals and crossover points are displayed)
    - Mu (Mutation): The genes were generated as a result of mutation (the number of the parent individual and the mutation point are displayed)

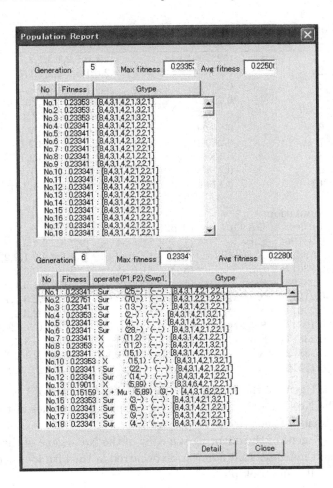

Fig. 2.75   Population Report window

- Sur (Survival): The genes are not elite, but were copied just as they were, without applying either crossovers or mutations (the number of the parent is displayed)

For example, assuming that the number of cities is 10 and the coding method is the ordinal representation, one execution of the TSP simulator produced the following:

Parent population:

No.	:	Fitness	:	GTYPE
No. 1	:	0.23706	:	[9,7,6,7,2,1,3,1,2,1]
No. 2	:	0.23674	:	[2,5,1,4,1,2,3,2,1,1]
No. 3	:	0.23674	:	[2,5,1,4,1,2,3,2,1,1]
No. 4	:	0.20897	:	[10,1,2,3,2,5,1,2,2,1]
No. 5	:	0.20897	:	[10,1,2,3,2,5,1,2,2,1]
No. 6	:	0.20286	:	[7,7,6,7,2,2,3,3,2,1]
No. 7	:	0.20022	:	[6,4,6,6,4,3,2,3,2,1]
No. 8	:	0.19595	:	[7,2,4,2,1,2,2,3,2,1]
No. 9	:	0.17859	:	[2,9,7,6,4,4,1,2,1,1]
No. 10	:	0.17485	:	[10,5,5,4,5,5,4,4,2,1]

Offspring population:

No.	:	Fitness	:	GA Op	:	p1,p2	:	sites	:	GTYPE
No. 1	:	0.23706	:	Elite	:	(1,-)	:	(-,-)	:	[9,7,6,7,2,1,3,1,2,1]
No. 2	:	0.19826	:	X + Mu	:	(3,4)	:	(8,-)	:	[2,1,1,4,2,2,1,2,2,1]
No. 3	:	0.23674	:	Sur	:	(3,-)	:	(-,-)	:	[2,5,1,4,1,2,3,2,1,1]
No. 4	:	0.23706	:	Sur	:	(1,-)	:	(-,-)	:	[9,7,6,7,2,1,3,1,2,1]
No. 5	:	0.21272	:	X + Mu	:	(2,3)	:	(2,-)	:	[2,6,1,4,1,2,3,2,1,1]
No. 6	:	0.23674	:	X	:	(2,3)	:	(-,-)	:	[2,5,1,4,1,2,3,2,1,1]
No. 7	:	0.19343	:	Sur+Mu	:	(4,-)	:	(5,-)	:	[10,1,2,3,6,5,1,2,2,1]
No. 8	:	0.23674	:	Sur+Mu	:	(2,-)	:	(5,-)	:	[2,5,1,4,1,2,3,2,1,1]
No. 9	:	0.18872	:	X	:	(5,3)	:	(-,-)	:	[2,1,1,4,1,2,1,2,1,1]
No. 10	:	0.15515	:	X	:	(5,3)	:	(-,-)	:	[10,5,2,3,2,5,3,2,2,1]

The No. 1 gene of the offspring is an elite copy of the No. 1 gene of the parent. The No. 3 and No. 4 genes of the offspring are copies of the No. 3 and No. 1 genes of the parent, respectively.

The No. 7 gene of the offspring is a copy of the No. 4 gene of the parent, but the result indicates that a mutation occurred at the fifth locus. In other words, the following took place:

No. 4   :   10, 1, 2, 3, 2, 5, 1, 2, 2, 1

↓ Mutation

No. 7   :   10, 1, 2, 3, 6, 5, 1, 2, 2, 1

where ^ was inserted to indicate the mutation point.

The No. 9 and No. 10 genes of the offspring were generated by means of crossover of the No. 5 and No. 3 genes of the parent. Uniform crossovers were used. Information about the crossover points is noted on the Excel

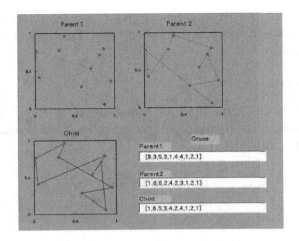

Fig. 2.76 PTYPE display

spreadsheet. In this case, we have the following:

$$0, 1, 0, 0, 0, 0, 1, 1, 0, 0$$

and the No. 2, No. 7, and No. 8 loci will be exchanged.

The result will look like this:

No. 5   : 10, 1, 2, 3, 2, 5, 1, 2, 2, 1
No. 3   : 2,   5, 1, 4, 1, 2, 3, 2, 1, 1
       ↓ **Crossover**
No. 10   : 10, 5, 2, 3, 2, 5, 3, 2, 2, 1
No. 9   : 2, 1, 1, 4, 1, 2, 1, 2, 1, 1

where the part to be exchanged is represented by ˆ.

The No. 5 gene of the offspring is generated by means of a crossover and mutation of the parent gene.

Clicking on a gene of the offspring under "Population Report" displays a window showing detailed information about the relationship between the GTYPE and PTYPE, as well as the behavior of the GA operators. The window can be opened at this point to see the PTYPEs of the parent and offspring on the map (Fig. 2.76). Looking at this, you can have a better idea about how the PTYPE changes as a result of crossovers and mutations. Pay particular attention to the following points:

- Mutations slightly change the structure of the parent.
- Crossovers carry over the partial structure of the parent.

Up to this point, we've been talking about ordinal representations. The following methods, however, are also proposed with respect to the traveling salesman problem.

Coding method

The sequence in which the cities are visited is used as the gene, just as it is. For instance, if the problem involves ten cities, the following would be the genotype (a candidate solution):

$$10\ 1\ 2\ 5\ 4\ 9\ 7\ 8\ 6\ 3$$

Crossover method

This method uses partially matched crossovers, or PMXs. This is an expanded version of the two-point crossover. The partial structure being crossovered is maintained, but other structures are changed so as to avoid producing lethal genes. It can be explained as follows: Suppose the arrays of the two genotypes are $A[1], A[2], \cdots A[n]$ and $B[1], B[2], \cdots B[n]$ where n is the gene length. Then the PMX crossover is performed by following the procedure given below:

Step 1 Two crossover points i and j ($1 \leq i \leq j \leq n$) are randomly selected. In **Step 4**, the section $A[i], A[i+1], \cdots A[j]$ is replaced by the section $B[i], B[i+1], \cdots B[j]$.

Step 2 When there are common elements in $\{A[1], A[2], \cdots A[i-1], A[j+1], \cdots A[n]\}$ and $\{B[i], B[i+1], \cdots B[j]\}$, let them be $A[k]$ and $B[m]$. At this point, the value of $A[k]$ will be changed to that of $A[m]$.

Step 3 When there are common elements in $\{B[1], B[2], \cdots B[i-1], B[j+1], \cdots B[n]\}$ and $\{A[i], A[i+1], \cdots A[j]\}$, let them be $B[k]$ and $A[m]$. At this point, the value of $B[k]$ will be changed to that of $B[m]$.

Step 4 The segment $A[i], A[i+1], \cdots A[j]$ will be replaced by the segment $B[i], B[i+1], \cdots B[j]$.

For example, let's consider the following two paths (GTYPEs):

P1 3 4 9 10 6 8 5 1 7 2
P2 2 10 6 5 1 7 4 9 8 3

The PMX execution example would be as described below:

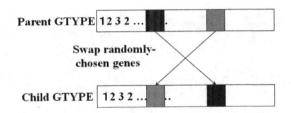

Fig. 2.77 Swap mutation

Step 1 Let's suppose that $i = 5$, $j = 7$ have been selected as the crossover points. In other words, the $A[5] = 6$, $A[6] = 8$ and $A[7] = 5$ of **P1** would be replaced by the $B[5] = 1$, $B[6] = 7$ and $B[7] = 4$ of **P2**.

Step 2 Since we now have $A[8] = B[5] = 1$, the value of $A[8]$ will be replaced by that of $A[5]$, or 6. Similarly, $A[9]$ and $A[2]$ will be replaced by $A[6]$ and $A[7]$, respectively. Replacing them all, **P1** will be as follows:

P1′ 3 5 9 10 6 8 5 6 8 2

Step 3 Since we now have $B[3] = A[5] = 6$, the value of $B[3]$ will be replaced by that of $B[5]$, or 1. Similarly, $B[9]$ and $B[4]$ will be replaced by $B[6]$ and $B[7]$, respectively. Replacing them all, **P2** will be as follows:

P2′ 2 10 1 4 1 7 4 9 7 3

Step 4 The segment $A[5] = 6$, $A[6] = 8$, $A[7] = 5$ will be exchanged with $B[5] = 1$, $B[6] = 7$, $B[7] = 4$. The GTYPE of the offspring generated as a result will be:

C1 3 5 9 10 1 7 4 6 8 2
C2 2 10 1 4 6 8 5 9 7 3

Check for yourself to see that no lethal genes are produced using this method.

Mutation method

In swap mutation (Fig. 2.77) the order of two randomly selected cities are switched. In particular, a greedy swap mutation method is used with the simulator, in which the swap mutation is carried out only if it results in a better tour.

Let's use the "Report" command of the TSP simulator to check the details of the PMX operation (see Appendix A.3 for details). As with ordinal representation, pressing the "Report" button opens a window similar to that shown in Fig. 2.78 and Fig. 2.79. Detailed information about the

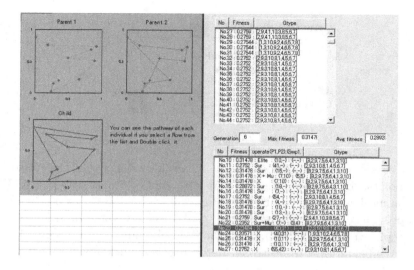

Fig. 2.78   Report Command (Crossover)

gene generation is displayed here. Also, clicking on the gene of an offspring shows the relationship between the PTYPE and GTYPE. Generally, the PMX method is known to produce better outcomes than the ordinal representation; the reason being that with ordinal representation, the useful partial structure that was generated in the previous generations may be destroyed by a crossover. Try setting various maps and parameters, and verify this empirically.

2.8.2   *Job shop scheduling problem (JSSP)*

In this section, we will try applying GA to a scheduling problem, as an example of a different type of application. Scheduling is needed in many everyday situations. Moreover, putting together an efficient schedule is a critical issue for businesses. To cite just a few examples:

- Schedules for nursing shifts (night shifts, day shifts, days off)
- Schedules for airline crews
- Creating timetables (educators and classrooms, student schedule management)

These and other tasks are issues that require an optimum schedule based on the appropriate constraints (avoiding overtime, overbooking, etc.). In

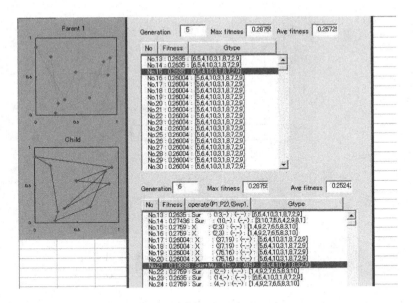

Fig. 2.79 Report Command (Mutation)

Table 2.7 Required time

Machine Job	M_1	M_2
A	3	8
B	6	4
C	2	9

general, these types of problems are extremely difficult to solve, and probabilistic search methods such as GAs and heuristics are frequently utilized to find solutions.

One classic scheduling problem is the job shop scheduling problem (JSSP). Suppose there are three jobs to be done, called A, B and C. If all of the jobs are to be done on two machines, M_1 and M_2, with M_1 being used first and subsequently M_2. In what order should the jobs be done on the machines to minimize the total processing time? The times required by jobs A, B, and C on machines M_1 and M_2 are as shown in Table 2.7.

If we try listing the possible sequences for the three jobs, A, B and C, we can see that the result would be $3! = 6$ possibilities, as shown below.

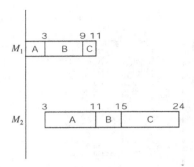

Fig. 2.80   Gantt chart example

$$A \to B \to C \quad A \to C \to B \quad B \to A \to C$$
$$B \to C \to A \quad C \to A \to B \quad C \to B \to A$$

Thus, if we run the jobs in the order of $A \to B \to C$, the total time required would be 24 hours, as shown in Fig. 2.80. The figure should be viewed as follows: Since processing is being done in the order of $A \to B \to C$, the first step would be to run Job A on Machine M_1. At the scale marking 3 on the M_1 time axis, Job A would be switched to M_2, and at the same time, Job B would begin running on M_1. We simply need to continue this process to find out the times at which the jobs would start and end sequentially. However, if execution ends on M_1 but a different job is still being run on M_2, which is in an earlier process, we would have to wait until that job finishes. A diagram such as this is called a Gantt chart. For the current problem, we would try drawing up six Gantt charts and see which one had the shortest total required time. If you actually tried doing a procedure such as this, you would see that executing the jobs in the order of $C \to A \to B$ or $C \to B \to A$ would achieve the shortest total required time (23 hours).

In a simple situation such as the above, we can enumerate all possible cases and arrive at the optimum solution. This is called the "complete enumeration method". As the number of jobs and/or machines increases, however, it becomes impossible to solve the problem using this method. With m machines and n jobs, the processing combinations would be $(n!)^m$ possibilities. For example, even if we have $n = 5$ and $m = 5$, the number of combinations would be $(5!)^5 \approx 25$ billion, making it impossible to search all

Table 2.8   Required times for JSSP instance

Job	Task (machine number, processing time)			
J0	$(M_0,5)$	$(M_1,7)$	$(M_2,3)$	$(M_3,9)$
J1	$(M_3,9)$	$(M_0,4)$	$(M_2,6)$	$(M_1,5)$
J2	$(M_1,3)$	$(M_3,2)$	$(M_2,5)$	$(M_0,1)$

of the combinations using a computer. This is known as a "combinatorial explosion".

For this reason, we would normally use heuristics and decide an appropriate sequence for executing the processing. This is called the "dispatching rule" (or "work allocation rule"). The following heuristics are frequently used:

- RANDOM: Jobs are selected at random.
- SPT (shortest processing time): The job with the shortest processing time is selected. This tends to reduce average delays, but it can also result in jobs being significantly delayed.
- EDD (earliest due date): The job with the earliest deadline is selected. This is effective in avoiding delays.
- SLACK: The job with the least slack time (= due time - current time - total remaining processing time) is selected. This is effective in avoiding delays.
- FIFO (first in first out): The first job that came in is selected. Results are more uniform than those from the RANDOM method.

The aim here is to obtain a solution that may not be ideal but is at least workable to some extent (a sub-optimal solution) in a reasonable amount of time.

Problems in which n jobs would be processed on m machines in order to minimize the total required time are called job shop scheduling problems (JSSP). In the above example (Table 2.7), the processing sequence for all of the jobs had already been determined as moving from M_1 to M_2, but generally, the processing order is different depending on the job.

Summarizing the above, the following constraints apply to the JSSP:

(1) Each job is only processed on one machine at a time.
(2) Each machine only processes one job at a time.
(3) The machine processing order and work time for each job are provided.

First, run the JSSP simulator. This should display an execution window similar to that shown in Fig. 2.81. This is a simulator that solves JSSP using GA.

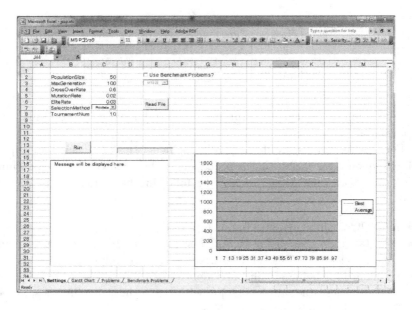

Fig. 2.81   JSSP simulator

You can note problems that you have defined yourself in the file and use the "Read File" command to read them. Files are ordinary text files and are added to a spreadsheet as shown in the "Problems" spreadsheet (see Fig. A.11). For example, the following notation defines a problem with three jobs × four machines:

$$
\begin{array}{cccccccc}
0 & 5 & 1 & 7 & 2 & 3 & 3 & 9 \\
3 & 9 & 0 & 4 & 2 & 6 & 1 & 5 \\
1 & 3 & 3 & 2 & 2 & 5 & 0 & 1 \\
\end{array}
$$

Job $J0$, which is noted on the first line, is done on machine M_0 and is carried out for a time 5, and it then moves to M_1, M_2, and then M_3. The same applies to $J1$ on the second line and $J2$ on the third line. The constraints for this JSSP are noted in Table 2.8.

Putting a checkmark on the "Use Benchmark Problem" checkbox makes it possible to use the $MT6 \times 6$, $MT10 \times 10$ and $MT20 \times 5$ problems. The problems are defined on the "Benchmark Problem" sheet. Here, "$MTi \times j$" indicates the JSSP of i jobs × j machines. These are famous benchmark tests put forth by [Muth and Thompson (1963)]. Of these problems, $MT10 \times 10$ is extremely difficult, and a solution found in 1988 showed that

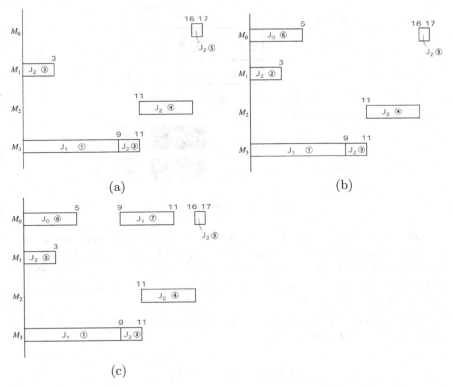

Fig. 2.82   Translation from GTYPE into PTYPE

the required time is 930 [Adams *et al.* (1988)]. That number was proven the following year to be the optimum solution [Carlier and Pinson (1989)]. It has also been found that the optimum solution for $MT6 \times 6$ is 55 and that for $MT20 \times 5$ is 1165 [Carlier and Pinson (1989)]. When these problems are used and the optimum solution is found, that information is displayed at the lower left of the screen.

Try using GA with various parameters and problems. How good are GAs for putting together schedules?

Now let's look at how GAs work. For example, let's take a JSSP with three jobs and four machines, like that shown in Table 2.8. Each cell of the table shows the machine used in the job and the required work times. Each row of the table shows the sequential order in which the machines are to be used, starting from the left.

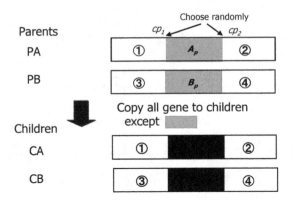

Fig. 2.83   Crossover for JSSP

Let's say that the GTYPE is a listing of the job numbers, to indicate which job should be subsequently placed on the Gantt chart. As a result, on the chromosome, the same job number will come up only as many times as the number of machines needed to process that job. This expression is called "sequential gene coding".

For example, let's consider a gene like the following when the JSSP shown in Table 2.8 is provided:

$$1\ 2\ 2\ 2\ 2\ 0\ 1\ 0\ 1\ 1\ 0\ 0$$

Note that the gene length will be the number of jobs multiplied by the number of machines. First, the machines and jobs are assigned on the Gantt chart as follows: The initial processing for job $J1$ (M_3) is carried out. Next, the initial processing for $J2$ (M_1) is done, followed by the second processing for $J2$ (M_3). In this manner, the Gantt chart shown in Fig. 2.82(a) is obtained when the assignment of the job at the fifth locus is finished. Now we consider the assignment of the job at the sixth locus ($J0$, M_0). The processing time is 5. Thus, you can assign this before the processing of $J2$ (immediately after starting) (Fig. 2.82(b)). The job at the seventh locus ($J1$, M_0), for which the processing time is 7, can be placed between $J0$ and $J2$ (Fig. 2.82(c)). In this way, when the jobs of all of the loci have been assigned, we will obtain the PTYPE from the GTYPE.

As with the TSP, swap mutation is used for the mutation. This switches the numbers of two jobs selected at random (see Fig. 2.77). Attention is required regarding crossover design, because we need to avoid producing lethal genes. Here, the following processing is carried out:

(1) The parent chromosomes PA and PB are selected (Fig. 2.83).

(2) Two crossover points, cp_1 and cp_2, are determined, and the segment between the cp_1 and cp_2 of each parent chromosome is taken as a partial chromosome A_p and B_p.

(3) Except A_p and B_p, all other corresponding genes are copied to the offspring chromosomes CA and CB (this corresponds to ① ~ ④).

(4) The partial chromosomes A_c and B_c of the offspring are configured from A_p and B_p in accordance with the following steps:

(a) Identical genes found in A_p and B_p are marked.

(b) The locations of marked genes are saved and transcribed to partial chromosomes of the offspring.

(c) For the remaining genes, the sequence from the same parent is saved and transcribed.

This sequence of steps makes it possible to avoid the production of lethal genes. An example of JSSP crossover is shown as follows:

Step 1: Mark * on the same gene values.

```
GTYPE1:  1  7  3  3   1   5   4
         *  *  * x1  x2  x3   *
GTYPE2:  2  7  3  1   4   7   6
        y1  *  *  *   *  y2  y3
```

Step 2: Move marked genes to children's GTYPE's, keeping them in the same positions.

```
GTYPE1:  1  7  3  3   1   5   4
         *  *  * x1  x2  x3   *
GTYPE2:  2  7  3  1   4   7   6
        y1  *  *  *   *  y2  y3
```

$$\Downarrow$$

```
GTYPE1': -  7  3  1  4  -  -

GTYPE2': 1  7  3  -  -  -  4
```

Step 3: Move the rest of genes.

```
GTYPE1': 3  7  3  1   4   1   5
        x1  *  *  *   *  x2  x3
GTYPE2': 1  7  3  2   7   6   4
         *  *  * y1  y2  y3   *
```

A number of other genotypes have also been proposed with respect to the JSSP (see [Mattfeld (1996)] for details).

Chapter 3

Real-valued GA and its Variants

3.1 Real-valued GA

Real-valued GAs are genetic algorithms that use real numbers (floating point numbers) as the genotype. They are known to be more efficient than binary expressions or gray expressions when optimizing real functions. The idea behind real-valued GA is simple: Generally, the solution of an optimization problem (the real function $f(x_1, x_2, \cdots x_n)$ of n variables) is encoded as a real vector as follows:

$$x_1, x_2, \cdots, x_n \tag{3.1}$$

In other words, a string of n real values just as they are, without modification, becomes a genotype. With real GA, special means are necessary to carry out crossover and mutation.

3.1.1 *Mutations in real-valued GAs*

The most straightforward way to mutate a real-valued GA individual is as follows. First, a coordinate (x_i) is selected at random that will undergo mutation with respect to a parent P. Next, x_i is mutated to a random value using the UD or ND methods explained below. When doing this, however, proper care should be taken to preserve the definition field of x_i.

3.1.1.1 *Uniform distribution (UD)*

Mutations are carried out by means of uniform random numbers. The procedure is as follows: Suppose the definition field of a selected gene is $[X_{MIN}, X_{MAX}]$, and the gene value of the selected coordinate is x_i.

- First, the direction (positive or negative) is selected with a probability of $1/2$.
- If the direction is positive, the offspring are selected in a uniformly random manner from a space $[x_i, min(x_i + M, X_{MAX})]$.
- If the direction is negative, the offspring are selected in a uniformly random manner from a space $[max(X_{MIN}, x_i - M), x_i]$.

Here M is a user-defined mutation size.

3.1.1.2 *Normal distribution (ND)*

The mutation is carried out by means of a normal distribution. The average value of the normal distribution is x_i, i.e. the gene value of the selected coordinate. The standard deviation is SD^2 which is defined by users. Generated individuals that exceed the definition field are adjusted to fit within the designated range.

3.1.2 **Crossovers in real-valued GAs**

In real valued GA, crossover is the fundamental operator for producing new candidate individuals. Therefore, several crossover operators have been proposed for real-valued GA, for example, the blend crossover (BLX-α) [Eshelman and Schaffer (1993)], the simulated binary crossover (SBX)[Deb and Agrawal (1995)], the unimodal normal distribution crossover (UNDX)[Ono and Kobayashi (1997)], the simplex crossover (SPX)[Tsutsui *et al.* (1999)], the parent centric crossover (PCX)[Deb *et al.* (2002)], etc. The BLX-α and UNDX operators, which are included in simulators, are explained below.

3.1.2.1 *BLX-α*

Let's take two parent-individual coordinates, a and b at index i. Then, the coordinate i of the offspring is decided in a uniformly random manner from a space $[A, B]$. A and B values are defined as follows:

$$A = \min(a, b) - \alpha d,$$
$$B = \max(a, b) + \alpha d,$$
$$d = |a - b|,$$

where α is a parameter defined by the user.

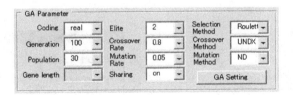

Fig. 3.1   Parameters for real-valued GA

3.1.2.2   *UNDX*

Ono and Kobayashi proposed the unimodal normal distribution crossover (UNDX) for real-valued GA [Ono and Kobayashi (1997)].   Let a and b be the i coordinates of two parent individuals.   Calculate the midpoint $m = (a + b)/2$ and the difference $d = (a - b)$. The offspring c is generated at this point according to the following formula:

$$c = m + \xi d,$$
$$\xi \sim N(0, \sigma^2),$$

where $N(0, \sigma^2)$ indicates a normal distribution with mean 0 and variance σ^2. In the simulator, σ is set as the standard deviation (SD) in the parameters. The recommended value for SD, based on empirical results, is 0.5.

3.1.3   *Let's try using real-valued GA*

We can use the same simulators for searching with real-valued GAs. These are executed by setting "real" in the "Coding" field. The crossover and mutation operators for real-valued GAs can be chosen from the "Crossover Method" and "Mutation Method" fields at the lower right of the GA parameters panel (Fig. 3.1). The following parameters for the crossover and mutation operators can be set by pressing the "GA Setting" button (Fig. 3.2):

- The α of BLX-α
- The standard deviation of UNDX
- The UD size
- The standard deviation of the ND

The "Step" and "Report" commands can be used to check detailed information regarding the operation of the real-valued GA. Try executing the GA-2D simulator, using the following settings.

- Function definition: $F(x) = 8 - 2 * \text{abs}(x - 4)$

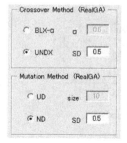

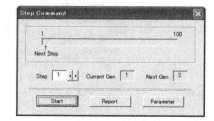

Fig. 3.2   Operators for real-valued GA   Fig. 3.3   Step Command window

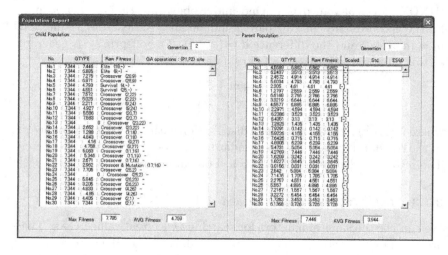

Fig. 3.4   Population Report window

- Definition field: $0 \leq x < 8$
- Search method: GA
- Coding: real
- Elite: 2
- Sharing: off

Press the "Step" button to open the "Step Command" window
(Fig. 3.3). Set "Step" to any value and then press the "Start"/"Continue"
button. This halts execution at the generation specified by the "Next Gen"
parameter. Now press the "Report" button. This opens a window like
that shown in Fig. 3.4, where you can see detailed information regarding
the population. The genes of the parent and offspring generations are dis-

played, along with the maximum fitness values and average fitness values. The gene information is as follows:

- No.: Gene number
- GTYPE: Genotype
- Raw Fitness: Fitness value
- GA operation: How the offspring gene was generated (for an offspring gene):
  - Elite: The gene was generated exactly as it was, as an elite individual (the number of the parent is displayed).
  - Crossover: The gene was generated by means of crossover operation (the two parent individuals are displayed).
  - Mutation: The gene was generated as a result of mutation (the number of the parent individual is displayed).

At a certain execution, for example, the following result was obtained:

Parent population:

No.	:	GTYPE	:	Raw Fitness
No. 1	:	(7.3852)	:	1.23
No. 2	:	(3.9424)	:	7.885
No. 3	:	(5.9188)	:	4.162
No. 4	:	(0.5458)	:	1.092
No. 5	:	(0.4963)	:	0.993
No. 6	:	(4.6501)	:	6.7
No. 7	:	(1.6725)	:	3.345
No. 8	:	(5.6537)	:	4.693
No. 9	:	(2.0652)	:	4.13
No. 10	:	(7.2657)	:	1.469

Offspring population:

No.	:	GTYPE	:	Raw Fitness	: GA Operations		
No. 1	:	(3.9424)	:	7.885	: Elite	(2,-)	-
No. 2	:	(4.6501)	:	6.700	: Elite	(6,-)	-
No. 3	:	(7.9920)	:	0.016	: Crossover	(9,1)	-
No. 4	:	(6.5382)	:	2.924	: Crossover	(9,1)	-
No. 5	:	(1.5464)	:	3.093	: Crossover	(5,2)	-
No. 6	:	(2.9494)	:	5.899	: Crossover	(5,2)	-
No. 7	:	(4.1228)	:	7.754	: Crossover	(6,2)	-
No. 8	:	(4.2216)	:	7.557	: Crossover & Mutation	(6,2)	-
No. 9	:	(3.9424)	:	7.885	: Survival	(2,-)	-
No. 10	:	(4.6501)	:	6.700	: Survival	(6,-)	-

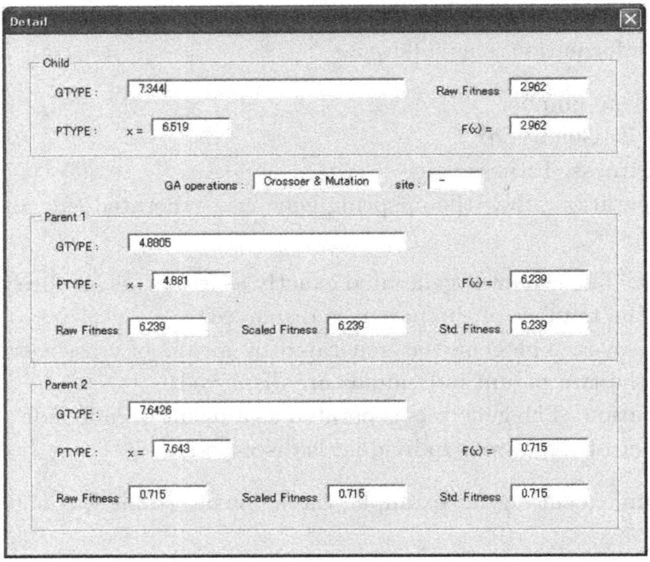

Fig. 3.5   Detailed information of gene codes

In function optimization using a real GA, the GTYPE and the PTYPE are the same; no GTYPE to PTYPE mapping is necessary.

The No. 1 and No. 2 genes of the offspring are copies of the No. 2 and No. 6 genes of the parent.

Let's take a look at the individuals generated by crossover. For example, the No. 5 and No. 6 genes of the offspring are generated by crossover of the No. 5 and No. 2 genes of the parents. Clicking on an offspring gene under "Population Report" displays a window showing its detailed information (Fig. 3.5).

Next, in order to closely examine how the real-valued GA operates with two-variable functions, try executing the GA-3D simulator with the following settings:

- Function definition: $F(x) = 32 - (x - 4) * (x - 4) - (y - 4) * (y - 4)$
- Definition field: $0 \leq x < 8,\ 0 \leq y < 8$
- Search method: GA
- Coding: real
- Elite: 2
- Sharing: off

Press the "Step" button to open the "Step Command" window. Set Step to any value and press the "Start"/"Continue" button. This interrupts execution at the generation specified by the "Next Gen" parameter. Now press the "Report" button. This opens a window like that shown in Fig. 3.6, where you can see detailed information about the population. For example, the following result was obtained in a particular run of the simulator:

Parent population:

No.	:	GTYPE	:	Raw Fitness
No. 1	:	(3.0148, 3.2885)	:	30.523
No. 2	:	(2.7394, 4.1707)	:	30.382
No. 3	:	(0.2333, 3.8089)	:	17.775
No. 4	:	(0.48, 4.4873)	:	19.372
No. 5	:	(7.4132, 4.3311)	:	20.24
No. 6	:	(2.3526, 4.3843)	:	29.138
No. 7	:	(2.7394, 4.1707)	:	30.382
No. 8	:	(3.0148, 3.2885)	:	30.523
No. 9	:	(6.1739, 4.7462)	:	26.717
No. 10	:	(7.2121, 4.8061)	:	21.032

Offspring population:

No.	:	GTYPE	:	Fitness	: GA Operations	
No. 1	:	(3.0148, 3.2885)	:	30.523	: Elite	(8,-) -
No. 2	:	(3.0148, 3.2885)	:	30.523	: Elite	(8,-) -
No. 3	:	(2.9986, 3.0882)	:	30.166	: Crossover	(1,7) -
No. 4	:	(5.4615, 7.1547)	:	19.912	: Crossover & Mutation (1,7) -	
No. 5	:	(7.8196, 4.7945)	:	16.779	: Mutation	(8,-) -
No. 6	:	(7.4132, 4.3311)	:	20.24	: Survival	(5,-) -
No. 7	:	(2.5623, 4.8628)	:	29.189	: Crossover	(6,8) -
No. 8	:	(2.0875, 4.6504)	:	27.919	: Crossover	(6,8) -
No. 9	:	(2.0816, 3.3056)	:	27.837	: Mutation	(6,-) -
No. 10	:	(6.1739, 4.7462)	:	26.717	: Survival	(9,-) -

Because this is a real GA, the GTYPE is the PTYPE (x and y coordinates) without any modifications.

Each of the No. 1 and No. 2 genes of the offspring is a (elite) copy of the No. 8 parent gene and the No. 6 gene of the offspring is a copy of the No. 5 parent gene.

Let's look at the individuals generated by crossover. For example, the No. 7 and No. 8 genes of the offspring are generated by crossover of the

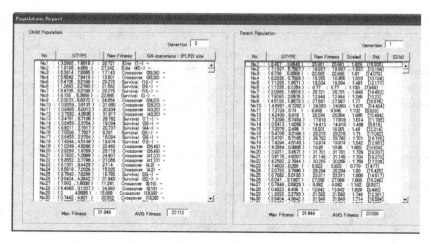

Fig. 3.6　Population Report window

No. 6 and No. 8 genes of the parent, and the No. 9 gene of the offspring is generated by a mutation of the No. 6 gene of the parent. The No. 4 gene of the offspring is generated from a crossover of the No. 1 and No. 7 genes of the parent and a mutation, and the No. 10 gene of the offspring is a copy of the No. 9 gene of the parent. Although this individual is not elite, the gene is copied just as it is, without applying crossover or mutation.

Detailed information regarding an offspring and its parent(s) can be found by clicking on its gene in the "Population Report" window (Fig. 3.7).

Try experimenting with real GAs using different crossover and mutation operators and various functions. Also study the effect of operator's parameters such as α, SD, size (Fig. 3.2). In particular, try running tests with the $F6$ and $F7$ functions shown below, in addition to De Jong's standard functions $F1$ through $F5$. These pre-defined functions can be loaded using the "Load" command.

$$F6(x, y) = 0.5 + \frac{\sin^2 \sqrt{x^2 + y^2} - 0.5}{[1.0 + 0.001(x^2 + y^2)]^2},$$

$$F7(x, y) = (x^2 + y^2)^{0.25}[\sin^2(50(x^2 + y^2)^{0.1}) + 1.0],$$

where the range of variables is $-100 \leq x, y \leq 100$. Schäfer's $F6$ and $F7$ rotate around the z axis, and the minimum value is $F6 = F7 = 0.0$ for $x = y = 0.0$ (see Fig. 3.8 and Fig. 3.9). These functions are complicated multi-peak (multi-modal) functions that have wells of differing depths and fences of differing heights. Consequently, this is a landscape that is extremely difficult to climb using the hill-climbing method.

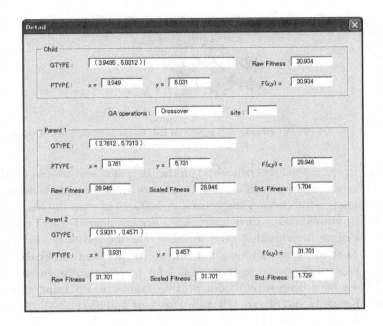

Fig. 3.7   Detailed information of gene codes

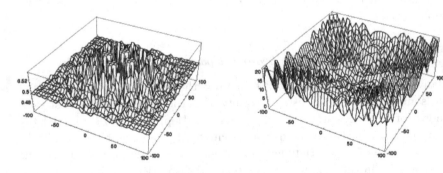

Fig. 3.8   Schäfer's *F*6 function

Fig. 3.9   Schäfer's *F*7 function

3.2   PSO: particle swarm optimization

This section introduces the optimization method "particle swarm optimization" (PSO), which slightly differs from GA and GP. PSO is an algorithm from the field of Swarm Intelligence. It was first described by Eberhart and Kennedy as an alternative to GA in 1995 [Kennedy and Eberhart (1995)].

Fig. 3.10   Do the movements of a school of fish follow a certain set of rules?

The algorithm for PSO was conceived on the basis of observations of certain social behavior in lower-class animals or insects. In contrast to the concept of modifying genetic codes using genetic operations as used in GA, in PSO the moving individuals (called "particles") are considered where the next movement of an individual is determined by the motion of the individual itself and that of the surrounding individuals. It has been established that PSO has capabilities equal to those of GA for function optimization problems. There have been several comparative studies on PSO and standard GA (see [Kennedy and Spears (1998a)],[Eberhart and Shi (1998)],[Angeline (1998)] and [Higashi and Iba (2003)]).

Below, we describe the origins of PSO, outline the procedure, compare its search efficiency with that of GA, and provide some examples of its application.

3.2.1   *Learning from the beautiful patterns of fish schools*

Many scientists have attempted to express the group behavior of flocks of birds and schools of fish, using a variety of methods. Two of the most well-known of these scientists are Reynolds and Heppner, who simulated the movements of birds. Reynolds was fascinated by the beauty of bird flocks [Reynolds (1987)], and Heppner, a zoologist, had an interest in finding the hidden rules in the instantaneous stops and dispersions of flocks [Heppner and Grenander (1990)]. These two shared a keen understanding of the unpredictable movements of birds; on the microscopic level, the movements were extremely simple, as seen in cellular automata, while on the macroscopic level, the motions were very complicated and appeared chaotic. This is what is called "emergent property" in the field of Artificial Life (Alife). Their model places a very high weight on the influence of individuals on each other. Similarly, it is known that the optimal distance is maintained among individual fish in a fish school (see Fig. 3.10).

This approach is probably not far from the mark as the basis for the social behavior of groups of birds, fish, animals and, for that matter, human beings. The sociobiologist E.O. Wilson made the following suggestion with respect to schools of fish [Wilson (1975)](p.890):

> In theory at least, individual members of the school can profit from the discoveries and previous experience of all other members of the school during the search for food. This advantage was documented earlier with reference to bird flocks. It can become decisive, outweighing the disadvantages of competition for food items, whenever the resource is unpredictably disturbed in patches. Thus larger fish that prey on schools of smaller fish or cephalopods might be expected to hunt in groups for this reason alone.

As one can understand from this quote, the most useful information to an individual is whatever is shared from other members of the same group. This hypothesis forms the basis for the method known as PSO.

3.2.2 *PSO algorithm*

The classic PSO proposed by Kennedy was intended to be applied to optimization problems. It simulates the motion of a large number of individuals (or "particles") moving in a multi-dimensional space [Kennedy and Eberhart (1995)]. Each individual stores its own location vector $(\vec{x_i})$, velocity vector $(\vec{v_i})$, and the position at which the individual obtained the highest fitness value $(\vec{p_i})$. All individuals also share information regarding the position with the highest fitness value for the group $(\vec{p_g})$.

As generations progress, the velocity of each individual is updated using the best overall location obtained up to the current time for the entire group and the best locations obtained up to the current time for that individual. This update is performed using the following formula:

$$\vec{v_i} = \chi(\omega\vec{v_i} + \phi_1 \cdot (\vec{p_i} - \vec{x_i}) + \phi_2 \cdot (\vec{p_g} - \vec{x_i})) \tag{3.2}$$

The coefficients employed here are the convergence coefficient χ (a random value between 0.9 and 1.0) and the attenuation coefficient ω, while ϕ_1 and ϕ_2 are random values unique to each individual and the dimension, with a maximum value of 2. When the calculated velocity exceeds some limit, it is replaced by a maximum velocity V_{max}. This procedure allows us to hold the individuals within the search region during the search.

The locations of each of the individuals are updated at each generation by the following formula:

$$\vec{x_i} = \vec{x_i} + \vec{v_i} \tag{3.3}$$

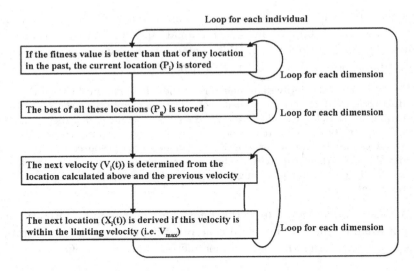

Fig. 3.11   Flow chart of the PSO algorithm

The overall flow of the PSO is as shown in Fig. 3.11. Let us now consider the specific movements of each individual (see Fig. 3.12). A flock consisting of a number of birds is assumed to be in flight. We focus on one of the individuals (Step 1). In the figure, the ◯ symbols and linking line segments indicate the positions and paths of the bird. The nearby ◎ symbol (on its path) indicates the position with the highest fitness value on the individual's path (Step 2). The distant ◎ symbol (on the other bird's path) marks the position with the highest fitness value for the flock (Step 2). One would expect that the next state will be reached in the direction shown by the arrows in Step 3. Vector ① shows the direction followed in the previous steps; vector ② is directed towards the position with the highest fitness for the flock; and vector ③ points to the location where the individual obtained its highest fitness value so far. Thus, all these vectors, ①, ② and ③, in Step 3 are summed to obtain the actual direction of movement in the subsequent step (see Step 4).

A simulator is available for investigating the PSO search process. Fig. 3.13 is a screenshot of the simulator. Interested readers are referred to the Appendix B.1 for a detailed description of how the simulator is operated.

The efficiency of this type of PSO search is certainly high because focused searching is available near optimal solutions in a relatively simple

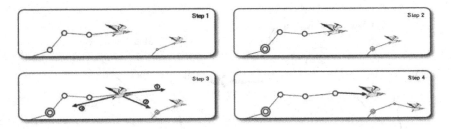

Fig. 3.12   In what way do birds fly?

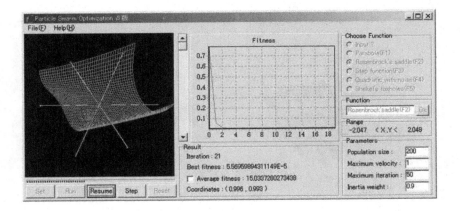

Fig. 3.13   PSO simulator

search space. However, the canonical PSO algorithm often gets trapped in local optimum in multimodal problems. Because of that, some sort of adaptation is necessary in order to apply PSO to problems with multiple sharp peaks.

To overcome the above limitation, a GA-like mutation can be integrated with PSO [Higashi and Iba (2003)]. This hybrid PSO does not follow the process by which every individual of the simple PSO moves to another position inside the search area with a predetermined probability without being affected by other individuals, but leaves a certain ambiguity in the transition to the next generation due to Gaussian mutation. This technique employs the following equation:

$$mut(x) = x \times (1 + gaussian(\sigma)), \tag{3.4}$$

where σ is set to be 0.1 times the length of the search space in one dimension. The individuals are selected at a predetermined probability and

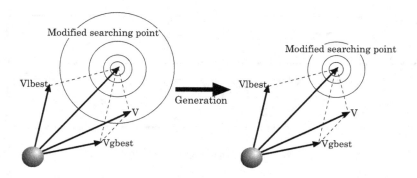

Fig. 3.14   Concept of searching process by PSO with Gaussian mutation

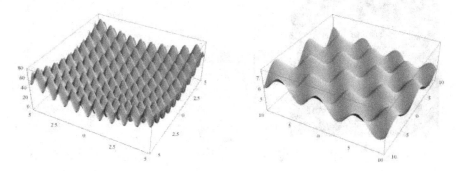

Fig. 3.15   Rastrigin's function ($F8$)   Fig. 3.16   Griewangk's function ($F9$)

their positions are determined at the probability under the Gaussian distribution. Wide-ranging searches are possible at the initial search stage and search efficiency is improved at the middle and final stages by gradually reducing the appearance ratio of Gaussian mutation at the initial stage. Fig. 3.14 shows the PSO search process with Gaussian mutation. In the figure, V_{lbest} represents the velocity based on the local best, i.e. $\vec{p_i} - \vec{x_i}$ in Eq. (3.2), whereas V_{gbest} represents the velocity based on the global best, i.e. $\vec{p_g} - \vec{x_i}$.

3.2.3   *Comparison with GA*

Let us turn to a comparison of the performance of the PSO with that of the GA using benchmark functions, to examine the effectiveness of PSO.

Table 3.1   Search space for test functions

Function	Search space
$F1$	$-5.11 \leq x_i < 5.12$
$F2$	$-2.047 \leq x_i < 2.048$
$F3$	$-5.11 \leq x_i < 5.12$
$F4$	$-1.27 \leq x_i < 1.28$
$F5$	$-5.11 \leq x_i < 5.11$
$F8$	$-65.535 \leq x_i < 65.536$
$F9$	$-10 \leq x_i \leq 10$

Table 3.2   PSO and GA parameters

Parameters	PSO,PSO with Gaussian	Real-valued GA
Population	200	200
V_{max}	1	
Generation	50	50
ϕ_1,ϕ_2	upper limits = 2.0	
Inertia weight	0.9	
Crossover ratio		0.7(BLX-α)
Mutation	0.01	0.01
Elite		0.05
Selection		tournament (size=6)

The benchmark functions $F1$–$F5$ described in Section 2.3 are used for the comparison. In addition, $F8$ (Rastrigin's function) and $F9$ (Griewangk's function) are also employed. These are defined as:

$$F8(x_1, x_2) = 20 + x_1^2 - 10\cos(2\pi x_1) + x_2^2 - 10\cos(2\pi x_2) \quad (-5.11 \leq x_i \leq 5.11)$$

$$F9(x_1, x_2) = \frac{1}{4000}\sum_{i=1}^{2}(x_i - 100)^2 - \prod_{i=1}^{2}\cos\left(\frac{x_i - 100}{\sqrt{i}}\right) + 1 \quad (-10 \leq x_i \leq 10)$$

Fig. 3.15 and Fig. 3.16 show the shapes of $F8$ and $F9$, respectively. The shapes of the other functions are shown in Section 2.3. As already noted, $F1$–$F5$, $F8$ and $F9$ seek the minimum value. Optimization of $F4$, $F5$, and $F8$ was particularly difficult for the following reasons: $F4$ incorporates noise at all points, $F5$ must negotiate valleys between steep peaks, and $F8$ contains a large number of peaks. The peak heights are not consistent in $F5$.

Comparative experiments were conducted with PSO and GA using the above benchmark functions. PSO and GA were repeatedly run 100 times. Search space ranges for the experiments are listed in Table 3.1. PSO and GA parameters are given in Table 3.2.

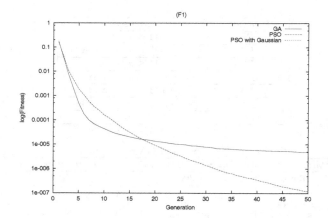

Fig. 3.17   Standard PSO versus PSO with Gaussian mutation for $F1$

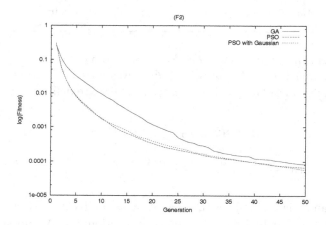

Fig. 3.18   Standard PSO versus PSO with Gaussian mutation for $F2$

The performance results are shown in Fig. 3.17–3.23 which plot the fitness values against the generations. With reference to the above results, PSO performed better than GA for $F1$ to $F4$ unimodals. On the other hand, PSO did not perform so well compared to GA for $F5$, $F8$ and $F9$ multimodals. One of the major causes is the interaction of the PSO algorithm acting inside the population. As for unimodals that have only one peak, individuals have effects on and pull each other, thereby finding the best fit values or those close to them. As for multimodals, when an in-

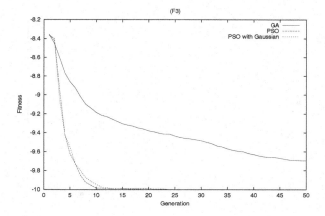

Fig. 3.19   Standard PSO versus PSO with Gaussian mutation for $F3$

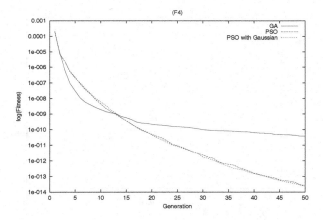

Fig. 3.20   Standard PSO versus PSO with Gaussian mutation for $F4$

dividual finds a spot with relatively good performance, other individuals are attracted by that individual, even if competitive fitness values exist for other individuals, resulting in a local minimum. It follows that getting away from this problem is very difficult because no means such as mutation is at hand.

Table 3.3 shows the averaged best fitness values over 100 runs. As can be seen from the table and the figures, the combination of PSO with Gaussian mutation allows us to achieve a performance that is almost equal to that of

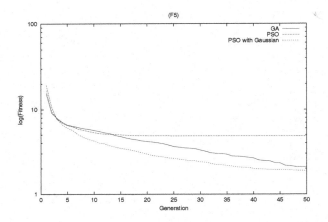

Fig. 3.21   Standard PSO versus PSO with Gaussian mutation for $F5$

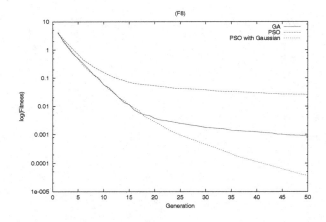

Fig. 3.22   Standard PSO versus PSO with Gaussian mutation for $F8$

the canonical PSO for the unimodals, and a better performance than the canonical PSO for the multimodals.

PSO is a stochastic search method, as are GA and GP, and its method of adjustment of $\vec{p_i}$ and $\vec{p_g}$ resembles crossover in GA. It also employs the concept of fitness, as in evolutionary computation. Thus, the PSO algorithm is strongly related to evolutionary computation (EC) methods. In conceptual terms, one could place PSO somewhere between GA and EP.

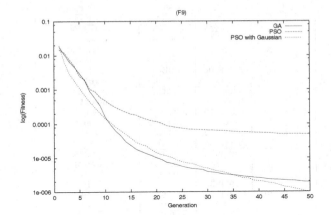

Fig. 3.23   Standard PSO versus PSO with Gaussian mutation for $F9$

However, PSO has certain characteristics that other EC techniques do not have. GA operators directly operate on the search points in a multi-dimensional search space, while PSO operates on the motion vectors of particles which in turn update the search points (i.e. particle positions). In other words, GA operators are position specific and the PSO operators are direction specific. One of the reasons PSO has gathered so much attention was the tendency of its individuals to proceed directly towards the target. This feature resembles the behavior of BUGS, which is described in Section 3.3.

In the chapter "The Optimal Allocation of Trials" in his book, Holland ascribes the success of EC on the balance of "exploitation", through search of known regions, with "exploration", through search, at finite risks, of unknown regions [Holland (1975)]. PSO is adept at managing such subtle balances. These stochastic factors enable PSO to make thorough searches of the relatively promising regions and, due to the momentum of speed, also allows effective searches of unknown regions. Theoretical research is currently underway to derive optimized values for PSO parameters by mathematical analysis, for stability and convergence (see [Kennedy *et al.* (2001); Clerc and Kennedy (2002)]).

3.2.4   *Examples of PSO applications*

PSO has been applied to an analysis of trembling of the human body [Eberhart and Hu (1999)]. Trembling has two types, ordinary shivering and the

Table 3.3   Average best fitness of 100 runs for experiments

	Gen	GA	PSO	PSO with gaussian
F1	1	0.176257	0.161864	0.163299
	10	4.33E-05	0.000161	0.000156
	20	1.32E-05	9.07E-06	8.25E-06
	30	7.68E-06	1.37E-06	1.44E-06
	40	5.71E-06	3.49E-07	3.44E-07
	50	4.80E-06	1.16E-07	1.10E-07
F2	1	0.266981	0.303957	0.295097
	10	0.009426	0.001758	0.001707
	20	0.001159	0.000335	0.000385
	30	0.000285	0.000152	0.000168
	40	0.000122	9.46E-05	9.48E-05
	50	8.48E-05	6.71E-05	5.65E-05
F3	1	-8.355	-8.306	-8.236
	10	-9.185	-9.976	-9.974
	20	-9.38	-9.998	-10
	30	-9.485	-10	-10
	40	-9.63	-10	-10
	50	-9.695	-10	-10
F4	1	1.81E-04	0.000189	0.00021
	10	1.92E-09	4.45E-09	5.95E-09
	20	2.17E-10	4.93E-11	4.49E-11
	30	9.82E-11	2.39E-12	1.74E-12
	40	6.25E-11	1.62E-13	1.53E-13
	50	3.76E-11	2.39E-14	2.69E-14
F5	1	11.36315	19.40166	13.23323
	10	5.660075	5.334231	4.849908
	20	4.161422	4.872864	3.668673
	30	3.29137	4.844246	2.865587
	40	2.646799	4.84	2.637028
	50	2.086842	4.84	2.246701
F8	1	4.290568	3.936564	3.913959
	10	0.05674	0.16096	0.057193
	20	0.003755	0.052005	0.002797
	30	0.001759	0.037106	0.000454
	40	0.001226	0.029099	0.000113
	50	0.000916	0.02492	3.61E-05
F9	1	0.018524	0.015017	0.019726
	10	0.000161	0.000484	0.000145
	20	1.02E-05	0.000118	1.43E-05
	30	3.87E-06	6.54E-05	4.92E-06
	40	2.55E-06	5.50E-05	2.04E-06
	50	1.93E-06	4.95E-05	1.00E-06

type of shaking that is caused by Parkinson's disease or other illnesses. The authors used a combination of PSO and a neural network to distinguish between the types. The sigmoid function given below was optimized with the PSO in a layered network with 60 input units, 12 hidden nodes, and 2 output units, thus:

$$output = \frac{1}{1 + e^{-k \sum w_i x_i}}$$

where x_i and w_i were the inputs and weights to each of the hidden layers and output layers, respectively. Optimization of the weight indirectly causes changes in the network structure. Ten healthy controls and twelve patients took part in this experiment. The system succeeded in distinguishing correctly between the types of shaking in the subjects with 100% accuracy.

It is common to apply PSO to problems of electric power networks [Miranda and Fonseca (2002)]. In their research, the experiments were conducted employing selection procedures that were effective for standard PSO and an extended version (EPSO) with a self-adaptive feature. The problem of "losses" in electric power networks refers to searching out the series of control actions needed to minimize the power losses. The objective function for this included the level of excitation of generators and adjustments to the connections to transformers and condensers, i.e. the control variables included both continuous and discrete types. The maximum power flow and the permitted voltage level were imposed as boundary conditions, and the algorithm searched for the solution with the minimum loss. Miranda *et al.* conducted a comparative experiment with EPSO and simulated annealing (SA), conducting 270 runs in each system and comparing the mean of the results. EPSO rapidly identified a solution that was close to the optimal one. SA converged more slowly. Comparison of the mean square errors indicated that SA did not have as high a probability of arriving at the optimal solution as EPSO. PSO has been also successfully applied to the economic load dispatch (ELD) problem for least cost power generation (see Section 6.3) [Gaing (2003); Park *et al.* (2005)]. These findings indicate that PSO can be trusted as a sufficiently robust method for solving real problems.

Practical research has also been conducted, applying PSO to optimize the mixing of materials for the production of valuable excretions by microorganisms [Kennedy *et al.* (2001)]. The authors compared PSO with traditional methods of experimental design, finding that the mixture indicated by PSO resulted in more than a doubling of the performance. When materials of low quality were used, the search efficiency was quite poor in the initial stages, but ultimately, PSO provided superior results. These findings confirmed that PSO offers good robustness against changes in the environment.

3.3   BUGS: a bug-based search strategy

This section describes another new approach to strategic learning, based on GA. Simple GAs optimize functions by adaptive combination (crossover) of coded solutions to problems (i.e. points in the problem's search space). In this approach, an analogy is made between the value (at a given point) of a function to be maximized, and the density of bacteria at that point. More specifically, the adaptive learning used in this system, called BUGS (a bug-based search strategy), is due to evolving choice of directions, rather than positions (as with previous real-valued GA methods) [Iba *et al.* (1993)]. The bugs evolved by the BUGS program learn to search for bacteria in the highest density regions and are thus likely to move towards those points where the function has a maximum value. This strategy combines a hill-climbing mechanism with the adaptive method of GA, and thus overcomes the usual weakness of simple GAs (which do not include such local search mechanisms).

3.3.1   *Evolution of predatory behaviors using genetic search*

This section introduces the fundamental idea of BUGS. We can experimentally verify the evolution of bugs which possess "predatory behaviors", i.e. the evolution of bugs that learn to hunt bacteria. The original motivation for these experiments was derived from [Dewdney (1989)]. Bugs learn to move to those regions in the search space where the bacterial concentration is highest. Since the bug concentration is set up to be proportional to the local value of the function to be maximized in the search space, the "stabilized" bug concentrations are proportional to these search space values. Hence the bugs learn (GA style) to be hill climbers. BUGS simulator is available for the readers' self-study. The details are given in Appendix B.2.

3.3.1.1   *Bugs hunt bacteria*

Fig. 3.24(a) illustrates the world in which bugs (large dots) live (a 512×512 cellular grid). They feed on bacteria (small dots) which are continually being deposited. Normal bacterial deposition rate is roughly 0.5 bacterium per (GA) generation over the whole grid. Each bug has its internal energy source. The maximum energy supply of a bug is set at 1500 units. When a bug's energy supply is exhausted, the bug dies and disappears. Each bacterium eaten provides a bug with 40 units of energy, which is enough to make 40 moves, where a move is defined to be one of six possible directional displacements of the bug as shown in Fig. 3.25.

A bug's motion is determined by coded instructions on its gene code. The six directions a bug can move are labeled F, R, HR, RV, HL and L

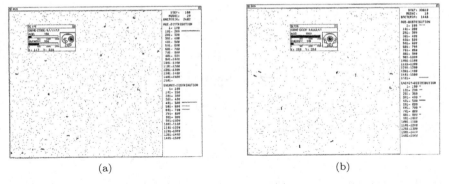

(a)　　　　　　　　　　　　　　　　(b)

Fig. 3.24　Bug world (a)166th generation (b) 39618th generation

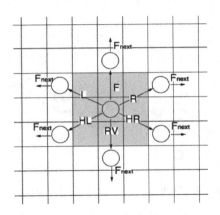

Fig. 3.25　Bug's gene code

for Forward, Right, Hard Right, Reverse, Hard Left, and Left, respectively. The GA chromosome format for these bugs is an integer vector of size six where the elements of the vector correspond to the directions in the following order (F,R,HR,RV,HL,L), e.g. (2,1,1,1,3,2) (as shown in the window in Fig. 3.24(a)). When a bug is to make a move, it will move in the direction d_i (e.g. $d_3 = HR$) with a probability $p(d_i)$, which is determined by the formula $p(d_i) = e^{ai}/\sum_{j=1}^{6} e^{aj}$, where a_i is the i-th component value of the chromosome vector (e.g. $a_5 = 3$ above). Once a move is made, a new directional orientation should be determined. Fig. 3.25 shows the new F_{next} directions, e.g. if the move is R, new forward direction will be to the right (i.e. east). For instance, a bug with a gene code of (1,9,1,1,1,1) turns frequently in direction R so that it is highly likely to move in a circle.

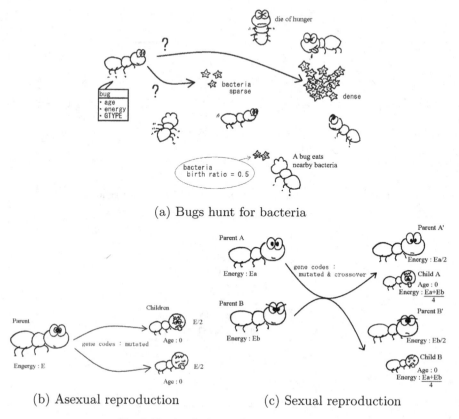

(a) Bugs hunt for bacteria

(b) Asexual reproduction   (c) Sexual reproduction

Fig. 3.26   A schematic illustration of bugs

After 800 moves (i.e. when it attains an "age" of 800), the bug is said to be "mature" and is ready to reproduce if it is "strong" (i.e. its energy is greater than a threshold value of 1000 energy units). There are two types of reproduction, asexual and sexual (see Fig. 3.26). With asexual reproduction, a strong mature bug disappears and is replaced by two new bugs (in the same cell on the grid). Each daughter bug has half the energy of its parent. The genes of each daughter bug are mutated as follows. One of the components of the directional 6-vector is chosen with uniform probability. The value of the direction is replaced by a new value chosen with uniform probability (over the integer range of e.g. [0,10]). Sexual reproduction occurs when two strong mature bugs "meet" (i.e. they move within a threshold distance from each other called the "reproductive radius"). The distance between two parents is defined as the Euclidean distance between the two parents. The reproductive radius is set at 10.0. The two parents continue to live and are joined by the two daughter bugs. Each parent loses half of its energy in the sexual reproductive process. As a result, two children are born, whose energies are half the average of the parents' energies. The children's genes are obtained by applying mutation and uniform crossover operators to the parents' genes. Thus these reproductions are constrained by probabilities.

Fig. 3.24(b) shows the results of the first simple evolutionary experiment. The simulation began with ten bugs with random genetic structures. Most of the bugs jittered from side to side unpredictably and are called "jitterbugs". They are likely to starve to death because they eat up most of the food in their immediate vicinity and are unable to explore widely. In time "cruiser" bugs evolve, which move forward most of the time and turn left or right occasionally (Note that if a bug hits an edge of the grid, it stays there until an appropriate move displaces it away from that grid edge). These "cruiser" bugs succeed in finding food and thus dominate the entire population. A typical chromosome for a "cruiser" bug is shown in the sub-window of Fig. 3.24(b); i.e. (9,6,0,2,4,1). The remarkable features of this chromosome vector are as follows:

(1) The forward gene (F) is large (9).
(2) The reverse gene (RV) is small (2).
(3) One of the Right (R), Left (L), Hard Right (HR) and Hard Left (HL) is of moderate size (6).

The second feature is important because bugs with large "reverse" (RV) gene values create "twirlers" which make too many turns in one direction. Such unfortunate creatures usually die. The third feature is also essential, because intelligent bugs have to avoid loitering around wall edges.

3.3.1.2 *Effectiveness of sexual reproduction*

Dewdney's original paper used only mutation operators, i.e. asexual reproduction. The sexual reproduction is introduced in bugs to increase the effective evolution of bugs [Iba *et al.* (1992)]. It can be experimentally shown that the speed of evolution is higher with sexual reproduction. In the first experiment, we can statistically compare the performance rates,

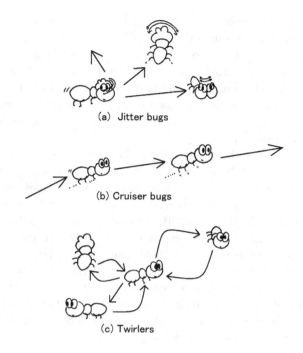

(a) Jitter bugs

(b) Cruiser bugs

(c) Twirlers

Fig. 3.27   Types of bugs

where the performance of bugs at generation t is defined as follows:

$$Performance(t) = \sum_{i=0}^{9} Perf(t-i), \qquad (3.5)$$

where

$$Perf(k) = \frac{\#Eaten(k)}{\#Bac(k) \times \#Bug(k)} \qquad (3.6)$$

$$\#Bug(k) = (\text{no. of bugs at the k-th generation}) \qquad (3.7)$$

$$\#Bac(k) = (\text{no. of bacteria at the k-th generation}) \qquad (3.8)$$

$$\#Eaten(k) = (\text{no. of bacteria eaten by bugs at k-th generation}) \qquad (3.9)$$

This indicates how many bacteria are eaten by bugs as a whole in the last ten generations. As can be seen in Fig. 3.28, sexual reproduction after the mature age (800) performs better than asexual reproduction, which is tested statistically.

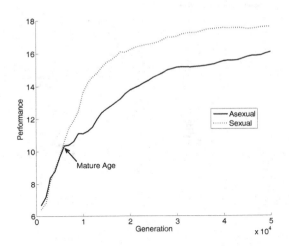

Fig. 3.28   Performance comparison

In a second experiment, the bacteria in the lower left-hand corner (called the Garden of Eden, a square of 75 × 75 cells) are replenished at a much higher rate than normal (Fig. 3.29(a)); normal bacterial deposition rate is roughly 0.5 bacterium per (GA) generation over the whole grid. In the Garden of Eden, this rate is 0.5 over the 75 × 75 area, i.e. a rate roughly $\frac{512 \times 512}{75 \times 75} \approx 47$ times greater than normal. As the (GA) generations proceeded, the cruisers evolved as before. But within the Garden of Eden, the jitterbugs were more rewarded for their jittering around small areas (see Fig. 3.27). Thus two kinds of "species" evolved (i.e. cruisers and twirlers) (Fig. 3.29(c)). Note how typical gene codes of these two species differed from each other. In this second experiment, three different strategies (asexual reproduction, sexual reproduction, and sexual reproduction within reproductive radius) are compared in four different situations. The aim is to evolve a mix of bugs, namely the cruisers and twirlers. Two initial conditions are tested: a) randomized initial bugs and b) cruisers already evolved. In addition, the influence of an empty area in which no bacteria exist is investigated. Obviously this empty-area condition makes the problem easier. The results of these experiments are shown in Table 3.4.

As shown in the table, the sexual reproduction with a reproductive radius is superior to the other two strategies and the performance improvement is significant for more difficult tasks such as non empty-area conditions.

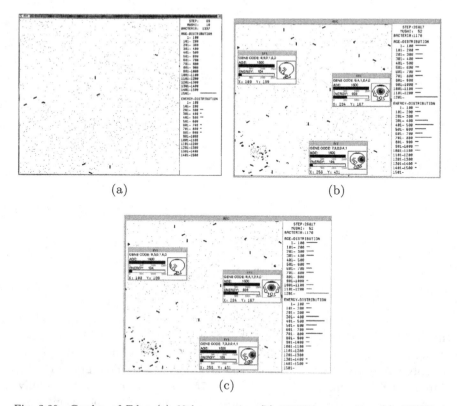

Fig. 3.29   Garden of Eden (a) 69th generation (b) 72337th generation (c) 478462nd generation

So it was confirmed that crossover is useful for the evolution of predatory behavior. The described method contrasts with traditional GAs in two ways: the bugs' approach uses search directions rather than positions, and selection is based on energy. This idea leads to a bug-based GA search (BUGS) whose implementation is described in the next section.

3.3.2   *A bug-based GA search*

Those individuals which perform the search in this scheme are called "bugs". The function that these bugs maximize is defined as:

$$f(x_1, x_2, \cdots, x_n) \qquad \text{where } x_i \in Dom_i. \tag{3.10}$$

Here Dom_i represents the domain of the i-th parameter x_i.

Table 3.4   Experimental results (sexual vs asexual selection)

Task		Asexual mutation	Sexual crossover mutation	Sexual Prox. crossover mutation
initial	empty area			
Random	○	○	○	⊙
Cruisers	○	○	○	⊙
Cruisers	×	△	△	○
Random	×	△	△	○
△ difficult		○ possible	○ fast	⊙ faster

Each bug in the BUGS program is characterized by 3 parameters:

$Bug_i(t)$:   position $\vec{X}_i(t) = \qquad (x_1^i(t), \cdots, x_n^i(t))$ (3.11)

direction $D\vec{X}_i(t) = \qquad (dx_1^i(t), \cdots, dx_n^i(t))$ (3.12)

energy $e_i(t)$ (3.13)

where t is the generation count of the bug, x_j is its j-th component of the search space, and $D\vec{X}_i$ is the direction in which the bug moves next. The updated position is calculated as follows:

$$\vec{X}_i(t+1) = \vec{X}_i(t) + D\vec{X}_i(t) \tag{3.14}$$

The fitness of each bug is derived with the aid of the function (3.10). The energy $e_i(t)$ of bug "i" at time (or generation) "t" is defined to be the cumulative sum of the function values over the previous T time steps or generations, i.e.

$$e_i(t) = \sum_{k=0}^{T} f(\vec{X}_i(t-k)) \tag{3.15}$$

The format of a bug's "chromosome" which is used in the BUGS program is the bug's real numbered DX vector, i.e. an ordered list of N real numbers.

With the above definitions, the BUGS algorithm can now be introduced:

Step 1 The initial bug population is generated with random values:
$Pop(0) = \{Bug_1(0), \cdots, Bug_N(0)\}$
where N is the population size.
The generation time is initialized to $t := 1$. The cumulative time period T (called the *Bug-GA Period*) is set to a user-specified value.

Step 2 Move each bug using Eq. (3.14) synchronously.

Step 3 The fitness is derived using (3.10) and the energy is accumulated using:
for $i := 1$ to N do $e_i(t) := e_i(t-1) + f_i(\vec{X}(t))$

Step 4 If t is a multiple of T (T-periodical), then execute the GA algorithm (described below) called $BUGS$-$GA(t)$, and then go to **Step 6**.

Step 5 $Pop(t+1) := Pop(t)$, $t := t + 1$, and then go to **Step 2**.

Step 6 for $i := 1$ to N do $e_i(t) := 0$
$t := t + 1$. Go to **Step 2**.

In **Step 1**, initial bugs are generated on conditions that for all i and j,

$$x_j^i(0) := \mathbf{Random}(a, b) \tag{3.16}$$

$$dx_j^i(0) := \mathbf{Random}(-|a - b|, |a - b|) \tag{3.17}$$

$$e_i(0) := 0 \tag{3.18}$$

where $\mathbf{Random}$(a,b) is a uniform random generator between a and b. The *Bug-GA Period* T specifies the frequency of bug reproductions. In general, as this value becomes smaller, the performance becomes better, but at the same time, the convergence time is increased. For the appropriate setting of this value, the entropy-based adaptation is used which is described in Section 3.3.3.2.

As mentioned in Section 3.1, for real-valued function optimization, real-valued GAs are preferred over the string-based GAs. Therefore, the real-valued GA approach is used in $BUGS$-GA. The BUGS version of the genetic algorithm, $BUGS$-$GA(t)$, is as follows (Table 3.5):

Step 1 $n := 1$.

Step 2 Select two parent bugs $Bug_i(t)$ and $Bug_j(t)$ using a probability distribution over the energies of all bugs in $Pop(t)$ so that bugs with higher energy are selected more frequently.

Step 3 With probability P_{cross}, apply the uniform crossover operation to the $\vec{DX}$ of copies of $Bug_i(t)$ and $Bug_j(t)$, forming two offspring $Bug_n(t+1)$ and $Bug_{n+1}(t+1)$ in $Pop(t+1)$. Go to **Step 5**.

Step 4 If **Step 3** is skipped, form two offspring $Bug_n(t+1)$ and $Bug_{n+1}(t+1)$ in $Pop(t+1)$ by making copies of $Bug_i(t)$ and $Bug_j(t)$.

Step 5 With probability P_{asex}, apply the mutation operation to the two offspring $Bug_n(t+1)$ and $Bug_{n+1}(t+1)$, changing each allele in $\vec{DX}$ with probability P_{mut}.

Step 6 $n := n + 2$.

Step 7 If $n < N$ then go to **Step 2**.

The aim of the $BUGS$-GA subroutine is to acquire bugs' behavior adaptively. This subroutine works in much the same way as a real-valued GA,

Table 3.5   Flow chart of reproduction process in *BUGS-GA*

Sexual reproduction :

	individual	energy	gene		individual	energy	gene
Parent$_1$	$Bug_i(t)$	E_1	G_1	$\Rightarrow$ Parent$'_1$	$Bug_n(t+1)$	$(E_1/2)$	G_1
Parent$_2$	$Bug_j(t)$	E_2	G_2	$\Rightarrow$ Parent$'_2$	$Bug_{n+1}(t+1)$	$(E_2/2)$	G_2
				Child$_1$	$Bug_{n+2}(t+1)$	$(E_1+E_2/4)$	G'_1
				Child$_2$	$Bug_{n+3}(t+1)$	$(E_1+E_2/4)$	G'_2

Reproduction condition $\Rightarrow$
    $(E_1 >$ Reproduction energy threshold$) \wedge (E_2 >$ Reproduction energy threshold$)$
            $\wedge$ (distance between Parent$_1$ and Parent$_2 <$ Reproduction Radius)
Recombination $\Rightarrow$
    G'_1, G'_2 : uniform crossover of G_1 and G_2 with P_{cross}, mutated with P_{mut}

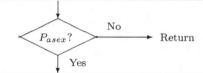

P_{asex}?   No $\longrightarrow$ Return

Yes

Asexual reproduction :

	individual	energy	gene		individual	energy	gene
Parent	$Bug_i(t)$	E	G	$\Rightarrow$ Child$_1$	$Bug_n(t+1)$	$(E/2)$	G'
				$\Rightarrow$ Child$_2$	$Bug_{n+1}(t+1)$	$(E/2)$	G''

Reproduction condition $\Rightarrow (E >$ producible energy$)$
    G', G'' : mutation of G with P_{mut}

Table 3.6   BUGS vs real-valued GA

	BUGS	**Real-valued GA**
Fitness evaluation	$\vec{X}$	$\vec{X}$
GA operator target	$\vec{DX}$	$\vec{X}$
Selection criteria	Energy	Fitness

except that it operates on the directional vector $(\vec{DX})$, not on the positional vector $(\vec{X})$. Positions are thus untouched by the adaptive process of the GA, and are changed gradually as a result of increment by Eq. (3.14). On the other hand, the fitness is evaluated using the positional potential (3.10), which is the same as for a real-valued GA. Furthermore, chromosome selection is based on the cumulative fitness, i.e. the energy. The summary of differences between real-valued GA and BUGS is presented in Table 3.6.

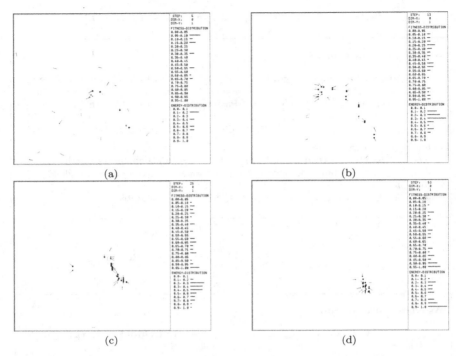

(a)   (b)

(c)   (d)

Fig. 3.30   Bugs' motions for $F2$ (a) 5th generation (b) 13th generation (c) 25th generation (d) 53rd generation

The main difference lies in the GA target (i.e. $\vec{X}$ vs $\vec{DX}$) and the selection criteria (i.e. energy vs fitness). Remember that the basic idea of this combination is derived from a paper [Dewdney (1989)] which simulated how bugs learn to hunt bacteria (as described in the previous section). We will show that the ideas contained in the BUGS program (particularly the idea of using the search direction vector, rather than the position vector, as the real-valued "chromosome" to be evolved) can be extended to other problems in functional optimization.

3.3.3   *Experiments with BUGS*

This section presents several experiments which show how the bugs of the BUGS program evolve, and how they can be used to solve different optimization problems.

3.3.3.1 *Standard set of test functions*

Fig. 3.30 shows the evolution (over 5 to 53 time steps) of the positions and directions of the bugs in the BUGS program. These bugs were used to optimize the following De Jong's $F2$ function (modified to maximization problem):

$$Maximize \quad f(x_1, x_2) = -(100(x_1^2 - x_2)^2 + (1 - x_1)^2)$$
$$where \quad -2.047 \leq x_i < 2.048. \quad (3.19)$$

The main window shows a bird's-eye view of a two-dimensional projection of the $F2$ function domain. The bugs are represented as black dots. The larger the black dot, the greater the bug's cumulative energy, and hence its fitness. The "tail" of a bug indicates the direction vector of its motion. The energy and fitness distributions are shown as bar graphs to the right of the windows. It is clear that each bug climbs the ($F2$) potential hill. As the generations pass (i.e. the time steps), the tails become shorter and shorter (as shown in Fig. 3.30(b),(c),(d)). This shows that the bugs evolved the correct directions in which to move, and thus "converged" to the top of the hill. It was confirmed that for optimizing all standard functions described in Section 2.3, the approach used in the BUGS program has the same or greater search power than real-valued GAs (from the viewpoint of online and off-line performance) [Iba *et al.* (1992, 1993)]. Moreover, the experiment in $F5$ (i.e. plateau with deep perforations) has made it clear that bugs can go beyond the valley to the next peak so as to avoid the local-extrema trap. This is realized with appropriate step sizes (i.e. tails of bugs) and *Bug-GA Period*. The next section describes this type of further improvement using an entropy-based adaptation.

Fig. 3.31 shows the results of the modified De Jong's $F4$ function (maximization problem), defined as follows:

$$Maximize \quad f(x_1, \cdots, x_n) = -(\sum_{i=1}^{n} ix_i^4 + GAUSS(0, 1))$$
$$where \quad -5.12 \leq x_i \leq 5.12. \quad (3.20)$$

Here GAUSS(0,1) is a normal distribution with mean 0.0 and variance 1.0. We performed experiments by varying n (as shown in Eq. (3.20)) to investigate the effect of using higher dimensions. Fig. 3.31 shows the online performance results for different numbers of generations. These curves are plotted using the average online performance of ten runs. Naturally, performance becomes worse in higher dimensions. However, as can be seen, at

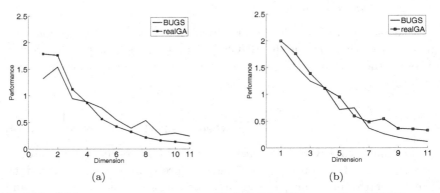

(a)   (b)

Fig. 3.31   Performance comparison on modified $F4$ (a) 300th generation (b) 500th generation

Table 3.7   BUGS vs real-valued GA (t-test)

	BUGS	real GA	BUGS	real-valued GA
Generation	300		500	
n	26		26	
Count	10	10	10	10
Average	0.4311	0.2827	0.5806	0.3249
Variance	0.0301	0.0165	0.0203	0.0059
f-value	1.8263		3.4660	
t-value	2.1728		4.9524	

higher dimensions, BUGS performs better than the real-valued GA, whereas for lower dimensions, the real-valued GA did as well or better. These results were tested for statistical significance using the t-test shown in Table 3.7.

If we compare two results in different generations with 18 degrees of freedom ($= 10 + 10 - 2$), we find that in each case, the difference in the averages (i.e. the superiority of BUGS's average to that of real-valued GA) is shown to be (t-test) significant ($t_{0.05;18} = 2.101$, $2.101 < 2.1728$, $2.101 < 4.9524$). Thus we can conclude that the BUGS program is an effective optimizer, especially at higher dimensions. However, the t-test hypothesis is somewhat questionable for the latter case (i.e. for 500 generations), because the requirement that the variances be almost equal is not accepted by the f-test ($F_{0.05;9,9} = 3.18$, $3.18 < 3.466$). This high-variance effect in BUGS is due to the fact that the bugs converge to the top of the hill well enough to be sensitive to random noise caused by GAUSS(0,1). This phenomenon might well be regarded as an advantage over real-valued GA, with its low variance.

3.3.3.2 *Recovery of superquadric primitives*

BUGS was then applied to more practical problems, such as those requiring geometric learning or reasoning. These areas are usually too complicated to be treated using traditional symbolic reasoning techniques, so other approaches have been proposed such as algebraic constraint-directed methods. In this section, we describe some experiments with curve fitting for computer vision. The original problem was presented in [Yokoya *et al.* (1992)], and is described as follows. The aim is to derive a model description using superquadric forms from vision data (normals and positions) (See Fig. 3.32(a) and Fig. 3.33(a)). More formally, the position vector $\vec{Y}$ and the normal vector $\vec{N}$ of a superellipsoid in canonical positions are explicitly represented using the north–south parameter η and the east–west parameter ω as follows:

$$\vec{Y}(\eta,\omega) = \begin{bmatrix} x(\eta,\omega) \\ y(\eta,\omega) \\ z(\eta,\omega) \end{bmatrix} = \begin{bmatrix} a_1 \cos^{\epsilon_1}\eta\cos^{\epsilon_2}\omega \\ a_2 \cos^{\epsilon_1}\eta\sin^{\epsilon_2}\omega \\ a_3 \sin^{\epsilon_1}\eta \end{bmatrix} \tag{3.21}$$

$$\vec{N}(\eta,\omega) = \begin{bmatrix} n_x(\eta,\omega) \\ n_y(\eta,\omega) \\ n_z(\eta,\omega) \end{bmatrix} = \begin{bmatrix} (1/a_1)\cos^{2-\epsilon_1}\eta\cos^{2-\epsilon_2}\omega \\ (1/a_2)\cos^{2-\epsilon_1}\eta\sin^{2-\epsilon_2}\omega \\ (1/a_3)\sin^{2-\epsilon_1}\eta \end{bmatrix} \tag{3.22}$$

where the parameters η and ω have the ranges of $-\frac{\pi}{2} \leq \eta \leq \frac{\pi}{2}$ and $-\pi \leq \omega \leq \pi$, respectively. Note that the cosine and sine function values can be negative for possible values of η and ω. Strictly speaking, the first component of $\vec{Y}$ in Eq. (3.21), for example, should be written as $a_1 \text{sign}\{\cos\eta\cos\omega\}|\cos\eta|^{\epsilon_1}|\cos\omega|^{\epsilon_2}$.

The above definition gives the following implicit representation of the superellipsoid:

$$f = \left(\left(\frac{|x|}{a_1}\right)^{\frac{2}{\epsilon_2}} + \left(\frac{|y|}{a_2}\right)^{\frac{2}{\epsilon_2}} \right)^{\frac{\epsilon_2}{\epsilon_1}} + \left(\frac{|z|}{a_3}\right)^{\frac{2}{\epsilon_1}} \tag{3.23}$$

This function is called "inside-outside" function. If $f(x,y,z) = 1$, the point (x,y,z) is on the superellipsoid; If $f(x,y,z) > 1$, the point (x,y,z) lies outside the superellipsoid; If $f(x,y,z) < 1$, the point (x,y,z) lies inside the superellipsoid. Several "inside-outside" functions have been proposed, which differ only in detail.

The superellipsoidal shape model is represented in total by 11 independent parameters, which include parameters for shape (ϵ_1, ϵ_2) and size

(a_1, a_2, a_3), as well as translation and rotation parameters. In order to use BUGS, these 11 parameters were considered as bug-positions:

$$\vec{X} = (a_1, a_2, a_3, \epsilon_1, \epsilon_2, \theta_1, \theta_2, \theta_3, l_1, l_2, l_3) \tag{3.24}$$

where a_i and ϵ_i are given as above, θ_i is the rotation angle and l_i is the translation length. In order to recover the superquadric primitives from an image, its fitness value is defined using the error-of-fit measure E as follows:

$$f = \frac{1}{1 + E} \quad \text{where} \quad E = E_1 + \lambda E_2 \left(\frac{V}{4\pi/3} \right)^{\frac{2}{3}}, \quad E_1 = \frac{1}{p} \sum_{i=1}^{p} \left| \vec{Y}_i - \vec{y}_i \right|^2 \tag{3.25}$$

$$E_2 = \frac{1}{q} \sum_{i=1}^{q} \left| \frac{\vec{N}_i}{\left| \vec{N}_i \right|} - \vec{n}_i \right|^2, \quad V = 2a_1 a_2 a_3 \epsilon_1 \epsilon_2 B(\frac{\epsilon_1}{2} + 1, \epsilon_1) B(\frac{\epsilon_2}{2}, \frac{\epsilon_2}{2}) \tag{3.26}$$

The vectors $\vec{y}_i$ and $\vec{n}_i$ represent the position and unit surface normal vectors at a point in a given range image. The vector $\vec{Y}_i$ represents the position vector of a point on the superellipsoid through which a straight line connecting the point $\vec{y}_i$ and the center O of the superellipsoid passes. The vector $\vec{N}_i$ represents the surface normal at the point $\vec{Y}_i$. The volume of the superellipsoid is denoted by V and is computed by using Eq. (3.26), where B represents the *beta function*. Note that E_1 evaluates the error-of-fit in depth and E_2 evaluates the error-of-fit in surface orientation. Both of these terms have a minimum value of zero when the given data points fit perfectly to a superellipsoid. A more detailed discussion can be found in [Yokoya *et al.* (1992)].

It is widely known that when performing a hill-climbing search, it is easy to fall into the trap of local extrema, especially when higher dimensions are involved. This is partly due to the difficulty of avoiding premature convergence. With BUGS, we try to avoid this problem by varying the step sizes and directions. The entropy-based adaptation of step sizes is realized in BUGS in order to generate a population variance in the bugs. This variance generation technique was originally introduced into GAs for classifier systems [Wilson (1987)]. The entropy of the bugs at generation t is defined as follows:

$$H(t) = -\frac{\sum_{i=1}^{N} p(i) log_2 p(i)}{log_2 N} \quad \text{where} \quad p(i) = \frac{f(i)}{\sum_{i=1}^{N} f(i)} \tag{3.27}$$

N is the population size, and $f(i)$ is the fitness of the i-th bug. With this entropy, we chose the following criteria for the step-size coordination at generation t:

$$\Delta(t) := H(t) - H(t - 1) \tag{3.28}$$

Table 3.8 Experimental condition and BUGS parameters

a_1, a_2, a_3	0.1~5.1	N (population size)	40	λ	1.0
ϵ_1, ϵ_2	0.1~3.1	P_{CROSS}	0.6	Δ_1	-5.0E-4
Rotation parameters	$-\pi \sim \pi$	$P_{MUTATION}$	0.0333	Δs_1	0.1
Translation parameters	$-5.0 \sim 5.0$	Bug-GA period	6	Δ_2	3.5E-4
		Selection period	3	Δs_2	0.1

$$\text{If } \Delta(t) \geq \Delta_1 \quad \text{then} \quad \text{for } i := 1 \text{ to } N \text{ do } \ \vec{DX}_i(t) := (1 + \Delta s_1)\vec{DX}_i(t) \tag{3.29}$$

$$\text{If } \Delta(t) < \Delta_2 \quad \text{then} \quad \text{for } i := 1 \text{ to } N \text{ do } \ \vec{DX}_i(t) := (1 - \Delta s_2)\vec{DX}_i(t) \tag{3.30}$$

We now present the experimental results of the use of BUGS for the recovery (or evolution) of superquadric shapes. In this experiment, the search ranges for the superellipsoid parameters and the parameters used in the BUGS program are given in Table 3.8.

Fig. 3.32 shows the evolutionary development of a cubic shape shown in Fig. 3.32(b) ($a_1 = a_2 = a_3 = 1.0, \epsilon_2 = \epsilon_1 = 0.1, \theta_1 = \theta_2 = \theta_3 = l_1 = l_2 = l_3 = 0.0$) from the normal and positional data given in Fig. 3.32(a). Fig. 3.32(c) shows the convergence of the error-of-fit measure of BUGS, as a function of the generation count. From Fig. 3.32(d) it is clear that the bugs converged to the cubic shape in superquadric form over the generations. In this case, the rotation angle around each axis was allowed to be multiples of 90. Once at 1079th generation, the shape seemed to converge to a cube. However, since its axis is a little different, this shape (i.e. local extreme) is abandoned so as to search for another cubic shape at generation 1106. In this way, local-extrema traps can be avoided by BUGS. In the same way, Fig. 3.33 shows the evolutionary development of a cylindrical shape ($a_1 = a_2 = a_3 = \epsilon_2 = 1.0, \epsilon_1 = 0.1, \theta_1 = \theta_2 = \theta_3 = l_1 = l_2 = l_3 = 0.0$). In this case, the rotation angle around the Z-axis (θ_1) was allowed to be arbitrary. Just as in the cubic model above, the local-extrema shape is abandoned at generation 89 in cylindrical model formation (since the size is a little different). Although the error-of-fit measure is nearly zero, the acquired shape at generation 689 is less similar to the target than in the cubic model experiment (Fig. 3.32). This may reflect the difficulty in defining the fitness of curved shapes such as cylinders. With these experiments we have shown the utility of the BUGS program as an effective search method which is suitable for practical applications.

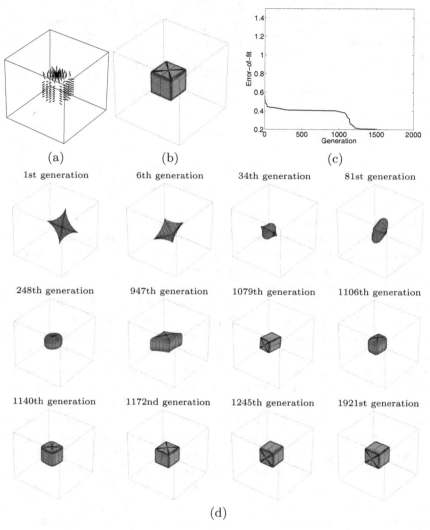

Fig. 3.32   Recovery of cubic model: (a) Input data, (b) Target model, (c) Performance (Error-of-fit vs Generation), (d) Experimental results.

3.3.3.3   *Multiple-line fitting problem*

This section presents another experiment for computer vision applications using BUGS. The aim is to derive multiple descriptors from noisy vision

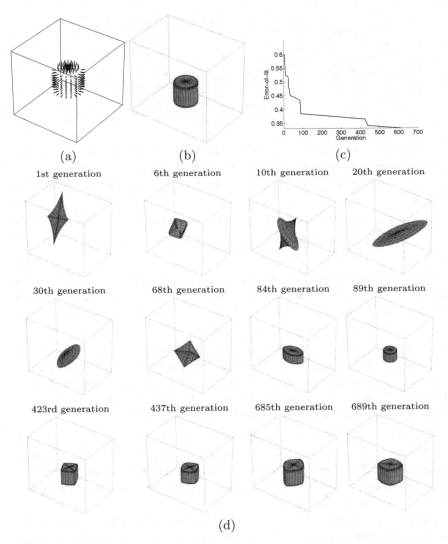

Fig. 3.33 Recovery of cylindrical model: (a) Input data, (b) Target model, (c) Performance (Error-of-fit vs Generation), (d) Experimental results.

data (See Fig. 3.34(a)). Multiple-line fitting problems are more difficult to solve than single-line fitting problems and cannot be solved easily with usual optimization techniques such as simulated annealing. This is because it is necessary to seek different local optima simultaneously. On the contrary,

Table 3.9   Experimental condition and BUGS parameters (2)

r (domain range)	0.0~1.0	P_{CROSS}	0.6
θ (domain range)	0.0~2π	$P_{MUTATION}$	0.033
Line points	30~80	P_{asex}	0.1
Random points	10~20	Selection period	100
Init. pop. size	40	Selection rate	0.8
Int. energy	5	Repr. energy	15
Aging decay	0.6	Repr. radius	0.1

BUGS can solve this type of problem naturally by introducing biologically realistic features, such as resource competition and resource sharing.

The bugs used to solve multiple-line fitting problems are defined as follows:

$$Bug_i(t) : \text{position } \vec{X}_i(t) = (r^i(t), \theta^i(t)) \tag{3.31}$$

$$\text{direction-code } \vec{DX}_i(t) = (dx_1^i(t), \cdots, dx_6^i(t)) \tag{3.32}$$

$$\text{energy } e_i(t) \tag{3.33}$$

Each bug position provides two parameters (r, θ) for the equation of a straight line, where r is the distance from the origin to the line, and θ is the angle of the normal to the line. With some simple trigonometry, it can be shown that the equation of the line is:

$$(cos\theta)x + (sin\theta)y = r \tag{3.34}$$

Hence there is a mapping (called "Hough transformation") from a bug's position (r, θ) to the equation of a line. The positions and energies of these bugs are derived as explained in the earlier bug simulations. The fitness of each "line-finding" bug in (r, θ) is defined as follows:

$$f(r, \theta) = \# \text{ of points on the line } (\cos\theta)x + (\sin\theta)y = r \tag{3.35}$$

Instead of raw vision data, we use data pre-processed by smoothing techniques such as the "median filter" [Nevatia (1982)]. A selection process was also applied to weed out hopeless (i.e. low fitness) bugs ("selection period" and "selection rate").

Fig. 3.34(d) shows the results for a three-line fitting problem, making use of the parameters in Table 3.9. Each small "streak" in the (r, θ)-plane represents one bug. The tail of each bug represents $\vec{DX}$ (length and direction) and the dot size indicates fitness (the larger the fitness, the bigger the dot). Bugs share resources and compete with each other appropriately, which means they hill-climb over the r-θ plane. Fig. 3.34(c) illustrates the approximate search space which maps the fitness $f(r, \theta)$ (vertical axis) in the r-θ plane. Note that different "species" of bugs correspond to these optima.

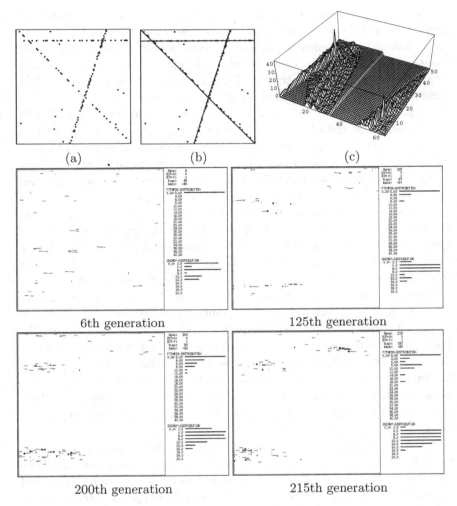

(a)   (b)   (c)

6th generation   125th generation

200th generation   215th generation

Fig. 3.34 Three-line fitting problem: (a) Noisy data, (b) Acquired lines, (c) Search space, (d) Experimental results.

3.3.4 *BUGS vs real-valued GA*

The experiments discussed above show that the BUGS approach is an effective optimization and search strategy, and is more efficient than the usual real-valued GA approach. What is the possible reason behind the search efficiency of bugs?

Real-valued GA-based optimization methods depend largely upon the phenomenon of data recombination (i.e. crossover), thus lack local search (hill-climbing) mechanisms. This lack makes it difficult for a real-valued GA to search initially in a "coarse-grained" manner, and later to switch to a "fine-grained" search strategy. BUGS, however, uses a combined hill-climbing method and a real-valued GA-like approach. This combination is made possible by the representation and selection scheme used in BUGS. More specifically, the adaptive learning used in BUGS is due to an evolving choice of directions, rather than positions (as with the real-valued GA methods). This direction based evolution is somewhat similar to the strategic learning of a meta-GA. Informally, a meta-GA's search control is regarded as a generalization of the adaptation of bugs' directions.

Just as with a real-valued GA, the adaptive behavior of BUGS is derived from the *Schema Theorem* and the building-block hypothesis [Goldberg (1989)] (see Chapter 4 in this book). The building blocks of BUGS are the direction components in the chromosome, whereas positions (as distinct from directions) are used only to determine the fitness for chromosome selection for the next generation. In the experiments mentioned earlier (Fig. 3.30) we discovered that this adaptive process occurred when two or more bugs moving in various directions collided with each other on the higher levels of the hill, and when they reproduced children with "averaged" directions (i.e. shorter-length vectors or middle-angles). Thus, the tails of the bugs become shorter as they climb up the hill and want to stay there. Generally reproductions occur everywhere in the search space, but these collisions on the higher levels are expected to be more frequent because of the gradual convergence of bugs.

As the generations proceed, the bugs in the BUGS program are converged to the top of the hill via position-based fitness selection (see Fig. 3.35). In the meantime, the motion directions are gradually refined by the GA mechanism. We consider this BUGS-type adaptation to be closely related to the building-block hypothesis and to schema-based adaptation. In some cases, such as in Fig. 3.31, the BUGS approach has been shown to be a more efficient search strategy than a real-valued GA. This is justified by the comments of [Rechenberg (1986)]. He claimed that, in general, the essential dimensions for search are relatively few in higher dimensions and that an effective optimization is realized by following the gradient curve in these essential dimensions. We think that direction-based (rather than position-based) building blocks produce a more efficient search strategy in the sense that essential dimensions are adaptively acquired in bugs' motions, similar to PSO search.

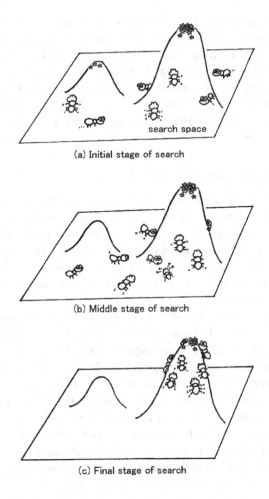

(a) Initial stage of search

(b) Middle stage of search

(c) Final stage of search

Fig. 3.35   Illustration of bug-based search

3.4   DE: differential evolution

The rest of this chapter presents another new generation EA called differential evolution (DE) for real parameter optimization. In the field of continuous optimization the DE algorithm has drawn much attention in the last few years after it was proposed by Rainer M. Storn and Kenneth V. Price in 1995 [Storn and Price (1995)]. Being a member of the EA family, it works with a population of solutions and stochastically searches through the search space. The beauty of the algorithm is its simple and compact structure which is very easy to understand and work with. In spite of its primitive architecture, it exhibits a powerful search capability which has brought it many real-world applications in diverse fields. Storn and Price proposed DE as a family of algorithms rather than as a single algorithm [Storn and Price (1995, 1997)]. In this section, first we present the key concepts of the algorithm class in the form of what is known as classic DE, and then we introduce the reader to the other versions of DE.

3.4.1　*The overall structure of DE*

Differential evolution was the outcome of the research by Kenneth Price and Rainer Storn for solving the Chebychev polynomial fitting problem. Using common concepts of EAs, they converted a combinatorial algorithm (the genetic annealing algorithm developed by Kenneth Price) to a numerical optimizer. Therefore, DE works with the general framework of EA and uses many of EA concepts such as multipoint searching, use of recombination and selection operators.

Like most of the EAs, DE starts to explore the search space by sampling at multiple, randomly chosen initial points [Storn (1999); Price *et al.* (2005)]. Thereafter, the algorithm guides the population towards the vicinity of the global optimum through repeated cycles of reproduction and selection. The generation alternation model used in "classic DE" for refining candidate solutions in successive generations is shown in Fig. 3.36. Looking at the overall framework of DE as shown in Fig. 3.36, it is not easy to differentiate the algorithm from any ordinary GA because it iterates with the same common components: *initialization, evaluation, reproduction* and *selection*. However, as we look inside these components in the following sections the distinct features of the algorithm will become apparent.

3.4.2　*DE population initialization*

One important concern in implementing any EA is the initialization of the population. Actually, there are two issues here: "How to initialize each gene of the individual?" and "How many individuals to be used in the population?" Here we will discuss only the first issue. The other issue, which is related to its population size, a critical parameter of DE, will be focused on in Section 3.4.7.3.

DE

Step 1 Generate a random initial population P^G

Step 2 Evaluate P^G

Step 3 **for** each individual I in P^G **do**

Step 4   Reproduce an offspring J from I

Step 5   Evaluate J

Step 6 $P^{G+1} = P^{G+1} \cup \text{Select}(I, J)$

Step 7 **end**

Step 8 Set $G = G + 1$

Step 9 **repeat Step 3** to **Step 8** until termination criteria is met

---

Fig. 3.36   Outline of the differential evolution algorithm

As we have seen in earlier sections, EA algorithms initialize each gene of each chromosome (individual) using a uniform random generator within the search ranges. And DE is not an exception in this regard. Suppose we are working in an N-dimensional problem. Then each individual of the DE population, P^G, would be an N-dimensional vector which can be initialized as follows:

$$x_{i,t}^{G=1} = Random_t(LB_t, UB_t) \qquad (3.36)$$

where $x_{i,t}^{G=1}$ denotes the t-th gene ($t = 1, 2, \cdots, N$) of i-th individual ($i = 1, 2, \cdots, P$) in generation $G = 1$. LB_t and UB_t denote the lower and upper limit of the search ranges for gene-j, respectively, and $Random_t(a, b)$ denotes the uniform random number generator that returns a uniformly distributed random number from [a, b). The subscript in $Random_t$ is used to clarify that a separate random number is drawn for each gene in each individual.

3.4.3   *DE selection*

Generally, two types of selection methods are applied in EC, selection for reproduction and selection for survival [Bäck *et al.* (2000)]. The first paradigm determines how to distribute the opportunity to reproduce among the individuals of the population; the latter paradigm determines how to administer the life span of different individuals for favoring the survival of promising individuals. Different EAs apply different combinations and implementations of these two selection criteria.

DE does not use the "selection for reproduction" mechanism, i.e. no individual is favored for reproduction compared to others [Price *et al.* (2005)]. In other words it can be said that in DE each individual gets an opportunity to spawn its own offspring by mating with other individuals. Section 3.4.3.1 explains how the auxiliary parents (to whom the principal parent mates for breeding) are chosen.

3.4.3.1 *Parent choice*

As shown in the DE model (Fig. 3.36), each individual in the current generation, irrespective of its fitness, becomes the principal parent for reproduction. Other individuals participating in reproduction, the auxiliary parents, are chosen randomly from the population. Specifically, for each individual x_i^G, where G denotes the current generation, three other random individuals x_j^G, x_k^G and x_l^G are selected from the population such that j, k and $l \in \{1, 2, \cdots, P\}$ and $i \neq j \neq k \neq l$. This way, a parent pool of four individuals is formed to breed an offspring.

3.4.3.2 *Selection for survival*

DE applies selection pressure only when picking survivors. A knockout competition is played between each individual x_i^G and its offspring u_i^G and the winner is selected deterministically based on objective function values and promoted to the next generation. So the survival criteria in DE can be described as follows:

$$x_i^{G+1} = \begin{cases} u_i^G & \text{if } f(u_i^G) \leq f(x_i^G) \\ x_i^G & \text{else} \end{cases} \tag{3.37}$$

where $f(\cdot)$ indicates the objective function that is being optimized (minimized here). The one-to-one replacement strategy used in DE is different from what is generally observed in EAs. However, practicing this one-to-one selection mechanism enables DE to exercise elitism on its population. In fact, this scheme preserves not only the global best (the best individual of the population) but also the local best (the best individual encountered at any index). However, the reader should note that the similar elitism is also used in PSO as described in Section 3.2.2.

On the other hand, using one-to-one survivor selection criteria, DE ignores many promising individuals, the exploitation of which could accelerate the search. Due to its positional elitism strategy it discards an offspring which is better than most of the current population but worse than its parent. However, such rejected individuals could be useful to accelerate the search for the global optimum (see [Noman and Iba (2006)]).

3.4.4 *DE operators*

In any EA, a set of operators are used to alter the genetic code of current individuals to improve their fitness. The success and failure of the evolutionary system depends on carefully chosen operators. The most commonly used operators found in EAs are mutation and crossover. DE also makes use of these two operators. However, as we will see, DE maintains its uniqueness in using these operators.

3.4.4.1 *Differential mutation*

DE derived its name from the mutation operator it applies to mutate its individual. The auxiliary parents selected for reproduction are engaged to generate the mutated individual. The scaled difference between two of the auxiliary parents are added to the third auxiliary parent to create the mutated individual. This operation is called "differential mutation" and generates the mutated individual v_i^G, for the principal parent x_i^G according to the following equation

$$v_i^G = x_j^G + F(x_k^G - x_l^G) \tag{3.38}$$

where F, commonly known as scaling factor or amplification factor, is a positive real number. The suggested range for F is $(0,1)$, based on empirical study [Price *et al.* (2005)]. Some studies suggest that the value of F less than 0.3 or 0.4 is less reliable and has no use at all [Zaharie (2002); Gämperle *et al.* (2002)]. However, there are examples where $F < 0.3$ proved to be the most suitable choice for optimization [Chakraborti *et al.* (2001); Noman and Iba (2008b)]. Nevertheless, it may be deduced that very small values of F are atypical but not impractical.

3.4.4.2 *Binomial crossover*

To complement the differential mutation search strategy, DE then uses a crossover operation, often referred to as "discrete recombination", in which the mutated individual v_i^G is mated with the principal parent x_i^G and generates the offspring or "trial individual" u_i^G. This crossover operation used in classic DE is also known as "binomial crossover" which is actually a slightly modified version of the uniform crossover operation. In uniform crossover, the trial individual is created by choosing genes from either of the parents with uniform random probability C_r. The DE version of uniform crossover, i.e. the binomial crossover, uses the same strategy with the exception that at least one gene is inherited from the mutated individual v_i^G.

Formally, the genes of u_i^G are inherited from x_i^G and v_i^G, determined by the parameter crossover probability C_r, as follows:

$$u_{i,t}^G = \begin{cases} v_{i,t}^G & \text{if } r(t) \leq C_r \text{ or } t = rn(i) \\ x_{i,t}^G & \text{if } r(t) > C_r \text{ and } t \neq rn(i) \end{cases} \tag{3.39}$$

where $(t = 1, 2, \cdots, N)$ denotes the t-th element of individual vectors. $r(t) \in [0,1]$ is the t-th evaluation of a uniform random number generator and $rn(i) \in \{1, 2, \cdots, N\}$ is a randomly chosen index which ensures that u_i^G gets at least one element from v_i^G. Originally, it was suggested that the value of C_r be chosen from [0,1]; later it was suggested that $0 \leq C_r \leq 0.2$ be used for decomposable functions and $0.9 \leq C_r \leq 1$ be used for inde-composable functions [Price *et al.* (2005)]. However, many different studies found that other settings of $C_r \in [0, 1]$ can also be effective for optimization [Noman and Iba (2005a); Krink *et al.* (2004)].

The way in which offspring are generated highlights another point of difference of DE from canonical GA. In GAs, mutation is generally stochas-tically applied to crossover-generated offspring to maintain the population diversity. On the other hand, in DE mutation is deterministically applied for generating each offspring and the mutated individual actually partici-pates in the crossover operation to breed the offspring. Here we introduced only the mutation and crossover used in classic DE, however, there are other mutation and crossover operators used by the DE algorithm which will be described in Section 3.4.6.

3.4.5   *Parameters of DE*

One problem often faced while using EAs is the choice of the appropriate values for its parameters. If a proper setting for the parameters is not used then the performance of EAs could be really disappointing. And a user could be easily confused with the optimum settings of so many parameters that some EAs work with. Here comes another advantage of DE over many other EAs – DE works with only three parameters: amplification factor F, crossover rate C_r and population size P.

Although DE works with only a handful of parameters, proper tuning of these parameters is very necessary for the reliable performance of the algorithm. In their original proposal, Storn and Price proposed that the population size P should be between $5 \times N$ and $10 \times N$ and not less than 4 to ensure the mutation operation in Eq. (3.38) can be carried out appropriately. However, many researchers have since reported that while for small dimensional optimization $N \leq 5$ this setting might be appropriate, in higher dimensions $P << 5 \times N$ would be a more appropriate setting for DE population size [Noman and Iba (2005a, 2006); Brest *et al.* (2006); Rahnamayan *et al.* (2008); Neri and Tirronen (2009)]. However, after some limit, it is not useful to increase the population size any more. Some results of population study on DE will be presented in Section 3.4.7.3.

Similar conclusions can be drawn about the proper settings of F and C_r. As we will show empirically in the benchmark study, for some settings DE can perform extraordinarily well on some problems, whereas with different settings of F and C_r the performance of DE can be really dull. So the careful and proper setting of parameters is important to work DE at its best.

3.4.6 *Standard DE family*

The above scheme is not the only variant of DE which has proven to be useful. Storn and Price have proposed at least ten variants of DE in their proposals. The generation alternation scheme in all of these variants are the same as presented in Section 3.4.1. The basic difference among them is how the mutation and crossover is performed. In order to distinguish among its variants the notation $DE/\alpha/\beta/\gamma$ is used, where α specifies the vector to be mutated which can be a random vector, the best vector or the current vector; β is the number of difference vectors used and γ denotes the crossover scheme, binomial or exponential. Using this notation, the DE strategy described above can be denoted as DE/rand/1/bin. Before we explain the other strategies, first we describe the "exponential crossover".

In exponential crossover, the mutated individual v_i^G participates with the principal parent x_i^G in the reproduction process – the same as in binomial crossover. Again, how the genes of the offspring u_i^G are inherited from these two parents is administered by the crossover rate (C_r). But here C_r regulates how many consecutive genes of the mutated individual on average are copied to the offspring.

To put it differently, in exponential crossover, the starting position of crossover is chosen randomly from $1, \cdots, N$, and then L consecutive elements (considering the chromosome is circular) are taken from the mutated individual v_i^G, where the value of L is determined randomly. The genes for the other positions are inherited from the principal parent. Therefore, the exponential crossover exchanges L adjacent elements, whereas the binomial version disperses the changed coordinates randomly over the dimensions $1, 2, \cdots, N$.

Now the mutated individual can also be generated using one of the following strategies replacing the mutation strategy given in Eq. (3.38):

$$\text{DE/best/1}: \qquad v_i^G = x_{best}^G + F(x_j^G - x_k^G) \qquad (3.40)$$

$$\text{DE/rand/2}: \quad v_i^G = x_j^G + F(x_k^G - x_l^G) + F(x_m^G - x_n^G) \qquad (3.41)$$

$$\text{DE/best/2}: \quad v_i^G = x_{best}^G + F(x_j^G - x_k^G) + F(x_l^G - x_m^G) \qquad (3.42)$$

$$\text{DE/curToBest/1}: \quad v_i^G = x_i^G + F(x_{best}^G - x_i^G) + F(x_j^G - x_k^G), \qquad (3.43)$$

where x_{best}^G represents the best individual in the current generation, and $l, m, n \in \{1, 2, \cdots, N\}$ and $i \neq j \neq k \neq l \neq m \neq n$. Changing the mutation operation in classic DE (DE/rand/1/bin) will result in different variants of DE which are referred to as DE/best/1/bin, DE/rand/2/bin, DE/best/2/bin, DE/current-to-rand/1/bin. Again, each of these variants can have an exponential version which is implemented by replacing the binomial crossover operation with the exponential crossover. And these variants are called DE/rand/1/exp, DE/best/1/exp, DE/rand/2/exp, DE/best/2/exp, DE/current-to-rand/1/exp, respectively, according to the nomenclature. As the reader can easily anticipate, more variants of DE like these can be created, some of which can be found in the code section of the Differential Evolution Homepage (http://www.icsi.berkeley.edu/~storn/code.html).

3.4.7   *Numerical study on DE*

In this section, we present the numerical results to illustrate the characteristics of DE as an optimizer. A complete study on the DE family under all experimental conditions does not fall within the scope of this book. But we want to present a brief sketch of the behavior of the algorithm as a new-generation optimization tool. Hence, the study was concentrated on classic DE (DE/rand/1/bin), and we also studied some other DE family members briefly.

Five test functions commonly used in the literature were used in this study. These functions are "sphere model" (f_{sph}), "generalized Rosenbrock's function" (f_{ros}), "Ackley's function" (f_{ack}), "Griewangk's function"

(f_{grw}), and "generalized Rastrigin's function" (f_{ras}). All benchmarks chosen are unconstrained minimization problems. It should be noted that four functions of this benchmark suite are actually generalized versions of the benchmark functions used in earlier sections. More specifically, f_{sph} is the generalized $F1$, f_{ros} is the generalized $F2$, f_{ras} is the generalized $F8$ and f_{grw} is the generalized $F9$, respectively. For the readers' convenience the generalized definitions of these functions are given as follows:

$$f_{sph}(\vec{x}) = \sum_{i=1}^{N} x_i^2; \qquad -100 \leq x_i \leq 100; \qquad f_{sph}^* = f_{sph}(0, \cdots, 0) = 0$$

$$f_{ros}(\vec{x}) = \sum_{i=1}^{N-1} (100(x_{i+1} - x_i^2)^2 + (1 - x_i)^2); \qquad -100 \leq x_i \leq 100;$$

$$f_{ros}^* = f_{ros}(1, \cdots, 1) = 0$$

$$f_{ack}(\vec{x}) = 20 + exp(1) - 20exp\left(-0.2\sqrt{\frac{1}{N}\sum_{i=1}^{N} x_i^2}\right) - exp\left(\frac{1}{N}\sum_{i=1}^{N} \cos(2\pi x_i)\right);$$

$$-32 \leq x_i \leq 32; \qquad f_{ack}^* = f_{ack}(0, \cdots, 0) = 0$$

$$f_{grw}(\vec{x}) = \sum_{i=1}^{N} \frac{x_i^2}{4000} - \prod_{i=1}^{N} \cos\frac{x_i}{\sqrt{i}} + 1; \quad -600 \leq x_i \leq 600;$$

$$f_{grw}^* = f_{grw}(0, \cdots, 0) = 0$$

$$f_{ras}(\vec{x}) = 10N + \sum_{i=1}^{N} (x_i^2 - 10\cos(2\pi x_i)); \quad -5 \leq x_i \leq 5;$$

$$f_{ras}^* = f_{ras}(0, \cdots, 0) = 0$$

Here, f_{sph}, and f_{ros} are unimodal functions, f_{ack}, f_{grw}, and f_{ras} are multimodal functions and f^* denotes the global minimum for the function.

3.4.7.1 *Experimental setup*

In this numerical study DE was allocated a fixed number of function evaluations to find the global optimum of each problem. For N-dimensional problems, $N \times 10000$ fitness evaluations were allowed at maximum. The

Table 3.10 Statistics of error values and fitness evaluations for DE/rand/1/bin
($N = 30$, $P = 30$, $F = 0.5$ and $C_r = 0.1$)

Fun	Best Error Values	Required Fitness Evaluations	Success (25)
f_{sph}	4.95E$-$149 $\pm$ 8.94E$-$149	21181.8 $\pm$ 334.8	(25)
f_{ros}	5.12E+01 $\pm$ 2.60E+01	–	(0)
f_{ack}	2.66E$-$15 $\pm$ 0.00E+00	30770.5 $\pm$ 401.8	(25)
f_{grw}	0.00E+00 $\pm$ 0.00E+00	23544.0 $\pm$ 1339.6	(25)
f_{ras}	0.00E+00 $\pm$ 0.00E+00	43633.2 $\pm$ 1251.8	(25)

final fitness value that DE can achieve using the maximum allowed fitness evaluations was recorded. If the best achieved fitness value was less than 10^{-6} then we assume that the global optimum was found for that function. And the number of fitness evaluations required to reach that optimum was also recorded.

All experiments were repeated 25 times. The average (AVG) and the standard deviation (SD) of the minimum fitness values (and the required fitness evaluations) in different trial runs were calculated. The number of trials in which the global optimum was reached was also recorded for each function.

3.4.7.2 *Study using DE/rand/1/bin*

Table 3.10 presents the statistical results of the numerical study on the benchmark for DE/rand/1/bin. Here the choice of parameters was as follows: $P = N = 30$, $F = 0.5$ and $C_r = 0.1$. These parameter settings were chosen based on the study presented in Section 3.4.7.3. The figures in Table 3.10 show that DE was successful in finding the optimum for four functions in every trial. Only for f_{ros} was DE not successful in locating the optimum in any trial run. But it does not mean that DE failed to reach the optimum for f_{ros}. With proper tuning of parameters, DE can find the global optimum of f_{ros} function easily [Price *et al.* (2005)]. The average convergence curve of DE for these benchmark functions are also shown in Fig. 3.37. These convergence curves show that overall, DE exhibits consistent performance in locating the global optimum and had almost no difficulty to reach it.

3.4.7.3 *Parameter study for DE/rand/1/bin*

It has already been mentioned that DE is very much sensitive to its parameter settings. In this section a brief study is presented to show how the performance of DE can vary with its parameter choice. In this study one of the DE parameters was varied while the other two were kept constant.

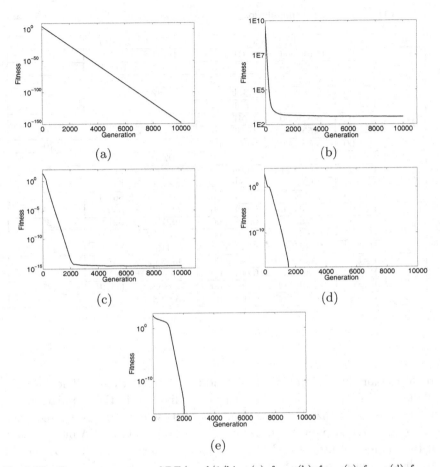

Fig. 3.37 Convergence curve of DE/rand/1/bin: (a) f_{sph}, (b) f_{ros}, (c) f_{ack}, (d) f_{grw}, (e) f_{ras}.

First, the effect of population size P was examined. For $N = 30$ dimensional problem space, different population sizes such as $P = 30$, $P = 50$, $P = 80$ and $P = 100$ were investigated. The summary of the results are shown in Table 3.11 and Fig. 3.38.

The data presented in Table 3.11 and the graphs in Fig. 3.38 show that the performance of DE is considerably affected by the choice of population size when the number of allowed fitness evaluations is limited. The presented results suggest that if too large a population size is chosen then DE

Table 3.11   Sensitivity to population size for DE/rand/1/bin ($N = 30$, $F = 0.5$ and $C_r = 0.1$)

Fun	P	Error Values	Fitness Evaluations	Success (25)
F_{sph}	P=30	4.95E−149 ± 8.94E−149	21181.8 ± 334.8	(25)
	P=50	3.42E−87 ± 3.43E−87	35595.8 ± 611.3	(25)
	P=80	7.62E−53 ± 2.67E−53	57024.2 ± 601.5	(25)
	P=100	2.06E−41 ± 9.31E−42	70982.8 ± 555.9	(25)
F_{ros}	P=30	5.12E+01 ± 2.60E+01	-	(0)
	P=50	3.61E+01 ± 1.74E+01	-	(0)
	P=80	3.55E+01 ± 1.46E+01	-	(0)
	P=100	3.39E+01 ± 9.06E+00	-	(0)
F_{ack}	P=30	2.66E−15 ± 0.00E+00	30770.5 ± 401.8	(25)
	P=50	2.66E−15 ± 0.00E+00	51499.4 ± 602.2	(25)
	P=80	3.09E−15 ± 1.18E−15	82321.6 ± 876.5	(25)
	P=100	3.09E−15 ± 1.18E−15	102985.9 ± 867.4	(25)
F_{grw}	P=30	0.00E+00 ± 0.00E+00	23544.0 ± 1339.6	(25)
	P=50	0.00E+00 ± 0.00E+00	39275.7 ± 1621.8	(25)
	P=80	0.00E+00 ± 0.00E+00	62515.2 ± 2314.0	(25)
	P=100	0.00E+00 ± 0.00E+00	78419.3 ± 1810.9	(25)
F_{ras}	P=30	0.00E+00 ± 0.00E+00	43633.2 ± 1251.8	(25)
	P=50	0.00E+00 ± 0.00E+00	74617.4 ± 2241.5	(25)
	P=80	0.00E+00 ± 0.00E+00	120866.9 ± 2647.0	(25)
	P=100	0.00E+00 ± 0.00E+00	152798.6 ± 2843.2	(25)

requires more fitness evaluations to find the global optimum. The reason is obvious – DE spawns offspring for every individual in the population. So if the population size is larger then more fitness evaluations are required. Although a larger population size may be used to make an EA more robust, if the number of fitness evaluations is limited, then for DE it is better not to choose a large population.

Now let's take a look at the effect of F and C_r on classic DE. We present a study on the benchmark suite varying the values of F and C_r choosing from [0.1, 0.3, 0.5, 0.7, 0.9]. The detailed results of this study is presented in Table 3.12. Analyzing these results, it was found that there is no best setting for all types of problems. For a specific function, a particular setting of these parameters was giving a very quick convergence and another setting was totally failing the algorithm. To give an idea on how these settings can affect the performance of the algorithm, we graphically compare the convergence curves for different parameter settings in Fig. 3.39. Based on these studies, it can be stated that for most of the cases the setting $F \geq 0.3$ is recommended and for C_r the setting $0.3 < C_r < 0.9$ is less effective.

Table 3.12   Parameter study for DE/rand/1/bin ($N = 30$, $P = 30$)

Sphere Function (f_{sph})

	CR=0.1	CR=0.3	CR=0.5	CR=0.7	CR=0.9
F=0.1	9.05E+01 ± 6.92E+01 (0)	5.11E+02 ± 3.12E+02 (0)	1.37E+03 ± 4.61E+02 (0)	3.59E+03 ± 1.87E+03 (0)	1.45E+04 ± 5.60E+03 (0)
F=0.3	9.34E-10 ± 4.67E-09 (25) [16223.2 ± 624.5]	2.30E-02 ± 7.94E-02 (21) [12401.5 ± 251.7]	2.00E+00 ± 6.43E+00 (4) [11182.0 ± 180.0]	3.08E+01 ± 4.00E+01 (0)	1.64E+03 ± 8.96E+02 (0)
F=0.5	4.95E-149 ± 8.94E-149 (25) [21181.8 ± 334.8]	7.67E-159 ± 1.67E-158 (25) [19826.4 ± 318.6]	2.09E-149 ± 2.97E-149 (25) [21029.4 ± 449.7]	1.19E-149 ± 3.38E-149 (25) [20972.5 ± 926.1]	4.51E+00 ± 1.65E+01 (6) [25473.5 ± 3766.0]
F=0.7	6.34E-104 ± 8.12E-104 (25) [29882.3 ± 445.2]	8.33E-78 ± 8.00E-78 (25) [38925.5 ± 905.0]	5.17E-51 ± 5.88E-51 (25) [57361.3 ± 1163.9]	1.19E-38 ± 1.62E-38 (25) [74170.2 ± 2653.7]	3.06E-63 ± 1.41E-61 (25) [47123.6 ± 1533.4]
F=0.9	2.25E-70 ± 2.59E-70 (25) [43003.2 ± 083.5]	8.62E-33 ± 6.13E-33 (25) [86435.2 ± 1889.2]	9.52E-12 ± 6.33E-12 (25) [201988.0 ± 4936.3]	2.84E-04 ± 2.38E-04 (0)	1.52E-17 ± 3.53E-17 (25) [145936.0 ± 8754.7]

Rosenbrock's Function (f_{ros})

	CR=0.1	CR=0.3	CR=0.5	CR=0.7	CR=0.9
AF=0.1	2.00E+06 ± 2.48E+06 (0)	3.23E+07 ± 5.54E+07 (0)	1.19E+08 ± 1.28E+08 (0)	4.11E+08 ± 3.03E+08 (0)	2.25E+09 ± 1.25E+09 (0)
AF=0.3	7.19E+01 ± 3.30E+01 (0)	5.47E+04 ± 1.40E+05 (0)	6.21E+05 ± 2.59E+06 (0)	6.93E+06 ± 1.20E+07 (0)	1.91E+08 ± 1.61E+08 (0)
AF=0.5	5.12E+01 ± 2.60E+01 (0)	2.88E+01 ± 1.68E+01 (0)	2.46E+01 ± 9.40E+00 (0)	2.73E+01 ± 1.88E+01 (0)	3.92E+05 ± 1.17E+06 (0)
AF=0.7	4.46E+01 ± 2.52E+01 (0)	2.88E+01 ± 2.21E+01 (0)	6.94E+01 ± 9.46E+01 (0)	8.35E-02 ± 9.15E-02 (0)	1.59E-01 ± 7.97E-01 (19) [271658.5 ± 22712.8]
AF=0.9	4.63E+01 ± 2.57E+01 (0)	3.41E+01 ± 2.23E+01 (0)	6.64E+01 ± 8.83E-01 (0)	4.45E+02 ± 6.92E+02 (0)	1.37E+02 ± 6.59E+00 (0)

Ackley's Function (f_{ack})

	CR=0.1	CR=0.3	CR=0.5	CR=0.7	CR=0.9
AF=0.1	2.72E+00 ± 8.64E-01 (0)	4.51E+00 ± 1.01E+00 (0)	6.28E+00 ± 1.54E+00 (0)	1.01E+01 ± 1.36E+00 (0)	1.55E+01 ± 1.10E+01 (0)
AF=0.3	2.31E-05 ± 1.02E-04 (23) [23377.3 ± 636.8]	1.30E-03 ± 4.98E-03 (15) [17840.9 ± 309.7]	3.36E-01 ± 4.80E-01 (2) [16069.5 ± 23.3]	1.78E+00 ± 1.39E+00 (0)	8.93E+00 ± 1.95E+00 (0)
AF=0.5	2.66E-15 ± 0.00E+00 (25) [30770.5 ± 401.8]	2.66E-15 ± 0.00E+00 (25) [28664.3 ± 444.1]	2.66E-15 ± 0.00E+00 (25) [30312.4 ± 587.6]	2.66E-15 ± 0.00E+00 (25) [30199.4 ± 794.8]	1.02E+00 ± 9.35E-01 (1) [31704.0 ± 0.0]
AF=0.7	4.37E-15 ± 1.81E-15 (25) [43478.0 ± 476.7]	4.51E-15 ± 1.81E-15 (25) [56911.7 ± 1054.0]	4.80E-15 ± 1.78E-15 (25) [85448.5 ± 1625.1]	5.36E-15 ± 1.55E-15 (25) [109511.6 ± 3165.9]	2.66E-15 ± 0.00E+00 (25) [69577.2 ± 2356.8]
AF=0.9	6.08E-15 ± 7.11E-16 (25) [62694.0 ± 691.9]	6.22E-15 ± 7.10E-16 (25) [125606.2 ± 1440.9]	7.04E-15 ± 2.72E-15 (23) [292089.7 ± 5043.7]	4.25E-03 ± 2.16E-03 (0)	6.07E-10 ± 4.89E-10 (25) [208962.0 ± 8601.8]

Griewangk's Function (f_{grw})

	CR=0.1	CR=0.3	CR=0.5	CR=0.7	CR=0.9
AF=0.1	1.82E+00 ± 1.04E+00 (0)	4.63E+00 ± 2.33E+00 (0)	1.26E+01 ± 5.83E+00 (0)	2.40E+01 ± 1.48E+01 (0)	1.10E+02 ± 4.61E+01 (0)
AF=0.3	9.76E-08 ± 4.88E-07 (24) [17907.0 ± 1042.8]	6.04E-03 ± 2.11E-02 (16) [13293.3 ± 926.1]	1.36E-01 ± 2.72E-01 (4) [11686.5 ± 330.9]	1.34E+00 ± 1.16E+00 (0)	2.11E+01 ± 1.06E+01 (0)
AF=0.5	0.00E+00 ± 0.00E+00 (25) [23544.0 ± 1339.6]	0.00E+00 ± 0.00E+00 (25) [21873.8 ± 1504.2]	0.00E+00 ± 0.00E+00 (25) [22594.0 ± 1677.8]	8.88E-04 ± 2.45E-03 (22) [21940.5 ± 1095.9]	3.98E-01 ± 1.03E+00 (2) [28203.5 ± 2682.1]
AF=0.7	0.00E+00 ± 0.00E+00 (25) [33313.8 ± 2037.6]	0.00E+00 ± 0.00E+00 (25) [43236.0 ± 2946.4]	6.90E-04 ± 2.41E-03 (23) [69415.3 ± 8923.7]	6.90E-04 ± 2.41E-03 (23) [81997.3 ± 6109.1]	6.90E-04 ± 2.41E-03 (23) [48985.0 ± 1898.8]
AF=0.9	0.00E+00 ± 0.00E+00 (25) [49298.3 ± 1883.1]	0.00E+00 ± 0.00E+00 (25) [106303.8 ± 5928.5]	2.12E-06 ± 4.58E-06 (19) [264515.2 ± 21717.0]	8.19E-02 ± 1.12E-01 (0)	2.46E-03 ± 4.66E-03 (19) [148714.8 ± 1588.1]

Rastigin Function (f_{ras})

	CR=0.1	CR=0.3	CR=0.5	CR=0.7	CR=0.9
RAS AF=0.1	8.28E+00 ± 2.93E+00 (0)	1.35E+01 ± 2.81E+01 (0)	2.04E+01 ± 3.96E+01 (0)	3.34E+01 ± 7.74E+01 (0)	1.01E+02 ± 2.80E+01 (0)
AF=0.3	4.26E-01 ± 6.99E-01 (11) [3.44E+04 ± 1.83E+03]	1.37E+00 ± 1.02E+01 (4) [9.89E+04 ± 3.44E+04]	4.84E+00 ± 3.81E+00 (0)	9.21E+01 ± 2.96E+01 (0)	3.79E+01 ± 6.18E+01 (0)
AF=0.5	0.00E+00 ± 0.00E+00 (25) [4.36E+04 ± 1.25E+03]	2.16E+00 ± 5.64E+00 (19) [2.62E+05 ± 2.28E+04]	7.59E+01 ± 7.57E+01 (0)	4.92E+01 ± 2.62E+01 (0)	2.08E+01 ± 5.70E+01 (0)
AF=0.7	1.19E-01 ± 3.30E-01 (22) [6.47E+04 ± 3.08E+03]	4.94E+01 ± 7.76E+01 (0)	1.12E+02 ± 8.56E+01 (0)	1.20E+02 ± 2.23E+01 (0)	2.89E+01 ± 9.08E+01 (0)
AF=0.9	0.00E+00 ± 0.00E+00 (25) [5.91E+04 ± 1.39E+03]	1.60E-06 ± 7.31E-06 (23) [2.80E+05 ± 1.17E+04]	1.03E+02 ± 1.16E+01 (0)	1.36E+02 ± 2.97E+01 (0)	2.51E+01 ± 8.37E+01 (0)

Table 3.13 Comparison among the DE variants ($N = 30$, $P = 30$, $F = 0.5$ and $C_r = 0.1$)

Fitness Value

	f_{sph}	f_{ros}	f_{ack}	f_{grw}	f_{ras}
Rand/1/Bin	4.95E−149 ± 8.94E−149	5.12E+01 ± 2.60E+01	2.66E−15 ± 0.00E+00	0.00E+00 ± 0.00E+00	0.00E+00 ± 0.00E+00
Rand/1/Exp	1.12E−137 ± 1.52E−137	8.28E+00 ± 8.53E+00	2.81E−15 ± 7.11E−16	0.00E+00 ± 0.00E+00	0.00E+00 ± 0.00E+00
Best/1/Bin	2.97E−216 ± 0.00E+00	4.53E+01 ± 3.48E+01	8.78E−15 ± 3.48E−15	2.07E−03 ± 3.88E−03	2.27E+00 ± 2.10E+00
Best/1/Exp	9.99E−152 ± 1.95E−151	1.58E+01 ± 2.51E+01	7.35E−15 ± 2.66E−15	0.00E+00 ± 0.00E+00	3.98E−02 ± 1.99E−01
Rand/2/Bin	2.12E−102 ± 2.63E−102	4.17E+01 ± 2.29E+01	4.65E−15 ± 1.80E−15	0.00E+00 ± 0.00E+00	0.00E+00 ± 0.00E+00
Rand/2/Exp	1.24E−110 ± 2.31E−110	6.68E+00 ± 9.69E+00	5.22E−15 ± 1.63E−15	4.44E−17 ± 2.22E−16	0.00E+00 ± 0.00E+00
Best/2/Bin	1.05E−137 ± 1.41E−137	4.58E+01 ± 2.89E+01	6.22E−15 ± 0.00E+00	0.00E+00 ± 0.00E+00	3.98E−02 ± 1.99E−01
Best/2/Exp	8.53E−121 ± 8.04E−121	1.07E+01 ± 1.18E+01	6.22E−15 ± 0.00E+00	4.44E−18 ± 2.22E−17	0.00E+00 ± 0.00E+00
CurToBest/1/Bin	1.08E−198 ± 0.00E+00	7.13E+01 ± 5.50E+01	1.01E−14 ± 4.09E−15	0.00E+00 ± 0.00E+00	1.19E−01 ± 3.30E−01
CurToBest/1/Exp	1.42E−114 ± 1.22E−114	7.50E−01 ± 1.44E+00	6.79E−15 ± 1.97E−15	0.00E+00 ± 0.00E+00	0.00E+00 ± 0.00E+00

Required Fitness Evaluation

	f_{sph}	f_{ros}	f_{ack}	f_{grw}	f_{ras}
Rand/1/Bin	21181.8 ± 334.8	−	30770.5 ± 401.8	23544.0 ± 1339.6	43633.2 ± 1251.8
Rand/1/Exp	23618.6 ± 521.8	−	35674.7 ± 551.0	37419.4 ± 7498.8	27952.6 ± 528.5
Best/1/Bin	14747.9 ± 353.1	−	21380.4 ± 316.0	16143.2 ± 875.6	29648.5 ± 55.9
Best/1/Exp	21398.7 ± 373.5	−	32219.2 ± 553.3	27047.8 ± 2644.5	24726.5 ± 424.1
Rand/2/Bin	30264.5 ± 493.2	−	44025.3 ± 681.6	35929.9 ± 2458.9	74109.8 ± 1836.4
Rand/2/Exp	28826.6 ± 517.7	−	43404.4 ± 472.0	61171.7 ± 11416.5	35471.1 ± 643.3
Best/2/Bin	22758.7 ± 523.3	−	33232.9 ± 434.5	27702.6 ± 2675.6	55711.3 ± 2664.4
Best/2/Exp	26447.0 ± 403.6	−	39625.4 ± 516.3	44982.8 ± 7888.4	32315.2 ± 524.5
CurToBest/1/Bin	15916.6 ± 316.7	−	23221.4 ± 390.1	19943.6 ± 1876.0	50858.3 ± 1679.2
CurToBest/1/Exp	27624.8 ± 488.6	−	44158.9 ± 1109.6	39609.0 ± 6191.7	39478.2 ± 2968.4

Success in Finding Optimum

	f_{sph}	f_{ros}	f_{ack}	f_{grw}	f_{ras}
Rand/1/Bin	25	0	25	25	25
Rand/1/Exp	25	0	25	25	25
Best/1/Bin	25	0	25	19	2
Best/1/Exp	25	0	25	25	24
Rand/2/Bin	25	0	25	25	25
Rand/2/Exp	25	0	25	25	25
Best/2/Bin	25	0	25	25	24
Best/2/Exp	25	0	25	25	25
CurToBest/1/Bin	25	0	25	25	22
CurToBest/1/Exp	25	0	25	25	25

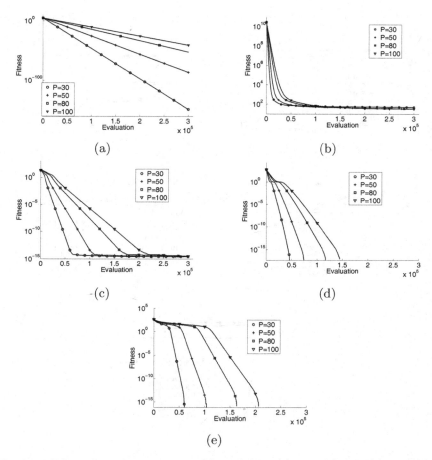

Fig. 3.38 Effect of population size on DE/rand/1/bin: (a) f_{sph}, (b) f_{ros}, (c) f_{ack}, (d) f_{grw}, (e) f_{ras}.

3.4.7.4 *Study on DE variants*

Finally we present a brief study on the different DE variants introduced in Section 3.4.6. Using the same benchmark suite, we studied ten DE variants under the same experimental conditions. The purpose of the study was to show that the performance of the algorithm may notably vary if the learning scheme or strategy is changed.

The experiments were done at $N = 30$ dimension with $P = 30$, $F = 0.5$ and $C_r = 0.1$. No parameter tuning was done to keep the experimental condition unbiased. All the experiments were repeated 25 times and the

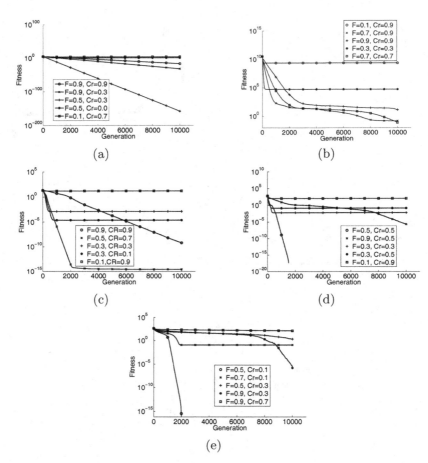

Fig. 3.39   Effect of F and C_r on DE/rand/1/bin: (a) f_{sph}, (b) f_{ros}, (c) f_{ack}, (d) f_{grw}, (e) f_{ras}.

results are presented in Table 3.13. The average convergence characteristics of different variants are also graphically presented in Fig. 3.40.

From the results presented in Table 3.13 and Fig. 3.40, it can be found that the choice of DE learning scheme can significantly affect the algorithm's performance. Under the same parameter settings one variant can repeatedly reach the global optimum, while another variant can fail to locate the optimum in maximum trials.

One important point is that we did not study the variants under their best parameter settings. Each variant can perform much better

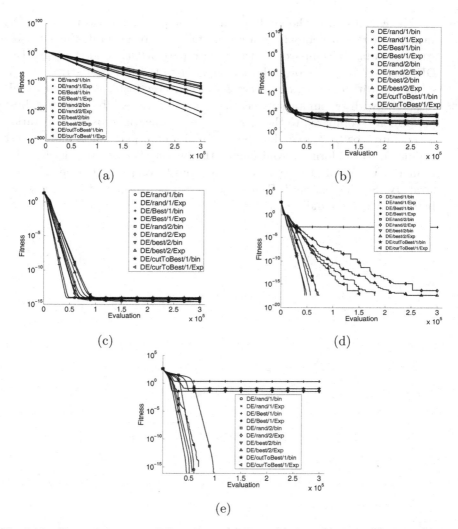

Fig. 3.40 Comparison among DE variants: (a) f_{sph}, (b) f_{ros}, (c) f_{ack}, (d) f_{grw}, (e) f_{ras}.

if their parameters are tuned accordingly. For example, if we used the DE/rand/2/exp strategy with $F = 0.5$ and $C_r = 0.8$ then convergence in trials in all functions is possible. However, we wanted to keep the comparison general and not biased for any particular variant. So we chose a parameter setting based on earlier studies on DE/rand/1/bin and used it as fixed for all the variants.

The conclusion of the analysis on the comparative performance of DE variants in this benchmark suite is as follows. In general, the DE/best strategy is faster compared to the counterpart of DE/rand strategy. But DE/rand strategy is more robust compared to the DE/best strategy. DE strategies with one mutation vector can converge faster compared to DE strategies with two mutation vectors, but the latter exhibit a more robust performance compared to the former. The exponential crossover operation is generally slower compared to the binomial counterpart, but is more robust compared to the former. And finally, the DE/curToBest strategy is faster than the DE/rand strategy, but more robust compared to the DE/best strategy. So the DE/curToBest strategy can be considered a compromise between DE/rand and DE/best.

Chapter 4

Theoretical Background of GA Search Performance

As we have seen in previous chapters, EA search mechanisms are basically dependent upon (1) genetic operation (i.e. crossover and mutation) and (2) selection. In this chapter we will see how GA operates in a search space through the use of these mechanisms. We make use of a binary string GTYPE (gene code) in the following explanation. These are fundamental concepts on theoretical GA. Recent research results on GA theory can be found in several literatures, e.g. the proceedings of the Foundations of Genetic Algorithms (FOGA) [Rawlins (1991); Whitley (1993)] etc. However, an understanding of these theories is not a mandatory requirement for working with EAs.

4.1 Schema theorem

The Schema theorem is Holland's original theoretical explanation of how GAs work. The theorem is based on the concept of a "schema". This is a sub-structure maintained in a population of GTYPEs. The GA search proceeds by combining those schemata with the crossover operation. For chromosomes of length l in an alphabet A, a schema is a subset of the space A^l in which all chromosomes share a particular set of defined values. Schema is generally represented as a string composed from the original alphabet augmented with "$*$", where $*$ represents the "don't care" symbol. For $A = \{0, 1\}$, the $*$ symbol represents either 1 or 0, and the schema

$$H = *11 * 0$$

represents the following four strings:

$$01100, \quad 01110, \quad 11100, \quad 11110.$$

Table 4.1   Parameters for the Schema theorem

n	population size, i.e. individuals (GTYPE's) are numbered as $1, 2, \cdots, n$.
$f_1, f_2, \cdots, f_n$	fitness value of each individual
$f(ij \cdots k)$	fitness value of a string $ij \cdots k$
$f(H)$	fitness value of a schema H, i.e. average of fitness values of strings included in H. For example, $f(1 * 1) = \frac{m(101,t) \times f(101) + m(111,t) \times f(111)}{m(101,t) + m(111,t)}$
$\overline{f}$	average of fitness values among the whole population, i.e. $\overline{f} = \frac{1}{n} \sum_{i=1}^{n} f_i$
$m(H, t)$	number of strings included in a schema H at the generation of t.
l	length of a string
$\delta(H)$	defining length of a schema H
$o(H)$	order of a schema H, i.e. number of non-* symbols
p_c	crossover probability
p_m	mutation probability

In this case, the above strings are said to be included in H or to belong to H. The defining length $\delta(H)$ of a schema H is the number of positions between its first and last specific positions. For instance,

$$\delta(*11 * 0 * *) = 4 - 1 = 3 \tag{4.1}$$

$$\delta(0 * * * *) = 0 \tag{4.2}$$

The order $O(H)$ of a schema H is the number of 0 or 1 (i.e. non-*) symbols.

$$O(*11 * 0 * *) = 3 \tag{4.3}$$

$$O(0 * * * *) = 1 \tag{4.4}$$

Let $m(H, t)$ be the number of individuals (i.e. GTYPEs) included in a schema H at generation t. Table 4.1 summarizes the parameters used in the following discussion. With this preparation, we can make the following inferences.

Inference 1. In case of selection without any crossover or mutation, each individual is forwarded to the next generation with the probability of $p_i = f_i / \sum f_i$. Therefore, the number of strings included in a schema H in the next generation is given as:

$$m(H, t + 1) = m(H, t) \cdot n \cdot \frac{f(H)}{\sum f_i} \tag{4.5}$$

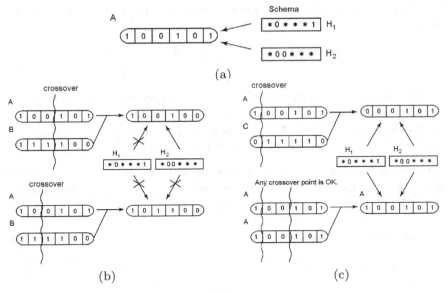

Fig. 4.1   Schema destruction by crossover

Thus, we obtain

$$m(H, t+1) = m(H, t) \times \frac{f(H)}{\bar{f}} \qquad (4.6)$$

Inference 2.   A schema of larger defining length is prone to destruction due to destructive crossover, whose crossover points happen to be inside the defining position of the schema. For instance, consider the following two schemata $H1$ and $H2$ including a string A (see Fig. 4.1(a)):

$$
\begin{aligned}
A &= 1 \quad 0 \quad 0 \quad 1 \quad 0 \quad 1 \\
H1 &= * \quad 0 \quad * \quad * \quad * \quad 1 \\
H2 &= * \quad 0 \quad 0 \quad * \quad * \quad *
\end{aligned}
$$

When the crossover point falls between the third and the fourth genes, the latter half of A is changed so that the offspring will not be included in the schema $H1$. This is called "schema destruction". On the other hand, the offspring will be still included in the schema $H2$ (the upper portion of Fig. 4.1(b)).

The crossover between the second and third genes will result in destructing both schemata $H1$ and $H2$ (the lower portion of Fig. 4.1(b)). In some other cases, the schema is not destructed in spite of the crossover operation (Fig. 4.1(c)).

We can mathematically formulate the above-mentioned destruction as follows:

$$m(H, t+1) \geq m(H, t) \cdot \frac{f(H)}{\overline{f}} \cdot \left[1 - p_c \cdot \frac{\delta(H)}{l-1}\right] \qquad (4.7)$$

This formula shows that a schema H is destroyed when crossover occurs with a probability of p_c and when the crossover point falls within defining positions of length $\delta(H)$. The inequality means that the schema may not be destroyed due to the opponent GTYPE (see Fig. 4.1(c)).

Inference 3.   A schema is destructed by a mutation when a non-* gene (i.e. 0 or 1) is mutated. Note that the number of non-* genes in a schema H is $O(H)$. Thus, we obtain the following theory:

Theorem 4.1. Schema theorem

$$m(H, t+1) \geq m(H, t) \cdot \frac{f(H)}{\overline{f}} \cdot \left[1 - p_c \cdot \frac{\delta(H)}{l-1} - O(H) \cdot p_m\right] \qquad (4.8)$$

Eq. (4.8) is called the "Schema theorem", which describes the fundamental mechanisms of GA. The implication of the Schema theory is that a short schema of low order is expected to increase exponentially if its fitness value is above average. Such a schema is called a "building block". GA is supposed to search in a space by combining those building blocks. This is what the theorem claims. However, it should be noted that this is just a hypothesis because the definition of building blocks is problem-dependent in general. As we will see in later sections, in some situations this hypothesis is not necessarily true.

4.2   Royal road functions

In this section, we present some experiments to see how schemata are generated and extinguished during GA search. We use royal road functions in the following examples. These functions were introduced by Stephanie Forrest, John Holland and Melanie Mitchell in order to analyze schema processing and have been widely used as benchmark functions for performance analysis [Forrest and Mitchell (1993)].

The fitness value of a royal road function $R_1(x)$ is defined using a series of schemata s_i $(i = 1, \cdots, 8)$:

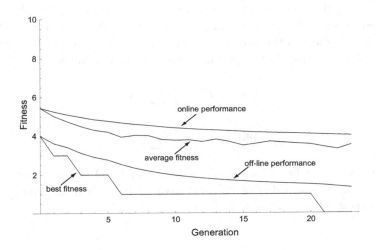

Fig. 4.2   Optimization of the royal road function R_1 using GA

```
s1 = 1111******************** ; c1 = 8
s2 = ****1111**************** ; c2 = 8
s3 = ********1111************ ; c3 = 8
s4 = ************1111******** ; c4 = 8
s5 = ****************1111**** ; c5 = 8
s6 = ********************1111 ; c6 = 8
```

Where R_1 is a 24-bit string of GTYPE. Each s_i schema has a cost of c_i. The fitness $R_1(x)$ of a string x is defined as follows:

$$R_1(x) = \sum_i c_i \delta_i(x), \text{ where } \delta_i(x) = \begin{cases} 1 \ (x \in s_i) \\ 0 \ (x \notin s_i) \end{cases}$$

For instance, if x is an instance of two four-order schemata, then $R_1(x) = 16$. In the same way, $R_1(111\cdots1) = 48$. The optimum solution is $111\cdots1$ (note that R_1 is to be maximized).

If the schema theorem is true, then GA will pave a "royal road" (i.e. an easy way) to the optimum string. This is the meaning of the objective function.

Now let's trace the schema processing in a GA by optimizing this $R_1(x)$ function. To suite the minimization task, we use the following fitness function by subtracting the $R_1(x)$ value from 48:

$$\text{Fitness}(x) = 48 - R_1(x) \tag{4.9}$$

where the optimum value is 0.0. Selected GA parameters are as follows: (1) population size 100, (2) crossover probability 0.7, (3) mutation probability 0.05. Fig. 4.2 shows the fitness transition against generation for a typical run. The online and off-line performance is defined as follows:

$$\text{Online}(T) = \frac{1}{T} \sum_{i=1}^{T} f(i)$$

$$\text{Off-line}(T) = \frac{1}{T} \sum_{i=1}^{T} f^*(i)$$

where $f(i)$ is the fitness value of the best individual at generation i and $f^*(i)$ is the fitness value of the best evolved individual at generation i. More precisely, $f^*(i) = Min(f(t))$, $t = 1, \cdots i$.

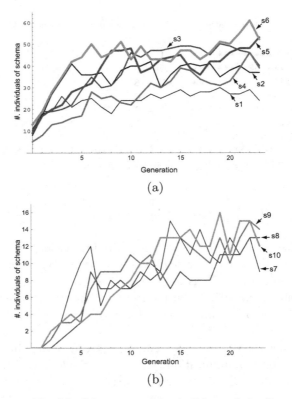

Fig. 4.3   Schema processing in GA search for R_1

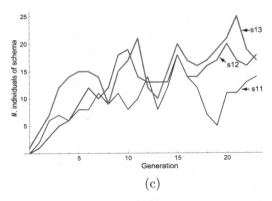

(c)

Fig. 4.3 (*Continued*)

In this case, the optimum value (1111 ··· 1111) is acquired at generation 21. Then, we try tracing the schema processing during this GA search. Fig. 4.3 shows the numbers of individuals included in the following schemata with generations.

```
s1  = 1111********************
s2  = ****1111****************
s3  = ********1111************
s4  = ************1111********
s5  = ****************1111****
s6  = ********************1111
s7  = 1111****1111************
s8  = 1111********1111********
s9  = 1111************1111****
s10 = 1111****************1111
s11 = ****1111************1111
s12 = ********1111********1111
s13 = ************1111****1111
```

Four-order schemata (s1, s2, s3, s4, s5, s6), which contribute to the fitness, were increasing almost monotonically with generations. On the other hand, schemata of longer defining length were easily destroyed so that their numbers did not become larger. For instance, s11 almost disappeared during the GA search. However, no schemata totally disappeared. As a result, the search was successfully terminated at generation 21.

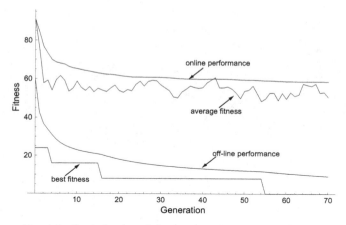

Fig. 4.4   Optimization of the royal road function R_2 using GA

Now let us consider the following royal road function $R_2(x)$:

```
s1 = 1111****************** ; c1 = 8
s2 = ****1111************** ; c2 = 8
s3 = ********1111********** ; c3 = 8
s4 = ************1111****** ; c4 = 8
s5 = ****************1111** ; c5 = 8
s6 = ********************1111 ; c6 = 8
s7 = 11111111************** ; c7 = 16
s8 = ********11111111****** ; c8 = 16
s9 = ****************11111111 ; c9 = 16
```

The maximum value of $R_2(x)$ is 96 (the optimum solution is $1111\cdots1111$). Thus, the fitness value of a string x is defined as follows:

$$\text{Fitness}(x) = 96 - R_2(x) \qquad (4.10)$$

We used the same GA parameters as was used in R_1. Fig. 4.4 shows the fitness transition against generations for a typical run. In this case, the optimum value $(1111\cdots1111)$ is acquired at generation 55. Fig. 4.5 shows the number of individuals included in the following schemata against generations.

```
s1 = 1111******************
s2 = ****1111**************
s3 = ********1111**********
s4 = ************1111******
s5 = ****************1111**
s6 = ********************1111
```

```
s7  =  1111****1111************
s8  =  1111********1111********
s9  =  1111************1111****
s10 =  1111****************1111
s11 =  ****1111************1111
s12 =  ********1111********1111
s13 =  ************1111****1111
s14 =  11111111****************
s15 =  ********11111111********
s16 =  ****************11111111
```

As can be seen from the figure, the increase and decrease were more drastic than with the previous R_1 function. Some schemata totally disappeared during the search. Note that the four-order schemata were divided into two classes, i.e. the large number (s1, s2, s3) vs the small number (s4,

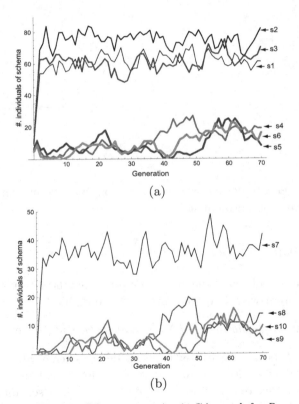

(a)

(b)

Fig. 4.5   Schema processing in GA search for R_2

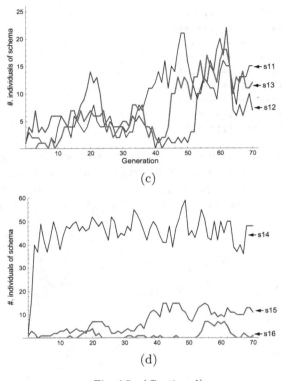

Fig. 4.5   (*Continued*)

s5, s6). This seems to be the reason why it took twice as many generations as R_1 to acquire the optimum solution.

4.3   Implicit parallelism

We first prove the following theorem. The proof may be difficult to understand. If you are new to GA, you may skip reading it.

Theorem 4.2. *A population P of N individuals keep at least N^3 schemata.*

Proof.   Let L be the gene length. Consider a schema which has r instances (i.e. strings belonging to that schema) in P. Let $k = \log_2(N/r)$. Then, for any choice of k positions, there are 2^k distinct schemata defined at those k positions, each of which can be expected to have r instances in

P. Therefore, the number of distinct schemata with r instances in P is at least $M_r = 2^k \cdot \binom{L}{k}$.

For most practical problems, we can assume that $L \geq 64$, $2^6 \leq N \leq 2^{20}$, $r \geq 8$. In this case, for instance, if $r = 8$, then $3 \leq k \leq 17$. By inspection of the value of M_r over this range, we can see that $M_r \geq N^3$. $\square$

The above proof is based on [Fitzpatrick and Grefenstette (1998)] (see [Goldberg (1989)] (p.41) for an alternative proof, which is more general in the sense that it needs no assumption about the value range).

The implication of this theorem is as follows. Though GA uses a relatively small population (of size N), it processes a large number (i.e. N^3) of schemata. Thus, sometimes higher-order schemata of a longer defining length may be destroyed by crossover or mutation. However, considering the implicit parallelism, we do not have to worry about the destruction so much.

4.4 Deceptive functions

However, GA does not always work well. We can define an objective (fitness) function artificially so as to refute the building-block hypothesis. These kind of functions are called "deceptive functions". Such functions are defined as follows. Consider the four schemata of order two:

Fitness	Schema								
f_{00}	*	*	*	0	*	*	*	0	*
f_{01}	*	*	*	0	*	*	*	1	*
f_{10}	*	*	*	1	*	*	*	0	*
f_{11}	*	*	*	1	*	*	*	1	*

Suppose that f_{11} gives the optimum value. In other words, the following equation holds true:

$$f_{11} > f_{00}, \; f_{11} > f_{01}, \; f_{11} > f_{10} \tag{4.11}$$

Then, in order to deceive GA, either of the following two inequalities should hold true for order-one schemata:

$$f(0*) > f(1*) \tag{4.12}$$

$$f(*0) > f(*1) \tag{4.13}$$

In the following explanation, we only show genes at defining positions. For instance, $f(* \, 0)$ represents $f(* * * * * * * 0 *)$. Then, the above two inequalities can be written as:

$$\frac{f(00) + f(01)}{2} > \frac{f(10) + f(11)}{2} \tag{4.14}$$

$$\frac{f(00) + f(10)}{2} > \frac{f(01) + f(11)}{2} \tag{4.15}$$

These two inequalities do not hold true simultaneously (if so, f_{11} cannot be maximum). Without the loss of generality, we assume that the first inequality, i.e. Eq. (4.14) holds true. For the sake of simplicity, we use normalization as follows:

$$r = \frac{f_{11}}{f_{00}}, \; c = \frac{f_{01}}{f_{00}}, \; c' = \frac{f_{10}}{f_{00}} \tag{4.16}$$

Then, Eq. (4.11) is translated into

$$r > 1, r > c, r > c' \tag{4.17}$$

In addition, Eq. (4.14) is given as:

$$r < 1 + c - c' \tag{4.18}$$

Therefore, we obtain

$$c' < 1, c' < c \tag{4.19}$$

In consideration of different cases of c, we have two types of deceptive functions:

TYPE I : $f_{01} > f_{00}(c > 1)$ (see Fig. 4.6)

TYPE II : $f_{00} \geq f_{01}(c \leq 1)$ (see Fig. 4.7)

These are called the "minimal deceptive problems (MDP)". "Minimal" means that there is no order-one deceptive function.

Fig. 4.8 shows a GA search result for the following TYPE I function [Goldberg (1989)]:

$$f_{11} = 1.1, \; f_{01} = 1.05, \; f_{01} = 1.0, \; f_{10} = 0.0 \tag{4.20}$$

Initially, the individuals included in the optimum schema (i.e. 11) were very few. However, as the number of instances included in schemata 10 and 00 were becoming smaller, a competition began between schemata 11 and schemata 01. As a result of this, the schemata 11 survived. This survival

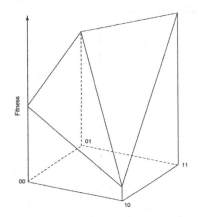

Fig. 4.6   Example of TYPE I deceptive function

Fig. 4.7   Example of TYPE II deceptive function

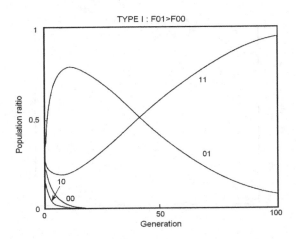

Fig. 4.8   Performance of GA for TYPE I deceptive function

of an optimum schema is true for other TYPE I functions. Thus, MDP of TYPE I is not essentially a difficult problem for GA, i.e. not "GA-hard".

On the other hand, GA search is not always successful for TYPE II functions. Both Fig. 4.9 and Fig. 4.10 show GA search results for the following function [Goldberg (1989)]:

$$f_{11} = 1.1, \quad f_{00} = 1.0, \quad f_{01} = 0.9, \quad f_{10} = 0.5 \tag{4.21}$$

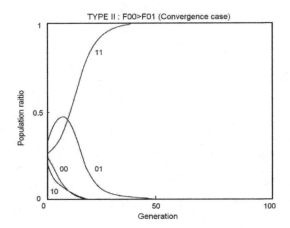

Fig. 4.9   Performance of GA for TYPE II deceptive function (convergence)

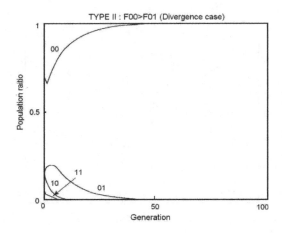

Fig. 4.10   Performance of GA for TYPE II deceptive function (divergence)

As we can observe in Fig. 4.10, when the number of individuals in schemata 00 was large in the initial population, the convergence did not occur to the optimal schema 11. It has been proven that the convergence to an optimal solution under TYPE II functions is as follows [Goldberg (1987)]:

Fig. 4.11   Two-armed bandit

$$P_{11}^0 > \frac{f_{00}}{f_{11}} P_{00}^0 \tag{4.22}$$

where P_{00}^0 and P_{11}^0 are the ratios of included individuals in the initial population.

4.5 k-armed bandit

Holland mathematically analyzed the GA search process using the analogy of a "k-armed bandit". We first explain the concept of a two-armed bandit (see Fig. 4.11), which is a slot machine with two arms (R and L) working under the following assumptions:

(1) Money is paid according to different pay-off rates for the two arms

(R and L). These rates are constrained according to averaged returns (μ_R, μ_L) and standard deviations or risks (σ_R^2, σ_L^2).

(2) There is no way to know whether $\mu_R > \mu_L$ or $\mu_R < \mu_L$.

(3) The total number of bets is limited to N.

Under these conditions, what betting strategy is the most profitable? To derive this, we need to consider the following two phases:

(1) **Exploration**: Decide whether $\mu_R > \mu_L$ or $\mu_R < \mu_L$.

(2) **Exploitation**: Bet on a better arm according to the above decision.

Since the number of N is limited, we face a dilemma. If the exploration is too much, the search tends to be local so that it is vulnerable to noise and hard to adapt to pay-off errors (i.e. standard deviations or risks). On the other hand, in case of too much exploitation, we will ignore the beneficial information gained from exploration [De Jong (1992)].

The optimum strategy for this two-armed bandit is to bet on the observed best arm according to the exponentially increasing number [Goldberg (1989)](p. 37).

More precisely, the following theorem has been proved (see [Holland (1975)] and [Mitchell (1998)](Ch. 4) for details).

Theorem 4.3 (Optimal strategy for a two-armed bandit).
If we pull a two-armed bandit N times, we should allocate

$$n^* \approx c_1 \ln\left(\frac{c_2 N^2}{\ln(c_3 N^2)}\right)$$

trials to the observed worse arm, where $\ln$ *denotes the natural logarithm.* c_1, c_2 *and* c_3 *are positive constants.*

Originally, Holland provided the following solution:

$$n^* \approx b^2 \ln\left(\frac{N^2}{8\pi b^4 \ln N^2}\right)$$

where $b = \frac{\sigma_L}{\mu_L - \mu_R}$ if $\mu_L > \mu_R$ and $b = \frac{\sigma_R}{\mu_R - \mu_L}$ if $\mu_R > \mu_L$.

Since $e^{\frac{n^*}{c_1}} \approx \left(\frac{c_2 N^2}{\ln(c_3 N^2)}\right)$ from the above equation, the optimal allocation of trials to the observed better arm is as follows:

$$N - n^* \approx e^{n^*/2c_1} \sqrt{\frac{\ln(c_3 N^2)}{c_2}} - n^*$$

Table 4.2   The analogy between GA and a k-armed bandit

	GA	k-armed bandit
Profit	fitness of schema	pay-off rate
Constraint	population size	total number of bets
Solution	betting on the observed best arm according to the exponentially increasing number	

Considering $e^{n^*/2c_1}$ is dominant as n^* becomes larger, we obtain:

$$N - n^* \approx e^{cn^*}$$

where $c = 1/2c_1$.

In other words, as Holland claimed, as more and more information is gained through sampling, the optimal strategy is to exponentially increase the probability of sampling the observed best arm relative to the probability of sampling the observed worst arm [Mitchell (1998)](p. 120).

Holland generalized GA schema processing using the model of k-armed bandit [Holland (1975)]. k-armed bandit is a slot machine of k arms. In the same way, the optimum strategy for this bandit is to bet on the observed best arm according to the exponentially increasing number.

Now we introduce the concept of competing schemata, by which we mean that at least one gene at defining positions (non-∗ symbols) is different. For instance, we have 8 competing schemata of length 7 and order 2:

$$
\begin{array}{ccccccc}
* & 0 & 0 & * & 0 & * & * \\
* & 0 & 0 & * & 1 & * & * \\
* & 0 & 1 & * & 0 & * & * \\
* & 0 & 1 & * & 1 & * & * \\
* & 1 & 0 & * & 0 & * & * \\
* & 1 & 0 & * & 1 & * & * \\
* & 1 & 1 & * & 0 & * & * \\
* & 1 & 1 & * & 1 & * & *
\end{array}
$$

We can regard k competing schemata as k arms of a bandit so that GA can be modeled as a k-armed bandit. Table 4.2 shows the analogy between GA and a k-armed bandit.

Furthermore, Holland proved the following points. Under the schema theorem and some assumptions, GA assigns individuals to schemata in the sense of the optimum strategy for the k-armed bandit. "Optimum" means that the individuals are assigned to the observed best schemata according to the exponentially increasing number. Thus, GA is able to find schemata of short defining length and of high fitness. This will be beneficial to GA for effectively searching for building blocks.

Is GA almighty then? However, the above argument has some serious problems. For instance:

(1) There are simultaneously many different competing schemata. Therefore, we may have to face contradictory assignment of individuals to schemata of a different order, just as in the case of solving deceptive functions.

(2) There is a slight gap between the bandit strategy and GA optimization [De Jong (1992)].

(3) There is not necessarily a direct relationship between GA schemata and bandit arms.

We explain the third point in detail. Grefenstette and Baker showed the following counter-example [Grefenstette and Baker (1989)]:

$$f(x) = \begin{cases} 2, & \text{if } x \in 111 * \cdots * \\ 1, & \text{if } x \in 0 * * * \cdots * \\ 0, & \text{otherwise} \end{cases} \qquad (4.23)$$

In this case, as generations proceed, $1 * * * \cdots *$ will prosper in the population. However, since $f(0 * * * \cdots *) = 1$ and $f(1 * * * \cdots *) = 1/2$, this prosperity is contradictory to the bandit's optimum strategy. In addition to this, the implicit parallelism (i.e. N^3) does not hold true in later generations. On the other hand, [Levenick (1990)] refuted that the above phenomenon is not contradictory to Holland's claim because the pay-off rate (i.e. the average fitness of a schema) is usually time-variant.

Arthur explored the dynamics of allocation under increasing returns in a context where increasing returns naturally arise, e.g. agents choosing between technologies competing for adoption in economics [Arthur (1994)]. He used the k-armed bandit analogy as the model for choosing which technologies to bet on. He showed that under increasing returns, rational expectations yield an absorbing random walk, which is called "lock-in" (or inflexibility).

4.6   No free lunch theorem

The no free lunch theorem (NFL) asserts that no search algorithm exists which can solve all problems efficiently. Wolpert and Macready

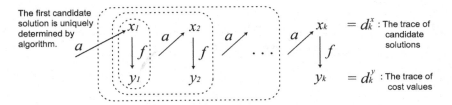

Fig. 4.12 The first candidate solution is uniquely determined by algorithm a. Subsequently, a new candidate solution x_{i+1} is output by algorithm a from the trace of candidate solutions and that of cost values. Thus, $d_k \in D_k$ is uniquely determined from a and f. We write this as $S(a, f)$.

mathematically proved NFL in 1995 [Wolpert and Macready (1995)]. This theorem, in other words, asserts that all search algorithms perform the same when averaged over all possible cost functions. According to NFL, the performance of genetic algorithm is the same as that of a random search when all problems are considered. Regarded as a basic principle for the performance of search algorithms, NFL had serious implications for the concept of generality of search algorithms and optimization.

4.6.1   *Overview of NFL theorem*

Let the candidate solution space be X, which is assumed to be finite[1]. Function f gives a cost value to solution $x \in X$ to describe how superior the solution is. This function is called a "cost function". When the space of solution cost values is assumed to be Y, the relation $f : X \to Y$ holds. Assume that search algorithm a is a function which outputs a next candidate solution $x_{i+1} \in X$ from the past search trace, more specifically, from the previously enumerated candidate solutions $(x_1, x_2, \cdots, x_i) \in X^i$ and the trace of their cost values $(y_1, y_2, \cdots, y_i) \in Y^i$ (see Fig. 4.12). For example, tabu search, a random search, genetic algorithm, and simulated annealing are included in this type of search algorithm.

NFL asserts that there is no efficient search algorithm that is applicable to any cost function. A cost function represents a problem to be solved. Therefore, this theorem means that no efficient search algorithm exists, which is applicable to every problem.

---

[1]The assumption that the candidate solution space is finite is not unnatural in that the numbers handled by computers are basically discrete ones.

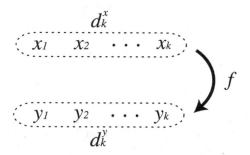

Fig. 4.13 Assume that a set of f which completely satisfies trace d_k is $F(d_k)$. More specifically, if $f \in F(d_k)$, we have $\forall i \; [y_i = f(x_i)]$.

4.6.2 *Definition*

We define notations as follows. More rigorous definitions are given in Appendix C.1. Let k be a natural number which satisfies $k < |X|$.

X A candidate solution space. A finite set.

Y A cost value space for a solution. A finite set.

F A set of all cost functions. $F = \{f : X \to Y\}$

D_k^X A set of all candidate solutions at the time when search has been put forward by k steps. However, $D_k^X \subsetneqq X^k$ holds without including any duplicate candidate.

D_k^Y A set of all cost values at the time when search has been put forward by k steps. $D_k^Y = Y^k$

D_k A set of all search traces at the time when search has been put forward by k steps. $D_k = D_k^X \times D_k^Y$

A A set of all search algorithms.

$F(d_k)$ A subset of F which completely satisfies search trace $d_k \in D_k$ (see Fig. 4.13).

Now note that D_k^X contains no duplicate candidate solution. Given $(x_1, x_2, \cdots, x_k) \in D_k^X$, we have

$$\forall i \; \forall j \; [i \neq j \to x_i \neq x_j]. \tag{4.24}$$

Therefore, search algorithm $a \in A$ references the traces of candidate solutions and then outputs one element of X, which has not been listed as a candidate solution. Since X and Y are finite sets, F is also a finite set.

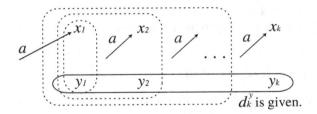

Fig. 4.14 Since y_i is given, sequentially determine x_i only. This will result in uniquely determining $d_k \in D_k$ from a and d_k^y. We write this as $R_k(a, d_k^y)$. The components of the trace of cost values for R_k are of identity mapping. $F(R_k(a, d_k^y))$ represents a set of cost functions which satisfy $R_k(a, d_k^y)$.

The sizes of sets are shown below:

$$|F| = |Y|^{|X|}$$
$$|D_k^Y| = |Y|^k$$
$$|F(d_k)| = |Y|^{|X|-k} \tag{4.25}$$

In particular, it should be noted that the size of set in $F(d_k)$ is only dependent on k and not dependent on d_k. Since d_k is given, the mapping of k elements in X is determined. The mapping the remaining $|X| - k$ elements should be considered. It is therefore found that $|Y|^{|X|-k}$ pieces of $f \in F$ satisfies d_k.

The search trace which has been obtained by putting forward search by k steps using algorithm a and cost function f is represented as $S_k(a, f) \in D_k$ (see Fig. 4.12). In contrast, when algorithm a and trace $d_k^y \in D_k^Y$ of the cost value for the solution are obtained, one $d_k^x \in D_k^X$ which does not contradict a and d_k^y as shown in Fig. 4.14 can be calculated. Thus one element of D_k can be uniquely determined from a and d_k^y. We write this as $R_k(a, d_k^y) \in D_k$. It is easily understandable that once one $f \in F(R_k(a, d_k^y))$ is given, we have (see Figs. 4.12 and 4.14):

$$R_k(a, d_k^y) = S_k(a, f) \tag{4.26}$$

This is called the "consistency" of S_k and R_k. We demonstrate in the proof given in Appendix C.2 that the consistency can be achieved rigorously.

Assume that the probabilistic variable which represents the trace of candidate solutions up to the k-th step is $\mathcal{D}_k^x$; the probabilistic variable which represents the trace of cost values for solutions up to k steps is $\mathcal{D}_k^y$; the probabilistic variable showing the search algorithm is $\mathcal{A}$; and the probabilistic variable denoting the cost function is $\mathcal{F}$. For example,

$$P(\mathcal{D}_3^y = (3, 7, 4) \mid \mathcal{A} = a) \tag{4.27}$$

shows a conditional probability which results in the trace of cost values being $(3, 7, 4)$ when the search algorithm is a.

4.6.3   *NFL by Wolpert* et al.

NFL by Wolpert *et al.* can be written as follows:

Theorem 4.4 (NFL). *Given $a_1, a_2 \in A$, $d_k^y \in D_k^Y$, we have:*

$$\forall a_1 \; \forall a_2 \; \forall d_k^y \; [\sum_{f \in F} P(\mathcal{D}_k^y = d_k^y \,|\mathcal{A} = a_1, \mathcal{F} = f)$$

$$= \sum_{f \in F} P(\mathcal{D}_k^y = d_k^y \,|\mathcal{A} = a_2, \mathcal{F} = f)] \qquad (4.28)$$

This means that once a search algorithm and a cost function are determined, the probability of obtaining the trace of a certain cost value is not dependent upon the algorithm when the sum is calculated for all cost functions. In other words, every algorithm outputs the trace of the same cost values when averaged.

When a solution is searched after a search algorithm and a cost function are determined, the search performance of that algorithm is determined by the trace of cost values for the solution. The simplest example is the method of determining the performance by the maximum of the cost value for the solution. More specifically, assuming that $d_m^y = (y_1, y_2, \cdots, y_m) \in D_m^Y$ has been obtained as the trace of cost values for the solution when the maximum step of the search is m, the search performance of the algorithm is frequently measured using:

$$\max_{k \leq m} y_k \qquad (4.29)$$

Alternatively, the search performance is measured by averaging cost values or studying the statistics of cost values. All these methods, however, only depend on the trace of cost values. Since the above NFL asserts that the distribution of traces of cost values is not dependent on the algorithm, it is found that the search performance does not depend on the algorithm whatever method is used to measure the search performance.

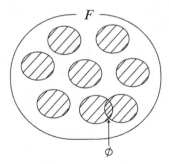

Fig. 4.15 Divide F and obtain the sum for each subset. If each subset can cover F without crossing, the lemma of dividing F holds.

4.6.4 *Proof*

We here present another simpler way to prove NFL. We start by proving the lemma of dividing cost function space F. The basic idea of this lemma is presented in [Sharpe (2000)], but not rigorously proved. In particular, it is not proved that f is unduplicated. The non-duplication of f is nonobvious. In the following lemma, assume V as any arbitrary vector space.

Lemma 1 (Lemma of dividing F). *Given $\varphi : F \to V$, $a \in A$, we have:*

$$\forall a \; \forall \varphi \; \forall k \; [\sum_{f \in F} \varphi(f) = \sum_{t \in D_k^Y} \sum_{f \in F(R_k(a,t))} \varphi(f)] \qquad (4.30)$$

The left side obtains the sum for every cost function, while the right side divides the cost functions and then obtains the sum for each subset (see Fig. 4.15). Each subset is parameterized by trace $t \in D_k^Y$ of cost values for the solution. What should be proven here is that all $f \in F$ come out without any duplication in the sum on the right side. Therefore, it should be demonstrated that no subset crosses the other and that the sum of elements in all subsets is $|F|$.

Proof. [Proof of lemma] Now assume $F(R_k(a,t_1)) \cap F(R_k(a,t_2)) \neq \phi$ for $t_1 \neq t_2$ $(t_1, t_2 \in D_k^Y)$. Hence

$$\exists f \; [f \in F(R_k(a,t_1)) \land f \in F(R_k(a,t_2))] \qquad (4.31)$$

Using this f, we have the following from the consistency between S_k and R_k:

$$R_k(a,t_1) = S_k(a,f) = R_k(a,t_2) \qquad (4.32)$$

The traces are completely consistent, but contradict $t_1 \neq t_2$ (the trace of cost values is distinct). Hence

$$F(R_k(a, t_1)) \cap F(R_k(a, t_2)) = \phi \qquad (4.33)$$

So $f \in F(R_k(a, t))$ is not duplicated for distinct $t \in D_k^Y$. Using the above, we have

$$\left| \bigcup_{t \in D_k^Y} F(R_k(a, t)) \right| = \sum_{t \in D_k^Y} |F(R_k(a, t))| \qquad (4.34)$$

$$= \sum_{t \in D_k^Y} |Y|^{|X|-k} \qquad (4.35)$$

$$= |D_k^Y| \times |Y|^{|X|-k} \qquad (4.36)$$

$$= |Y|^k \times |Y|^{|X|-k} \qquad (4.37)$$

$$= |Y|^{|X|} = |F| \qquad (4.38)$$

Consequently, this means that all $f \in F$ are summed. Now the proposition has been presented. $\qquad \square$

Using the above lemma, we prove NFL.

Proof. [Proof of NFL] The lemma holds for any arbitrary $a \in A$. So divide F by a_1

$$\sum_{f \in F} P(\mathcal{D}_k^y = d_k^y \,|\, \mathcal{A} = a_1, \mathcal{F} = f)$$

$$= \sum_{t \in D_k^Y} \sum_{f \in F(R_k(a_1, t))} P(\mathcal{D}_k^y = d_k^y \,|\, \mathcal{A} = a_1, \mathcal{F} = f) \qquad (4.39)$$

When the search is performed using $f \in F(R_k(a_1, t))$ and a_1, the trace of cost values will become t due to the consistency between S_k and R_k. Thus, given $f \in F(R_k(a_1, t))$, we have:

$$P(\mathcal{D}_k^y = t \,|\, \mathcal{A} = a_1, \mathcal{F} = f) = 1 \qquad (4.40)$$

$$P(\mathcal{D}_k^y \neq t \,|\, \mathcal{A} = a_1, \mathcal{F} = f) = 0 \qquad (4.41)$$

(see Lemma 3 in Appendix C.2). Hence

$$\sum_{f \in F(R_k(a_1, t))} P(\mathcal{D}_k^y = d_k^y \,|\, \mathcal{A} = a_1, \mathcal{F} = f)$$

$$= \begin{cases} 0 & d_k^y \neq t \\ |F(R_k(a_1, t))| = |Y|^{|X|-k} & d_k^y = t \end{cases} \qquad (4.42)$$

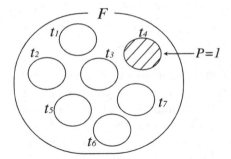

Fig. 4.16 Image of proof. The size of each subset is equal and the probability that the trace of cost values might become d_k^y $(= t_4)$ always 1 in the subset of F determined by t_4.

Therefore

$$\sum_{f \in F} P(\mathcal{D}_k^y = d_k^y \,|\, \mathcal{A} = a_1, \mathcal{F} = f) = |Y|^{|X|-k} \qquad (4.43)$$

Now it has been proved that the sum of $P(\mathcal{D}_k^y = d_k^y \,|\, \mathcal{A} = a_1, \mathcal{F} = f)$ for every cost function f is not dependent on algorithm a_1. Hence NFL holds.
$\square$

4.6.5 Interpretation of the proof

In Section 4.6.4, function space F is divided and then the sum is calculated for each subset $F(R(a, t))$ of each F which is parameterized by $t \in D_k^Y$. However, the probability of resulting in $d_k^y \in D_k^Y$ takes $F(R_k(a, d_k^y))$ as a support and is always 1 on $F(R_k(a, d_k^y))$. Therefore, when the sum is obtained in the whole function space, the size of $F(R_k(a, t))$ is equal to the frequency at which the trace of cost values t occurs. The way of dividing F varies depending on the algorithm. However, so far as k is constant, the size of divided set $|F(R_k(a, t))|$ is invariable regardless of algorithm a and trace of cost values t. Thus F is equally divided and the number of divisions is constant. Hence the frequency of any $d_k^y \in D_k^Y$ is constant regardless of the algorithm. The above proof image is illustrated in Fig. 4.16.

Assume that the probability distribution of cost functions is uniform distribution as follows:

$$P(\mathcal{F} = f) = \frac{1}{|F|} \qquad (4.44)$$

When both sides of NFL are multiplied by the above equation, we have:

$$\forall a_1 \; \forall a_2 \; \forall d_k^y \; [\mathrm{P}(\mathcal{D}_k^y = d_k^y \, | \mathcal{A} = a_1)$$
$$= \mathrm{P}(\mathcal{D}_k^y = d_k^y \, | \mathcal{A} = a_2)] \qquad (4.45)$$

This is the very equation that asserts that the distribution of cost values is independent of the algorithm. As you can find from this transformation, NFL requires the assumption that the distribution of cost functions is uniform when NFL asserts that there is no ideal search algorithm. As intuitively clear enough, when considering only the class of monotonically increasing functions in the defined range as a cost function space, the algorithm which returns the maximum in the defined range will be the best algorithm. When the cost functions otherwise belong to the class of unimodal functions, the hill-climbing method will achieve a good result[2].

Whether NFL holds is dependent on how to calculate the sum in the function space. Schumacher *et al.* (2001) present the condition under which NFL holds in a smaller function space. However, we should rather consider mainly a reverse case to see when a difference arises between two certain algorithms.

For example, when we consider an actual problem, we may exclude the cost functions which are monotonically increasing in the defined range from the function space. The function space can be narrowed down through a variety of other prior knowledge. As a result, the function space becomes distorted. If the sum is obtained in the distorted space, NFL will not hold. If the algorithm is different, the way of dividing F also differs. When the function space is narrowed down, the part that is excluded in the division of F determines whether the algorithm is effective in the solution space. Once one criterion for performance is established, it gives one order relation to D_k^y. As low-order functions are excluded when the function space is narrowed down, the algorithm proves to be superior (see Fig. 4.17). In contrast, the performance of two algorithms has no significant difference if the excluded parts are similar to each other.

Based on the above interpretation, the role of algorithms lies in determining the way of dividing cost function space F. The superiority or inferiority of algorithms in a certain problem space can be theoretically determined by studying what shape the function space takes in an actual problem and how the algorithm divides the function space. For example, the landscape of a search space in TSP has been analyzed. However, when

---

[2]The hill-climbing method comes in various forms depending on parameters. NFL may be effective for determining which form of the hill-climbing method should be used.

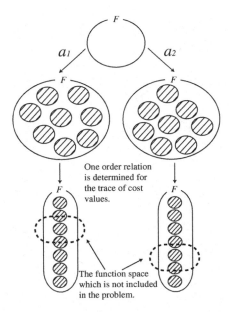

Fig. 4.17 The algorithm determines how to divide F. When one order relation is determined for D_k^y, the order of subsets in F is established. Now the superiority of the algorithm is determined by what function space is actually created by problems.

referring to the performance of an algorithm for a problem, we will have to consider how the algorithm addresses the problem. One of the possible approaches is to study how the algorithm divides the function space and what shape of the function space is formed by the class of the problem.

Only when the whole function space is taken into consideration[3], can NFL be interpreted as "the search efficiency of every algorithm is the same". The book *Artificial Intelligence: A Modern Approach* [Russell and Norvig (1995)],[p. 621] states that: "GA is the third best way of doing just about anything." This implicitly assumes that the problem we address does not uniformly cover the entire function space. However, this assumption cannot be accepted as self-evident. If no premise is made for the problem, NFL will hold.

---

[3]Specifically, NFL holds for a set of functions if and only if the set of functions forms a permutation set. The permutation set is the closure of a set of functions with respect to a permutation operator.

Chapter 5

The Memetic Computing Approach

5.1 From meme to memetics

Because of some inherent advantages, like robustness, parallelism, global search capability, ease of implementation, etc., many researchers have been studying EAs particularly for real-world optimization problems over the past few years. However, continued development in the community has established that canonical genetic algorithms (GAs) are often not good enough for fine-tuning in complex search spaces. Additionally, new developments have shown, hybridization with other strategies, such as meta-heuristics or local searches, can greatly improve the efficiency of the search [Davis (1991); Goldberg and Voessner (1999)].

According to the NFL theorem (see Section 4.6 for details), the performance of any two search algorithms, without incorporating problem specific knowledge, is the same if taken over the set of all possible optimization problems. It also suggests that a search algorithm performs proportionally to the quality and quantity of domain knowledge incorporated in it. Experimental studies show that if some sort of domain knowledge is incorporated into EAs it can perform better or competitively with other domain specific optimization techniques. These hybrid EAs are similar to traditional EAs, although their principles are more similar to the evolution in human culture rather than the evolution in nature. Therefore, these hybrid EAs are commonly referred to as "memetic algorithms".

The term "meme" was coined by the British scientist Richard Dawkins in his book about evolution, *The Selfish Gene* [Dawkins (1976)]. A meme is an idea or behavior one person can pass on to another. The examples of memes, given by Dawkins, are tunes, ideas, catch phrases, clothing fashion, ways of making pots or of building arches. According to Dawkins, what meme is to cultural evolution is the same as what gene is to biological evolution. In cultural evolution, information is not passed unaltered among individuals. Because humans do not always copy memes perfectly, and because they may process, refine, combine or otherwise modify them with other memes to create new memes, they can change over time. The field of memetics emerged to explore the concepts and transmission of memes in terms of an evolutionary model. Memetic algorithms can be defined as an amalgamation of the population-based global search paradigm inspired by Darwinian principles of natural evolution and local improvement process inspired by Dawkins' concept of meme [Krasnogor and Smith (2005)]. More commonly, GAs hybridized with local refinement procedures are commonly known as memetic algorithms (MAs) [Moscato (1989); Moscato and Norman (1992)]. In MAs this local refinement is often achieved by incorporating heuristics, approximation algorithms, truncated exact methods, specialized recombination operators, etc., that are used to improve individuals [Glover and Kochenberger (2003)].

5.2 The memetic algorithm framework

The term "memetic algorithm" (MA) was first introduced by Moscato in his technical report [Moscato (1989)] where he regarded MA as a form of population-based hybrid genetic algorithm coupled with a local refinement procedure. Although, there is some disagreement regarding using the term MA for a more extended class of algorithms, most in the community use the term "memetic algorithm" to refer to an EA that includes one or more local refinement procedures within its evolutionary framework.

A general framework of memetic algorithms is shown in Fig. 5.1. Note that in this framework no details about the evolutionary algorithm and the nature of the local refinement process is given. This is because there are numerous types of EAs and many different types of local refinement processes can be hybridized with EAs in several ways. Therefore, instead of using any particular genetic or local search approach, we used this abstract framework to express the algorithmic structure. The most crucial and distinctive feature of this MA framework is the use of local search procedure for refining the individuals in every generation. Many different variants of MA are possible within the most generalized structure as will be clear from the subsequent discussion in this chapter.

MA
Step 1 P = initialize population randomly
Step 2 P = applyLocalSearch(P)
Step 3 **repeat until** (termination_criteria)
Step 4   Select parent individuals from P
Step 5   Apply crossover and mutation to generate offspring C from parents
Step 6   Add offspring C to Q
Step 7 Q = applyLocalSearch(Q)
Step 8 P = Select (P,Q)
Step 9 **end repeat**

Fig. 5.1   Memetic algorithm framework

To illustrate the concept, we may think about an MA that applies local search procedure on every individual. So, after initializing every random individual and after breeding every offspring it will be refined by a local search process. And if the characteristics of the local search is such that it always returns a local optimum, then this particular MA will always work with a population of locally optimum solutions.

5.2.1 *Design issues of MA*

From the outline of MA, presented in the previous section, the reader can immediately identify that there are many issues to be solved for the successful design of MAs. The work of Q.H. Nguyen *et al.* [Nguyen *et al.* (2007)] and N. Krasnogor and J. Smith [Krasnogor and Smith (2005)] has highlighted several important issues that must be taken into consideration when designing a memetic algorithm. The major issues outlined by them and other researchers can be summarized as follows:

- What is the best tradeoff between global search and the local search? And how to strike a balance between them?
- Where and when should the local refinement be applied within the evolutionary cycle?
- How and which individuals should be selected for local refinement?
- How much computational budget should be allocated for local refinement?
- How to choose local search process to complement the genetic operators?

It is easy to understand that the answer to each of these questions can be chosen from a wide spectrum but the correct choice is possible only through theoretical reasoning and empirical evidence. In subsequent sections we will discuss and analyze some of the issues mentioned above. More details about the other issues can be found in [Hart (1994); Goldberg and Voessner (1999); Krasnogor and Smith (2000, 2005); Ong et al. (2006)].

5.2.2 *The choice of local refinement heuristics*

Generally, heuristics can be broadly classified as construction heuristics and improvement heuristics. As the nomenclature suggests the construction paradigm starts without a solution to the problem and builds up a feasible solution working from scratch. On the contrary, the improvement paradigm starts with a feasible solution and improves it through strategic transformations. It is obvious that the local refinement procedure to be used in the MA framework should be an improvement heuristic that intermittently refines the solutions that are uncovered by the global search process, i.e. the EA.

A shortcoming of using local improvement heuristics is their inherent problem-dependent characteristic. There is no local improvement procedure available that can be used for all types of problems where EAs are preferred. Therefore, MAs can be criticized to be more problem dependent compared to EAs. Nevertheless, there are a couple of local improvement procedures that can be applied for a wide range of problems, such as: hill-climbing, simulated annealing, tabu search, iterated local search. Here, we briefly introduce these local search procedures.

Hill-Climbing (HC): This is the simplest local search procedure that iteratively tweaks the current solution and replaces it with the modified solution only if the new one is better than the original one. The algorithmic description is given in Fig. 5.2. Here S is the solution chosen to be refined by the local improvement procedure.

The "Tweak()" operation means "a small bounded but random change" to the candidate solution. Note that the "Tweak()" operation is largely problem and representation dependent. It may range from a single bit alternation to complex, intensive computation. Many popular variations to this simple hill-climbing procedure are possible – a few of which were mentioned in Section 2.1.

Simulated Annealing (SA): Simulated annealing [Kirkpatrick et al. (1983)] derives its name and inspiration from the annealing process – a way

---

Hill-Climbing(S)

Step 1 repeat

Step 2 $R = \text{Tweak}(S)$

Step 3   **if** Quality(R) > Quality(S) **then**

Step 4 $S = R$

Step 5   **end**

Step 6 until S is optimal or iteration exhausted

Step 7 return S

Fig. 5.2   Hill-climbing algorithm

Simulated Annealing(S)

Step 1 $t =$ temperature, initially a larger value

Step 2 $Best = S$

Step 3 repeat

Step 4 $R = \text{Tweak}(S)$

Step 5   **if** Quality(R) > Quality(S) **or**
$$\text{RAND}(0,1) < e^{\frac{Quality(R)-Quality(S)}{t}}$$
then

Step 6 $S = R$

Step 7   **end**

Step 8   Decrease t using annealing schedule

Step 9   **if** Quality(S) > Quality($Best$)

Step 10 $Best = S$

Step 11   **end**

Step 12 until $Best$ is optimal or iteration exhausted

Step 13 return $Best$

Fig. 5.3   Simulated annealing algorithm

of cooling and freezing metal into a minimum-energy crystalline structure. SA varies from HC depending on when to replace the current solution, S, with the newly tweaked solution, R. Like HC, in simulated annealing S is always replaced by R if the new solution is of a higher quality. But if R is of a lower quality then SA stochastically replaces S by R with the following condition:

$$p(t,R,S) = e^{\left(\frac{\text{Quality}(R)-\text{Quality}(S)}{t}\right)} > \text{RAND}(0,1) \qquad (5.1)$$

where $t \geq 0$, the controlling parameter, often called the system

---

Tabu Search(S)

Step 1 $L = \{\}$ a tabu list of maximum length l

Step 2 $Best = S$

Step 3 **repeat**

Step 4   Find the best solution $R \in N(S)$ such that $R \notin T$

Step 5 $S = R$

Step 6 $L = L \cup S$

Step 7   **if** Quality(S) > Quality($Best$) **then**

Step 8 $Best = S$

Step 9   **end**

Step 10 **until** $Best$ is optimal or iteration exhausted

Step 11 **return** $Best$

Fig. 5.4   Tabu search procedure

"temperature" and RAND(0,1) is a random number in the interval [0,1]. If t is a large number then $p(t, R, S)$ is close to 1 and if t is close to zero then $p(t, R, S)$ is close to 0. By analogy with the physical process, the temperature t is initially high. Therefore, the probability of accepting lower-quality solution is initially high which allows the algorithm to move to every newly created solution regardless of how good it is. As the temperature gradually decreases (according to the "annealing schedule") the system is cooled slowly. And at the end, the probability of accepting a lower-quality solution becomes vanishingly small. At this point the algorithm is doing nothing more than plain HC. The working principle of SA is summarized in Fig. 5.3.

Tabu Search (TS): A distinctive feature of Tabu Search, proposed by Fred Glover [Glover (1989)], is the use of memory of the search. While most search methods keep track of the best solution found so far, TS keeps track of the recent itinerary of the search process. TS keeps a history of the recently considered candidate solutions (known as "tabu list") and refuses to return to those candidate solutions until they are sufficiently far in the past.

The simplest form of TS is shown in Fig. 5.4. As with SA, the acceptance criteria in TS is deterministic, i.e. TS always selects neighbors with higher quality. To prevent cycling back to previously visited solutions, TS maintains a tabu list of some maximum length l. When the tabu list overflows, the oldest candidate solution is removed and it is no longer a tabu to reconsider.

Iterated Local Search(S)	
Step 1	$H=S$
Step 2	$Best = S$
Step 3	**repeat**
Step 4	t=random time
Step 5	**repeat**
Step 6	$R = \text{Tweak}(S)$
Step 7	**if** Quality$(R) >$ Quality(S) **then**
Step 8	$S = R$
Step 9	**end**
Step 10	**until** S is optimum or t is finished or total time exhausted
Step 11	**if** Quality$(S) >$ Quality$(Best)$ **then**
Step 12	$Best = S$
Step 13	**end**
Step 14	$H = \text{NewHomeBase}(H, S)$
Step 15	S=Perturb(H)
Step 16	**until** $Best$ is optimal or total time exhausted
Step 17	**return** $Best$

Fig. 5.5   Iterated local search

However, the maintenance of the tabu list for the solutions and the searching within the list is often too time-consuming to be practical. Instead of keeping a tabu list of solutions we can keep a tabu list of moves. In other words, for each possible move a tabu flag in the data structure can be used to signal whether that move is allowed or not. But this procedure can sometimes be too restrictive in a sense that they may prohibit attractive moves, even when there is no danger of cycling. Therefore, to override/revoke tabus, "aspiration criteria" have been incorporated. The simplest and most commonly used aspiration criterion consists in allowing a move, though it is tabu, if it results in a solution with an objective value better than that of the current best-known solution.

Iterated Local Search (ILS): This heuristic is actually an intelligent version of the hill-climbing search that repeatedly performs HC search with random restarts. Since each HC is expected to return a local optimum, the ILS can be thought of as doing random walking through the space of local optimum. However, ILS actually works in a more intelligent way, as Fig. 5.5 shows.

As the work flow shows, instead of absolute random restarts, ILS applies some heuristics in selecting new restart points. The initial solution from where the search starts is considered to be a home base (H) for the search. When the embedded HC restarts, a new home base is chosen based on the current H and the recent local optimum solution S. And this process is indicated by the "NewHomeBase(H, S)" function. Then, the "Perturb(H)" function selects the new restart location by tweaking the current home base position. Finally, to randomize the search operation more, the iteration loop of the embedded HC operation is selected randomly.

The local heuristics work pretty well in discrete search space. And it is easy to conceive how to design the "Tweak()" operation in discrete space or how to compare two solutions for equality. But what if the search space is real-valued? The most straightforward implementation of "Tweak()" could be to add small random values to some members of the candidate solution vector – in the same way mutation is done to real-valued GA. And the equality of two solutions can be estimated based on their Euclidean distance. It will be unrealistic to expect that the distance will be exactly zero between two solutions. So a small value ϵ may be used as a threshold for equality. There are many efficient local improvement processes for continuous domains, for example, a few to mention are: Newton's methods [Fletcher (2000)], bit-climbing algorithm [Davis (1991)], Davies, Swann and Campey's strategies [Schwefel (1995); Swann (1964)], Powell's strategy [Schwefel (1995)], conjugate gradient [Hestenes and Stiefel (1952)], sequential quadratic programming (SQP) [Fletcher (2000)] and the simplex algorithm [Chvatal (1983)].

The local refinement heuristics, as a standalone search process, have some serious limitations. First, these are basically improvement heuristics, hence their performance is essentially dependent on the starting solution. Hence, there is a high risk that these local search processes will end in a local optimum. Then, the convergence speed of these local search processes is very slow. In a population-based search algorithm, multiple search points are explored in parallel. So they are comparatively faster but blamed for not being able to fine-tune the result. So if these two paradigms are to be blended in a single framework then they can complement each other and thereby work as an effective search process. And this is the motivation behind the memetic algorithms.

TSP
Step 1 Initialize population P with Nearest-Neighbor heuristic
Step 2 **for each** individual $i \in P$ **do** Local-Improvement(i)
Step 3 **repeat**
Step 4   **for** $i = 0$ to #crossovers **do**
Step 5   Select two parents $i_a, i_b \in P$ randomly
Step 6 $i_c = \mathrm{DXP}(i_a, i_b)$
Step 7   Local-Improvement(i_c)
Step 8   With predefined probability do Mutation(i_c)
Step 9   Replace an individual of P by i_c
Step 10   **end**
Step 11 **until** converged

Fig. 5.6   The MA for TSP in [Freisleben and Merz (1996a)]

5.2.3 *Solving TSP using MA*

TSP is one of the combinatorial optimization problems that has received many applications of MA. An overview of the early MAs, known as genetic local search, applied in TSP can be found in [Aarts and Verhoeven (1997)]. In [Holstein and Moscato (1999)] an MA is used that uses a local search procedure based on guided local search (GLS) heuristics. This MA uses a framework in which the local refinement is applied after each application of genetic operators rather than once in every EA iteration as shown in Fig. 5.1. Freisleben and Merz proposed a couple of efforts in solving TSP with specialized genetic operators and local search methods [Freisleben and Merz (1996a,b); Merz and Freisleben (1997)]. Their proposed MAs have probably been most successful in solving the TSP.

Here we briefly review the MA used by Freisleben and Merz in [Freisleben and Merz (1996a)] for solving TSP. They considered both symmetric TSP (STSP) and asymmetric TSP (ATSP) in their work. The symmetry depends on whether the distance between two cities is the same in both directions or not. The overall structure of the MA used for solving TSP is shown in Fig. 5.6.

The first step of the algorithm was to initialize the population using a simple "Nearest-Neighbor" heuristic. p different starting points were chosen randomly and then the nearest-neighbor heuristic was applied on them for initial population creation. Then each of the initial solutions were improved using the Local-Improvement process. For STSP, the "Lin-

Kernighan" (LK) tour improvement heuristic was applied, and for ATSP the "fast-3-Opt" tour improvement heuristic was used. The details about these LK and fast-3-Opt heuristics, which are different implementations of the k-Opt procedure, can be found in [Lin and Kernighan (1973)] and [Bentley (1992)], respectively.

Then a specialized crossover operation, called "distance preserving crossover" (DPX) is applied to randomly selected parents. In order to allow the GA to jump in the search space, the DPX was designed to produce an offspring which has the same distance to each of its parents as that one parent has to the other. Implementation details of the DPX operator which is a little different for STSP and ATSP problems, can be found in [Freisleben and Merz (1996a)]. Then the offspring is refined by the Local-Improvement procedure. Mutation is then performed with a small probability on the locally optimum offspring by modifying the tour by a random non-sequential 4-change. This mutation operator also varies for STSP and ATSP problems.

Besides TSP, MAs have been very successful in solving many other combinatorial optimization problems arising in scheduling, manufacturing, telecommunications and bioinformatics. For further information about MA applications, the reader can check these works [Moscato and Cotta (2003); Moscato *et al.* (2004)].

5.3   A memetic version of DE

As mentioned in Chapter 2, one key difficulty faced by all search algorithms is the "curse of dimensionality" [Bellman (1961)]. This expression refers to the exponential growth of the search space volume as a function of dimensionality. Thus even if there is an evolutionary computation solution to a problem of a particular size, with increased dimension the same problem might be completely intractable. And DE, which has been introduced in Chapter 3 as one of the most promising new generation EAs, can not escape this curse. Despite having a relatively high convergence performance in comparison with other EAs for nonlinear optimization of multi-modal functions, DE's convergence velocity is still low for optimizing computationally the most expensive objective functions, especially at higher dimensions [Fan and Lampinen (2003); Noman and Iba (2005a)]. In this section, we show how hybridization with a local improvement procedure can accelerate the convergence velocity of DE so that better solutions can be obtained with higher speed and increased robustness.

5.3.1 *Crossover-based local search (XLS)*

In order to design a memetic version of DE, the first decision is to choose a local improvement process. Several local improvement processes were introduced in Section 5.2.2. Recently, another type of local search (LS), called the "crossover-based LS" (XLS) has been used in real-coded MAs. The crossover operator is a recombination operator that produces offspring around the parents. For this reason, it may be considered to be a move operator for an LS strategy [Lozano *et al.* (2004)]. This is particularly attractive for real coding, since there are real-parameter crossover operators that have a self-adaptive nature in that they can generate offspring adaptively according to the distribution of parents without any adaptive parameter [Beyer and Deb (2001)].

Over the past few years, considerable research effort has been spent on developing efficient crossover operators that use probability distributions around the parents for creating offspring adaptively. Among such numerous approaches, the BLX-α crossover [Eshelman and Schaffer (1993)], the simulated binary crossover (SBX) [Deb and Agrawal (1995)], the unimodal normal distribution crossover (UNDX) [Ono and Kobayashi (1997)], the simplex crossover (SPX) [Tsutsui *et al.* (1999)], and the parent-centric crossover (PCX) [Deb *et al.* (2002)] deserve specific mention. And these types of crossover operators can be employed to create offspring distributed densely around the parents, favoring local tuning.

In order to make the best use of this characteristic of these crossover operators a specific model of GA has also been suggested. This model of GA actually performs a local search by generating many offspring around the parents, mating the participating parents repeatedly using the crossover operator. The most common examples of XLS-based MAs in the literature are minimal generation gap (MGG) [Satoh *et al.* (1996)] and generalized generation gap (G3) [Deb *et al.* (2002)]. Both of them employ the same parents to spawn multiple offspring. The idea is to induce an LS on the neighborhood of the parents involved in the crossover. The above-mentioned crossover operators with inherent adaptive nature show promise for building effective XLS for a continuous search space [Lozano *et al.* (2004)] and have received much attention recently. Another model of XLS has been proposed by Yang and Kao [Yang and Kao (2000)], where they search the neighborhood of each individual – they have named it "family competition" (FC). Here, we study a memetic version of DE hybridizing with XLS strategy.

DEFIR

Step 1 Generate a random initial population P^G

Step 2 Evaluate P^G

Step 3 $P^G = \text{FIR}(P^G)$

Step 4 **for** each individual I in P^G **do**

Step 5   Reproduce an offspring J from I

Step 6   Evaluate J

Step 7 $P^{G+1} = P^{G+1} \cup \text{Select}(I, J)$

Step 8 **end**

Step 9 $P^{G+1} = \text{FIR}(P^{G+1})$

Step 10 Set $G = G + 1$

Step 11 **repeat Step 4** to **Step 10** until termination criteria is met

---

Fig. 5.7   DEFIR – a memetic version of DE

5.3.2 *DE with XLS*

As mentioned earlier, XLSs are applied to search the neighborhood of parents to locally improve their fitness. The same strategy can be applied to the neighborhood of a single individual selected from each generation of DE [Noman and Iba (2005a)]. In other words, we can use XLS for exploring the neighborhood of an individual by mating it repeatedly with different individuals. In their proposed scheme of DE with XLS, Noman and Iba extend DE (DE/rand/1/exp) by applying some crossover-based local search (XLS) for exploring the neighborhood of the best individual [Noman and Iba (2005a)]. That is, in their XLS procedure the best individual x_{best}^G becomes the family father and its family is explored. This family father and other individual(s), randomly chosen from the rest of the current population, are mated to generate offspring. And this procedure is repeated L times. Finally, L solutions $(C_1, C_2, \cdots, C_L)$ are produced and among these offspring and the family father x_{best}^G, the individual with the best score replaces the family father in the next generation. This crossover-based local search process was named "fittest individual refinement" (FIR). The augmented version of DE with FIR in the general template of MA is called "DEFIR". The formal algorithm for DEFIR is given in Fig. 5.7.

The only structural difference between basic DE (Fig. 3.36) and the DEFIR algorithm is the application of FIR in each generation for refining the best individual. Two alternative implementations of DEFIR, presented in [Noman and Iba (2005a)], are DEfirDE and DEfirSPX.

In FIR strategy of DEfirDE scheme, the offspring is generated using the recombination operation of DE/rand/1/exp. In each generation G, for the best individual x_{best}^G three individuals x_j^G, x_k^G and x_l^G are selected such that j, k and $l \in \{1, \cdots, P\}$ and $best \neq j \neq k \neq l$. Then a mutated individual v_i^G is generated using the differential mutation operation (see Section 3.4.4.1). Finally, the offspring $C = u_i^G$ is generated using the exponential crossover operation between the mutated individual v_i^G and the best individual x_{best}^G. This procedure is repeated L times and then selection is performed.

On the other hand, the local search in DEfirSPX scheme generates offspring using the simplex crossover (SPX) operation. SPX is a multi-parent crossover operator that spawns the offspring from p parental vectors as follows:

(1) Choose p parents x_i^G, $i = 1, \cdots, p$ according to the generational model and calculate their center of mass O

$$O = \frac{1}{p} \sum_{i=1}^{p} x_i^G \tag{5.2}$$

(2) Generate random numbers r_i

$$r_i = u^{\frac{1}{i+1}}, (i = 1, \cdots, p-1) \tag{5.3}$$

where u is a uniform random number $\epsilon\ [0, 1]$

(3) Calculate y_i and C_i

$$y_i = O + \varepsilon(x_i^G - O), \quad (i = 1, \cdots, p) \tag{5.4}$$

$$C_i = \begin{cases} 0, & (i = 1) \\ r_{i-1}(y_{i-1} - y_i + C_{i-1}), & (i = 2, \cdots, p) \end{cases} \tag{5.5}$$

where ε is the "expansion rate", a control parameter of SPX.

(4) Generate an offspring C

$$C = y_p + C_p \tag{5.6}$$

SPX has many good characteristics, e.g. it does not depend on a coordinate system, the mean vector of parents and offspring generated with SPX are the same and SPX can preserve a covariance matrix of the population with an appropriate parameter setting. These properties make SPX a suitable operator for neighborhood searching. More details about the SPX crossover can be found in [Tsutsui *et al.* (1999)].

In FIR of DEfirSPX scheme the best individual and other $(p-1)$ random individuals are selected from the current generation. Then SPX is applied on these p parents to generate offspring. Selection is performed after repeating this procedure L times.

The justification for the design of DEFIR is as follows. The basic strategy of EAs is "many points, few neighbors", i.e. they work by searching the single neighborhood of multiple individuals in parallel over successive generations. On the other hand, the XLS-based MAs work with the "few points, many neighbors" strategy, i.e. they work by searching on a greater neighborhood of one individual in successive generations. In MAs, often LS is applied to a selected portion of the population. This is because each application of LS for exploring the neighborhood of an individual requires additional function evaluations. But there is no straightforward way of selecting the most promising individual for applying LS. However, the solution with the best fitness value is possibly in the proximity of a promising basin of attraction. Therefore, some extra fitness evaluations can be allowed to search the neighborhood of this solution for a better solution. DE applies a more directive search in a greedy way. Augmenting this FIR process in the structure of DE the search can be made more directive or greedier. In the context of continuous search space, it can be assumed that the solutions close to the current best individual are also potential candidates that form the neighborhood of the current best solution. With the progress of the search, by exploring the potential candidate solutions in the vicinity of the best individual, it is expected to reach the global optimum at a higher speed. This is similar to the "few points, many neighbors" strategy but is a greedier one. Hence, analogously it can be called the "best-point neighborhood" strategy. Using the above analysis it can easily be observed that the FIR strategy makes DE greedier by replacing the fittest solution of the generation with the best individual in its neighborhood through local refinement and thus accelerating the search.

In designing an XLS method several decisions are involved, like LS application strategy, length of the LS and selecting parents for crossover operation. Here, a very simple approach has been selected for applying the FIR strategy, i.e. only on the best individual of each generation. However, the FIR strategy can also be applied selectively where some other random individuals too will undergo LS. The length L of the FIR strategy was kept fixed, whereas it can be varied dynamically with the progress of the search. At the beginning of the search, the individuals are randomly scattered in the search space; hence an extended local search will be useful to identify a better solution. However, in later generations, as the individuals come closer, brief local searches will suffice to explore the neighborhood. In the current implementation the other parents participating in the FIR strategy were selected randomly. In order to promote a high degree of population diversity, other mating schemes such as "assortative mating", or selection methods such as roulette wheel can be used. In current implementation effort was taken to keep the model as simple as possible and in all cases the most straightforward decision was made.

5.3.3 Benchmarking DEFIR

In this section, the results of different experiments on DEfirDE and DEfir-SPX using the test suite described in Section 3.4.7 are presented. These minimization experiments were carried out in order to analyze the performance of DEfirDE and DEfirSPX algorithms comparing with DE. As mentioned in Section 5.3.2, DEfirDE and DEfirSPX algorithms are implemented by augmenting FIR with DE/rand/1/exp. In order to contrast the studies on DE presented in Chapter 3 using binomial crossover, exponential crossover was deliberately chosen.

5.3.3.1 *Experimental setup*

In this section, the general setup for different experiments to measure the performance of DE, DEfirDE and DEfirSPX is explained. Targeting high dimensional optimization, $N = 100$ was chosen for most experiments. Each experiment was repeated 30 times. The maximum number of evaluations allowed for each algorithm was 500,000. For DEs the most commonly used parameter settings were chosen and were not tuned to the best parameter values for each problem. The value of F was set to 0.5 and C_r was set to 0.8 [Noman and Iba (2005a)]. Experimenting with $L = 4,8,10,15,18,24,30$, and 40, it was found that the best setting for L was in the range $[4, 14]$ and generally for $L \geq 20$ performance of both DEfirSPX and DEfirDE schemes deteriorates. Based on these results, $L = 10$ was chosen for both FIR algorithms. For simplex crossover operation, the number of parents, p, was taken as 3. The algorithms were evaluated by calculating the average (AVG) and the standard deviation (SD) of their attained minimum fitness value within the maximum number of allowed evaluations.

Notation: The following three notations are used in result tables:

(1) **AVG ± SD**: Represents the average and standard deviation of the best fitness values obtained after 500,000 evaluations of multiple trials.

(2) **0.0 [AVG ± SD]**: Represents the average and standard deviation of the number of fitness evaluations required to reach the optimal value (when all trials reach optimal).

(3) **AVG ± SD (c%)**: Represents the average and standard deviation of the best fitness values obtained after 500,000 evaluations and the percentage of trials that reached the optimal value.

In all tables the best results are shown in bold type.

5.3.3.2 *Effect of problem dimensionality*

As specified earlier, the DEfirDE and DEfirSPX schemes were designed to speed up DE in high-dimensional optimization; and therefore, the effect of problem dimensionality on the performance of DE, DEfirDE and DEfirSPX algorithms was studied. Here, the benchmarks were studied in six dimensions: $N=50$, 100, 200, 300, 400, and 500 with population size $P = N$. Other parameter settings are the same as mentioned in Section 5.3.3.1. In these experiments if the fitness value was less than 10^{-6} range of actual optimum point, it is assumed that the solution was detected. The results are shown in Table 5.1 and some representative graphs from different functions in different dimensions are presented to illustrate the convergence properties of the algorithms.

By inspecting Table 5.1 it can be found that DEfirDE and/or DEfirSPX strategy succeeded to reach the optimal value in all trials for some functions (e.g. f_{Sph} (N=100), f_{Ack} (N=100)) for which DE failed in some trials (also showed in Fig. 5.8(a) and 5.8(c)). Even in those cases where DE could reach the optimal value in all trials, it took a higher number of function evaluations compared to that needed for DEfirDE and/or DEfirSPX. This can also be verified by looking at the graphs in Fig. 5.8(d) and 5.8(e). And if those cases where none of the three schemes could hit the global optimal are considered, then it is found that DEfirDE and DEfirSPX schemes attained AVGs which are significantly better than that achieved by their parent algorithm (Fig. 5.8(b)). For example, in Rosenbrock's function none of the above schemes were able to reach the optimal value within the maximum number of evaluations. Additionally, in all experiments DEfirDE and/or DEfirSPX were able to reach the lower average fitness values compared to DE. Another observation from Table 5.1 is that with the increase of dimensionality the minimum fitness achieved by all algorithms after 500,000 fitness evaluations increased polynomially. Nevertheless, with the increase of dimension, the performance difference between the memetic DE schemes

Table 5.1   The effect of problem dimensionality (N)

	N	DE	DEfirDE	DEfirSPX
f_{sph}	50	0 [145703.7 ± 22113.7]	0 [137500.5 ± 31588.9]	0 [101649.4 ± 14842.6]
	100	1.75E−5 ± 8.95E−5 (93.3%)	0 [392370.7 ± 27285.6]	0 [345124.5 ± 22515.7]
	200	5.00E+01 ± 1.64E+01	3.67E+01 ± 2.05E+01	1.50E+00 ± 8.46E−01
	300	7.95E+03 ± 8.67E+02	2.16E+03 ± 3.75E+02	2.82E+02 ± 6.60E+01
	400	7.20E+04 ± 3.68E+03	2.08E+04 ± 2.41E+03	3.09E+03 ± 2.89E+02
	500	2.59E+05 ± 7.06E+03	7.97E+04 ± 6.29E+03	1.16E+04 ± 1.53E+03
f_{ros}	50	7.99E+01 ± 1.03E+02	7.25E+01 ± 7.56E+01	6.81E+01 ± 4.23E+01
	100	1.30E+02 ± 4.78E+01	1.20E+02 ± 3.74E+01	1.08E+02 ± 2.69E+01
	200	9.37E+03 ± 3.67E+03	4.58E+03 ± 2.96E+03	1.48E+03 ± 4.72E+02
	300	1.98E+07 ± 5.28E+06	3.58E+06 ± 2.24E+06	6.39E+04 ± 1.70E+04
	400	4.88E+08 ± 5.74E+07	6.54E+07 ± 1.66E+07	1.20E+06 ± 3.30E+05
	500	3.55E+09 ± 2.34E+08	4.98E+08 ± 9.53E+07	8.54E+06 ± 1.48E+06
f_{ack}	50	0 [161401.9 ± 17471.5]	0 [153469.2 ± 20731.4]	0 [138447.6 ± 9712.1]
	100	1.08E−6 ± 4.87E−7 (90%)	9.37E−7 ± 1.23E−7 (96.7%)	0 [404276.2 ± 10553.6]
	200	4.52E−01 ± 4.86E−02	1.46E−01 ± 2.10E−02	4.90E−02 ± 5.50E−03
	300	7.02E+00 ± 1.07E−01	4.39E+00 ± 1.40E−01	3.02E+00 ± 1.06E−01
	400	1.42E+01 ± 8.30E−02	9.70E+00 ± 2.70E−01	5.84E+00 ± 2.41E−01
	500	1.79E+01 ± 7.50E−02	1.38E+01 ± 2.60E−01	7.94E+00 ± 3.16E−01
f_{grw}	50	0 [129545 ± 28418.3]	0 [129092.6 ± 23006.7]	0 [114993.8 ± 17656.1]
	100	0 [340765.7 ± 35477.28]	0 [318334.9 ± 43484.5]	0 [297807.5 ± 50001.4]
	200	7.80E−01 ± 8.00E−02	2.29E−01 ± 8.38E−02	5.20E−02 ± 2.80E−02
	300	4.14E+01 ± 1.54E+00	1.05E+01 ± 1.17E+00	3.17E+00 ± 2.56E−01
	400	6.03E+02 ± 1.68E+01	1.68E+02 ± 1.82E+01	3.39E+01 ± 4.06E+00
	500	2.32E+03 ± 5.55E+01	7.01E+02 ± 5.20E+01	1.16E+02 ± 9.33E+00
f_{ras}	50	0 [98840.0 ± 26608.2]	0 [98333.7 ± 29017.8]	0 [79041.6 ± 14065.3]
	100	0 [261150.7 ± 17976.1]	0 [243793 ± 24529.1]	0 [204120.8 ± 19879.2]
	200	3.95E−01 ± 1.68E−01	3.77E−02 ± 3.62E−02	4.54E−04 ± 6.65E−04
	300	6.74E+02 ± 2.83E+01	1.17E+02 ± 2.12E+01	5.07E+01 ± 9.40E+01
	400	2.86E+03 ± 5.30E+01	8.67E+02 ± 9.09E+01	4.01E+02 ± 1.80E+02
	500	7.65E+03 ± 2.45E+02	2.57E+03 ± 1.23E+02	1.35E+03 ± 1.91E+02

and the canonical DE becomes more significant. This testifies the claim that the FIR schemes will speed up DE for higher-dimensional function optimization.

Looking at the graphs of Fig. 5.8, it can be found that in every case DEfirSPX started with the steepest convergence curve and continued to produce the best fitness value compared to other strategies with the progress of the search. At the beginning of the search, SPX performs local searching using individuals randomly scattered in the search space and becomes very successful in generating offspring with high fitness, but at later generations it generates individuals around the dense populations slowing down the effect of the local search. On the other hand, the DEfirDE strategy, using the operators of DE, starts slowly compared to DEfirSPX, but continues to improve the fitness with the progress of the search; eventually its performance reaches close to that of DEfirSPX at the end of the search. Results presented in Table 5.1 imply that, for both multimodal (f_{Grw}, f_{Ras} and f_{Ack}) and unimodal (f_{Sph} and f_{Ros}) functions, DEfirDE and DEfirSPX exhibited superior performance compared to DE.

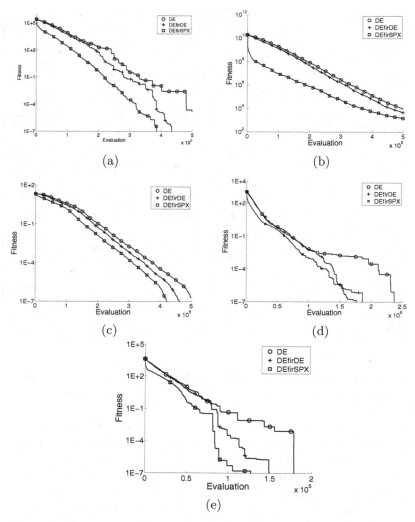

Fig. 5.8   Convergence graphs for (a) f_{sph} (N=100), (b) f_{ros} (N=200), (c) f_{ack} (N=100), (d) f_{grw} (N=50) and (e) f_{ras} (N=50).

5.3.3.3   *Sensitivities to control parameters*

Some experiments were conducted to assess the robustness of DEFIR schemes to the variation of population size and other control parameters. In these experiments, one of the three parameters from P, C_r and F was

Table 5.2   Sensitivity of DE and DEFIR to population size (P)

	N	DE	DEfirDE	DEfirSPX
f_{sph}	100	9.15E−09 ± 3.04E−08	1.92E−10 ± 4.42E−10	**1.56E−12 ± 6.00E−12**
	400	9.23E+00 ± 2.92E+00	2.23E+00 ± 1.16E+00	**2.47E−01 ± 1.00E−01**
	700	4.44E+02 ± 3.68E+01	1.14E+02 ± 2.91E+01	**1.87E+01 ± 7.59E+00**
	1000	2.50E+03 ± 2.33E+02	6.95E+02 ± 1.63E+02	**1.41E+02 ± 3.80E+01**
f_{ros}	100	1.30E+02 ± 4.78E+01	1.20E+02 ± 3.74E+01	**1.08E+02 ± 2.69E+01**
	400	5.73E+03 ± 1.88E+03	1.98E+03 ± 8.74E+02	**7.59E+02 ± 2.28E+02**
	700	3.35E+05 ± 1.40E+05	7.07E+04 ± 3.07E+04	**5.45E+03 ± 2.12E+03**
	1000	4.17E+06 ± 8.65E+05	7.56E+05 ± 3.18E+05	**3.41E+04 ± 1.26E+04**
f_{ack}	100	2.06E−07 ± 8.26E−08	1.67E−07 ± 1.51E−07	**8.56E−08 ± 7.20E−08**
	400	3.36E−01 ± 2.30E−02	1.28E−01 ± 2.70E−02	**5.50E−02 ± 1.33E−02**
	700	4.16E+00 ± 6.90E−02	2.63E+00 ± 1.40E−01	**1.69E+00 ± 1.52E−01**
	1000	7.74E+00 ± 1.53E−01	5.16E+00 ± 2.96E−01	**3.57E+00 ± 1.95E−01**
f_{grw}	100	1.92E−09 ± 9.06E−09	4.80E−12 ± 1.80E−11	**4.44E−14 ± 1.64E−13 (30%)**
	400	6.52E−01 ± 6.90E−02	1.95E−01 ± 6.50E−02	**3.00E−02 ± 1.26E−02**
	700	3.32E+00 ± 2.06E−01	1.61E+00 ± 1.28E−01	**1.14E+00 ± 2.70E−02**
	1000	1.96E+01 ± 1.36E+00	6.43E+00 ± 1.04E+00	**2.29E+00 ± 2.94E−01**
f_{ras}	100	0 [356115.4 ± 13528.2]	0 [330468.7 ± 18951.1]	**0 [284680.4 ± 15508.1]**
	400	5.03E−02 ± 2.20E−02	3.00E−03 ± 2.00E−03	**4.17E−05 ± 3.36E−05**
	700	6.18E+01 ± 7.42E+00	8.38E+00 ± 3.48E+00	**1.72E+00 ± 1.67E+00**
	1000	2.32E+02 ± 1.70E+01	5.04E+01 ± 1.21E+01	**3.63E+01 ± 3.91E+01**

Table 5.3   Sensitivity of DE and DEFIR to crossover rate (C_r)

	N	DE	DEfirDE	DEfirSPX
f_{sph}	0.1	1.49E+03 ± 2.30E+03	1.13E+03 ± 1.24E+03	**1.94E+00 ± 3.83E+00**
	0.3	1.74E+02 ± 3.15E+02	1.03E+02 ± 1.95E+02	**6.90E−02 ± 2.90E−01**
	0.6	2.80E−02 ± 6.00E−02	1.99E−02 ± 9.50E−02	**3.35E−08 ± 1.75E−07**
	0.8	9.15E−09 ± 3.04E−08	1.92E−10 ± 4.41E−10	**1.56E−12 ± 5.99E−12**
	1.0	1.43E+04 ± 3.07E+03	1.41E+04 ± 2.93E+03	**1.23E+04 ± 3.13E+03**
f_{ros}	0.1	3.00E+06 ± 2.66E+06	2.06E+06 ± 2.81E+06	**5.25E+04 ± 3.42E+04**
	0.3	1.87E+05 ± 3.08E+05	1.47E+05 ± 2.47E+05	**4.98E+03 ± 5.09E+03**
	0.6	6.77E+02 ± 5.80E+02	3.87E+02 ± 1.63E+02	**2.35E+02 ± 1.17E+02**
	0.8	1.30E+02 ± 4.78E+01	1.20E+02 ± 3.74E+01	**1.08E+02 ± 2.69E+01**
	1.0	2.51E+07 ± 7.97E+06	2.64E+07 ± 1.01E+07	**2.50E+07 ± 1.01E+07**
f_{ack}	0.1	1.70E−02 ± 1.50E−02	1.40E−02 ± 2.60E−02	**2.00E−03 ± 3.00E−03**
	0.3	7.00E−03 ± 1.40E−02	9.85E−04 ± 7.57E−04	**1.87E−04 ± 1.33E−04**
	0.6	2.16E−04 ± 4.80E−04	2.12E−05 ± 4.68E−05	**1.57E−06 ± 2.43E−06**
	0.8	2.06E−07 ± 8.26E−08	1.67E−07 ± 1.51E−07	**8.56E−08 ± 7.20E−08**
	1.0	1.17E+01 ± 5.36E−01	1.18E+01 ± 6.99E−01	**1.14E+01 ± 8.30E−01**
f_{grw}	0.1	6.00E−03 ± 2.10E−02	2.60E−03 ± 8.00E−03	**1.80E−03 ± 5.50E−03**
	0.3	1.50E−03 ± 4.60E−03	2.79E−04 ± 7.47E−04	**5.42E−05 ± 1.12E−04**
	0.6	2.97E−05 ± 1.36E−04	1.25E−05 ± 6.30E−05	**7.38E−06 ± 2.77E−05**
	0.8	1.92E−09 ± 9.06E−09	4.80E−12 ± 1.80E−11	**4.43E−14 ± 1.64E−13 (30%)**
	1.0	1.17E+02 ± 2.39E+01	1.29E+02 ± 3.00E+01	**1.13E+02 ± 1.92E+01**
f_{ras}	0.1	3.33E−4±1.70E−3 (6.7%)	1.80E−5±5.83E−5 (16.7%)	**9.07E−7±4.57E−6 (23.3%)**
	0.3	1.71E−7±8.22E−7 (16.7%)	7.74E−8±2.75E−7 (40%)	**1.84E−12±9.25E−12 (80%)**
	0.6	6.22E−15±2.40E−14 (93.3%)	0 [389469.9 ± 26722.2]	**0 [356382.9 ± 29942.0]**
	0.8	0 [356115.4 ± 13528.2]	0 [330468.7 ± 18951.1]	**0 [284680.4 ± 15508.1]**
	1.0	3.05E+02 ± 4.15E+01	**3.04E+02 ± 3.41E+01**	3.11E+02 ± 3.79E+01

varied within a certain range keeping the remaining two constant at values specified in Section 5.3.3.1. For all the experiments in this section, the problem dimension N=100 was used. The results are shown in Tables 5.2 to 5.4.

Table 5.4   Sensitivity of DE and DEFIR to amplification factor (F)

	N	DE	DEfirDE	DEfirSPX
f_{sph}	0.1	1.07E+04 $\pm$ 4.32E+03	1.12E+04 $\pm$ 4.15E+03	**4.24E+03 $\pm$ 1.91E+03**
	0.5	9.15E−09 $\pm$ 3.04E−08	1.92E−10 $\pm$ 4.41E−10	**1.56E−12 $\pm$ 5.99E−12**
	0.8	8.60E−03 $\pm$ 7.00E−03	4.20E−03 $\pm$ 4.60E−03	**1.40E−04 $\pm$ 3.25E−04**
	1.2	2.96E+01 $\pm$ 1.29E+01	2.24E+01 $\pm$ 1.41E+01	**9.82E−01 $\pm$ 5.45E−01**
	1.6	8.12E+02 $\pm$ 2.65E+02	5.40E+02 $\pm$ 3.38E+02	**2.95E+01 $\pm$ 1.16E+01**
	1.9	3.41E+03 $\pm$ 1.09E+03	2.01E+03 $\pm$ 8.03E+02	**1.16E+02 $\pm$ 5.58E+01**
f_{ros}	0.1	1.91E+07 $\pm$ 1.49E+07	3.99E+07 $\pm$ 2.23E+07	**1.07E+07 $\pm$ 8.12E+06**
	0.5	1.30E+02 $\pm$ 4.78E+01	1.20E+02 $\pm$ 3.74E+01	**1.08E+02 $\pm$ 2.69E+01**
	0.8	3.04E+02 $\pm$ 1.26E+02	2.81E+02 $\pm$ 1.21E+02	**1.44E+02 $\pm$ 5.06E+01**
	1.2	3.75E+04 $\pm$ 1.89E+04	2.19E+04 $\pm$ 1.38E+04	**2.52E+03 $\pm$ 1.20E+03**
	1.6	2.85E+06 $\pm$ 1.74E+06	1.34E+06 $\pm$ 9.72E+05	**3.49E+04 $\pm$ 4.63E+04**
	1.9	1.35E+07 $\pm$ 8.34E+06	5.77E+06 $\pm$ 3.51E+06	**1.02E+05 $\pm$ 5.58E+04**
f_{ack}	0.1	4.37E+00 $\pm$ 7.79E−01	5.72E+00 $\pm$ 1.14E+00	**3.71E+00 $\pm$ 6.81E−01**
	0.5	2.06E−07 $\pm$ 8.26E−08	1.67E−07 $\pm$ 1.51E−07	**8.56E−08 $\pm$ 7.20E−08**
	0.8	7.00E−03 $\pm$ 1.80E−03	4.00E−03 $\pm$ 1.50E−03	**6.52E−04 $\pm$ 1.94E−04**
	1.2	9.40E−01 $\pm$ 1.88E−01	5.78E−01 $\pm$ 1.60E−01	**1.25E−01 $\pm$ 4.10E−02**
	1.6	4.25E+00 $\pm$ 2.70E−01	2.37E+00 $\pm$ 2.64E−01	**1.53E+00 $\pm$ 1.82E−01**
	1.9	6.68E+00 $\pm$ 4.29E−01	3.72E+00 $\pm$ 4.71E−01	**2.67E+00 $\pm$ 2.54E−01**
f_{grw}	0.1	1.16E+01 $\pm$ 6.39E+00	1.73E+01 $\pm$ 6.94E+00	**1.06E+01 $\pm$ 8.96E+00**
	0.5	1.92E−09 $\pm$ 9.06E−09	4.80E−12 $\pm$ 1.80E−11	**4.43E−14 $\pm$ 1.64E−13 (30%)**
	0.8	2.40E−03 $\pm$ 5.30E−03	1.70E−03 $\pm$ 3.60E−03	**1.39E−04 $\pm$ 6.31E−04**
	1.2	6.65E−01 $\pm$ 1.13E−01	3.95E−01 $\pm$ 1.23E−01	**8.70E−02 $\pm$ 7.10E−02**
	1.6	1.88E+00 $\pm$ 2.51E−01	1.28E+00 $\pm$ 1.36E−01	**9.78E−01 $\pm$ 7.70E−02**
	1.9	6.20E+00 $\pm$ 1.02E+00	2.64E+00 $\pm$ 9.10E−01	**1.23E+00 $\pm$ 6.90E−02**
f_{ras}	0.1	1.15E+01 $\pm$ 4.72E+00	2.91E+01 $\pm$ 1.88E+01	**9.55E+00 $\pm$ 4.35E+00**
	0.5	0 [356115.4 $\pm$ 13528.2]	0 [330468.7 $\pm$ 18951.1]	0 [284680.4 $\pm$ 15508.1]
	0.8	6.52E−09 $\pm$ 2.09E−08	1.61E−09 $\pm$ 2.66E−09	**2.21E−12 $\pm$ 3.18E−12**
	1.2	3.80E−02 $\pm$ 2.90E−02	3.20E−02 $\pm$ 1.04E−01	**8.23E−05 $\pm$ 8.50E−05**
	1.6	1.45E+01 $\pm$ 5.21E+00	3.01E+00 $\pm$ 2.48E+00	**1.14E+00 $\pm$ 3.54E+00**
	1.9	6.40E+01 $\pm$ 1.62E+01	**1.45E+01 $\pm$ 5.58E+00**	1.86E+01 $\pm$ 2.06E+01

The effect of population size on DEFIR algorithms is similar to what was observed in the case of classic DE (see Section 3.4.7.3). The results show that in high-dimensional search spaces DE works better with a population size close to the dimension of the problem (in this case P=N). Since DEfirDE and DEfirSPX are just augmentations of basic DE with XLS, it is expected that their sensitivity to the variation of population will be more or less similar to that in basic DE and the results shown in Table 5.2 prove that. However, the performance of DEfirDE and DEfirSPX were found less susceptible to population variation compared to that of DE (Table 5.2). So it can be stated that the use of FIR has increased the robustness of DE against the variation of population size.

Experimental results obtained by varying the "crossover rate" (C_r) and "amplification factor" (F) are shown in Table 5.3 and Table 5.4, respectively. From these tables it can be seen that at any parameter setting the FIR scheme can be effective and DEFIR can produce better results than basic DE. So it can be stated that DEFIR schemes show lower sensitivity to variations in control parameters than canonical DE. Between the two DE-

FIR schemes, DEfirSPX is found to be more robust to parameter changes. The DEfirDE scheme also exhibited less sensitivity compared to DE against parameter changes. Only for $F = 0.1$ and in some cases where $C_r = 1.0$, was DEfirDE's performance slightly inferior to DE and for all other cases it showed superior performance. Additionally, it should be remembered that none of these values (i.e. $F = 0.1$ and $C_r = 1.0$) are recommended settings for DE (see Section 3.4.7.3). So it can be concluded that overall, for all control parameters, P, C_r, and F, DEFIR schemes showed less performance fluctuation compared to DE. In other words, because of hybridization with FIR strategy the overall robustness of DE has improved.

5.3.3.4 *Comparison with other hybrid GAs*

A performance comparison, of the DEFIR algorithms and some other hybrid GAs that have been proposed for solving real-parameter optimization problems, is presented in this section. Since MGG and G3 are two of the most prominent models of EAs and one of the FIR schemes uses the simplex crossover operator, it is well justified to compare these memetic DEs with MGG+SPX (MGG with simplex crossover) and G3+SPX (G3 with simplex crossover). Recently Lozano *et al.* [Lozano *et al.* (2004)] proposed a real-coded memetic algorithm (RCMA) that uses a real-parameter crossover hill-climbing (XHC) method and using an extensive study the authors have shown that their proposed RCMA+XHC algorithm can outperform or compete with many well-known models of RCMAs like hybrid steady-state RCMA, G3, family competition (FC) and hybrid CHC. Therefore, this RCMA+XHC model was also included in this comparative study. All the benchmarks were studied at dimension N=100. The control parameters of each algorithm were set according to the recommended parameters of each algorithm. For G3 and MGG population size P = 1500, the number of children generated by the simplex crossover per selection = 50, the number of parents participated in the crossover operation = N+1. For RCMA+XHC algorithm, P=300 was chosen and all other parameters were set to the values used in [Lozano *et al.* (2004)]. The maximum function evaluations allowed for each algorithm was 500,000 and the optimum was considered to be found only when the best fitness value was within 10^{-6} error.

Table 5.5 shows the results of the comparison. In this study none of the MGG or G3 models with simplex crossover could reach the global optima for any of the objective functions in any run using 500,000 function evaluations.

Table 5.5 Comparison of DEFIR with other MAs (N=100)

Alg	f_{Sph}	f_{Ack}	f_{Grw}
MGG+SPX	3.37E+02±4.57E+01	3.76E+00±1.48E−01	3.88E+00±4.01E−01
G3+SPX	2.87E+02±4.17E+01	3.67E+00±1.41E−01	3.68E+00±3.30E−01
RCMA+XHC	0 [421451.0±22622.9]	4.24E−04±2.82E−04	2.70E−2±4.61E−2 (56.67%)
DE	1.75E−5±8.95E−5 (93.3%)	1.08E−6±4.87E−7 (90%)	0 [340765.7±35477.3]
DEfirDE	0 [392370.7±27285.6]	9.37E−7±1.23E−7 (96.7%)	0 [318334.9±43484.5]
DEfirSPX	0 [345124.5±22515.7]	0 [404276.2±10553.6]	0 [297807.5±50001.4]

Alg	f_{Ras}	f_{Ros}
MGG+SPX	4.01E+00±7.44E−01	2.59E+04±6.60E+03
G3+SPX	3.13E+00±9.41E−01	1.88E+04±4.81E+03
RCMA+XHC	0 [355635.8±43611.3]	1.57E+02±7.32E+01
DE	0 [261150.7±17976.1]	1.30E+02±4.78E+01
DEfirSPX	0 [243793.0±24529.1]	1.20E+02±3.74E+01
DEfirSPX	0 [204120.8±19879.2]	1.08E+02±2.69E+01

Comparatively the performance of RCMA+XHC was better. However, RCMA+XHC could perform better than DE only for the simplest function f_{sph}. And both of the memetic DE algorithms DEfirSPX and DEfirDE outperform MGG+SPX, G3+SPX and RCMA+XHC for each benchmark function.

5.3.4 *Experiments with landscape generator*

According to the no free lunch (NFL) theorems [Wolpert and Macready (1997)] no algorithm is superior to others when their average performance over all possible problems is considered. Therefore, any general comment made about the performance of any algorithm based on results of experiments with a couple of test problems is similar to a general conclusion made about a very large data set depending on a few samples; and such a conclusion is often incomplete and misleading. In fact, algorithms operate on landscapes, not on problems, so the information about how an algorithm interacts with landscapes and the relationship between its performance and properties of landscapes will be more useful to predict its performance on other problems [Yuan and Gallagher (2003)]. Therefore, it is more useful to use landscape generators which do not take into account any specific problem rather than landscapes on which an algorithm will conduct searching as the test-bed for algorithm evaluation and testing. Another advantage of using landscape generators is that they can remove the opportunity to hand-tune algorithms to a specific problem. Furthermore, by allowing a large number of problem instances to be randomly generated, the predictive power of the simulation results can also be increased [Kennedy and Spears (1998b)].

5.3.4.1 *The Gaussian landscape generator*

To further highlight the effectiveness of the memetic framework, here we present a comparison between the memetic DE algorithms and the canonical DE algorithm using a continuous landscape generator proposed by Yuan and Gallagher [Yuan and Gallagher (2003)]. The basic component of this landscape generator is an N-dimensional Gaussian function (GF). Each landscape contains M GFs, each representing a "hill" in the landscape. The fitness of an individual is given by the maximum value of any of the Gaussian components at that point. So individuals are evaluated using the following fitness function:

$$F(X) = \max_{i=1}^{M} \left[\frac{1}{(2\pi)^{n/2} \mid \sum_i \mid^{1/2}} exp\left(-\frac{1}{2}(X - \mu_i)\sum_i^{-1}(X - \mu_i)^T \right) \right] \quad (5.7)$$

where X is the N-dimensional individual to be evaluated and $\sum_i$ and μ_i are the N-dimensional vector of mean and $(N \times N)$ dimensional covariance matrix of i-th $[i = 1, \cdots, M]$ Gaussian component, respectively. According to Eq. (5.7), given a point X in the search space, its value is calculated with regard to each GF and its fitness is set to the highest value returned from the GFs. Therefore, the mean vector of each GF corresponds to an optimum and the mean vector of the GF that has the highest peak value corresponds to the global optimum.

Multivariate Gaussian functions often produce very small values (i.e. probability) in high-dimensional spaces. Since test problems in high-dimensional spaces were desirable the original fitness function was transformed as follows:

$$F(X) = \max_{i=1}^{M} \left\{ \left[\frac{1}{(2\pi)^{n/2} \mid \sum_i \mid^{1/2}} exp\left(-\frac{1}{2}(X - \mu_i)\sum_i^{-1}(X - \mu_i)^T \right) \right]^{1/n} \right\}$$
$$(5.8)$$

So the parameters of the landscape generator are the number of GFs (M), the dimensionality of the landscape (N), the range of the search space, the mean vector and the covariance matrix of each GF. Again, a Gaussian function with arbitrary valid covariance structure can be conveniently generated through a series of rotations of the variable coordinate system [Salmon (1996)]. Hence, each $\sum_i$ is parameterized using rotation angles and variance values. Using these parameters the landscape can be tuned to have specific geometric characteristics, e.g. hills, valleys or other landscape features.

5.3.4.2 *Experimental setup*

As specified earlier, the motivation for experimenting with the landscape generator is to gain insight on the performance of different algorithms by evaluating them using random test problems. In these experiments, the above specified landscape generator was employed for investigating the performance of DE, DEfirDE and DEfirSPX using one set of randomly generated problem instances with similar structural features. Here the dimensionality $N = 50$ and number of GFs $M = 100$ was chosen. The rest of the parameters were chosen randomly. The search space was restricted to the interval [-10.0, 10.0] in each dimension. For covariance matrices the range of variance values was set to [0.50, 5.50] in order to avoid very sharp peaks and too many flat areas, and the range of rotation angles was set to [-$\pi/4$, $\pi/4$] (as suggested by [Yuan and Gallagher (2003)]). Ten random maximization problems were generated using the above configuration. Then each algorithm was run for 20 trials on each of these problems. The parameter settings for the algorithms were $P = N = 50$, $F = 0.5$, $C_r = 0.8$ and $L = 10$. Each algorithm was allowed to evolve for a maximum of 10,000 fitness evaluations.

5.3.4.3 *Results*

The fitness value of the best individual found during the run of each algorithm was used for performance evaluation. Different landscapes may have different global optima in terms of fitness value. Therefore, in order to have a uniform representation for different landscapes, raw fitness values were normalized in the range [0, 1]. Box-plots were used to represent the performance of each algorithm where each box shows the fitness distribution of an algorithm on a specific landscape over 20 runs.

The graphs in Fig. 5.9 show the performance of DE, DEfirDE and DEfirSPX on different landscapes, respectively. From these graphs it is clear that after an equal number of evaluations the best fitness attained by DEfirDE and DEfirSPX algorithms are significantly better than that attained by DE. In Figs. 5.9(a), 5.9(b) and 5.9(c) the fitness distribution of the same landscape takes the same position in the graph. So if these three graphs are compared then it will be found that if some landscape was comparatively

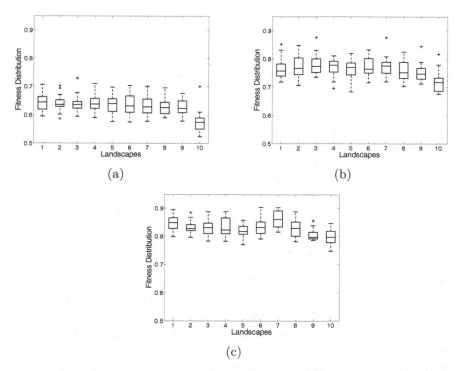

Fig. 5.9 Experimental results on landscapes using (a) DE, (b) DEfirDE and (c) DEfir-SPX.

difficult for DE (e.g. landscape 10), it was also difficult for DEfirDE and DEfirSPX. This is not unlikely as the FIR schemes work within the general framework of DE. Still, by searching locally in the neighborhood of the best individual of each generation, the memetic versions of DE were successful in reaching a better fitness value compared to that attained by DE. Therefore, from these results it is obvious that FIR schemes can improve the performance of DE.

Fig. 5.10 shows the convergence curve of different algorithms for the first landscape. This graph can be taken as a representative graph for all other landscapes. As shown in this graph, the performance of all algorithms saturated with time, but starting with a steeper curve DEfirDE and DEfirSPX, attained better fitness compared to DE. The convergence curve of DEfirSPX is especially notable. Because of the superiority of the simplex crossover operation, the FIR strategy generated offspring of very high qual-

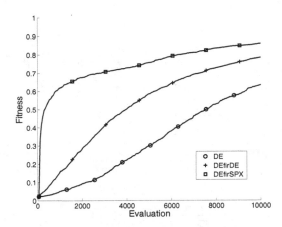

Fig. 5.10   Mean performance of DE, DEfirDE and DEfirSPX on landscape no. 1

ity, resulting in a sharp increase in fitness at the beginning of the search. The DEfirDE scheme also showed better convergence velocity than DE. Moreover, the relative performance of DEfirDE and DEfirSPX is similar to what was observed in benchmark studies. However, the results of these experiments were helpful to establish the claim that the use of local search such as the FIR strategy can improve the performance of DE for highly multimodal problems.

5.4   Adaptation in memetic algorithms

Depending on whether their strategic parameters are changed over the course of evolution, EAs are broadly classified as static and adaptive. Adaptive EAs are designed to alter their control parameters according to some rule during the run of the algorithm. The purpose of adaptation is to tune the algorithm parameters online so that it can perform more effectively over a broader range of problems or even at different stages of evolution. The adaptation in EAs may take place at different levels such as environment, population, individual or component [Hinterding *et al.* (1997)].

Hence, design of MAs that employ parameter and/or operator adaptation has become one of the most important and promising areas of research. Ong and Keane proposed meta-Lamarckian learning in MAs for adaptation of local search (LS) operators [Ong and Keane (2004)]. They presented two algorithms, MA-S1 and MA-S2, both of which work with a pool of LS operators. During the course of evolution the algorithms keep track of the effectiveness of different LS operators and adapt the subsequent selection of LS operators depending on their previous performance. Using an empirical study, they showed that their MAs with the adaptation of LS operators are effective in producing search performances close to MAs with the best chosen LS operators. An excellent taxonomy and comparative study on the adaptive choice of memes in MAs is presented in [Ong *et al.* (2006)]. In order to balance between local and genetic search, Bambha *et al.* proposed simulated heating that systematically integrates parameterized LS (both statically and dynamically) into EAs [Bambha *et al.* (2004)]. In the context of combinatorial problems, Krasnagor and Smith showed that self-adaptive hybridization of GA and LS/diversification process gives rise to a better global search meta-heuristic [Krasnogor and Smith (2000)].

Due to the superior performance of adaptive MAs, in this section the performance of an adaptive XLS hybridized with DE will be investigated. But before that we briefly present some other contemporary efforts taken to make DE adaptive.

5.4.1 *Adaptive differential evolution algorithms*

As discussed in Section 3.4.5 and empirically shown in Section 3.4.7.3, the performance of DE is very much sensitive to its parameter settings. Due to this well-known issue of DE's sensitivity to its control variables, a couple of studies have been conducted to design adaptive DE that does not require setting of F and C_r.

For example, Zaharie [Zaharie (2003)] proposes a feedback update rule for F that is designed to maintain the population diversity at a given level and thereby stops the premature convergence of the search. However, in order to obtain adequate behavior in the update rule for F, tuning of another parameter γ is required. Therefore, as the author points out himself, although the algorithm seems to perform better, in fact the problem merely changes from that of choosing F to choosing γ and there is little real advantage in a practical sense.

Liu and Lampinen proposed "fuzzy adaptive differential evolution" (FADE) that uses a fuzzy knowledge-based system to dynamically control DE parameters, such as F and C_r [Liu and Lampinen (2005)]. The parameters of FADE respond to the population's information, i.e. parameter vectors, function values, and their changes. Based on human knowledge and expertise, FADE is designated to expedite the convergence velocity of DE by the use of adaptive parameters. A set of benchmark functions were used to explore the performance of FADE which showed that FADE resulted in faster convergence in higher problem dimensions.

Jason Teo made an effort to self-adapt the population size parameter of DE in addition to self-adapting crossover and mutation rates [Teo (2006)]. The proposed algorithm was called "differential evolution with self-adapting populations" (DESAP) and it came in two versions depending on the encoding method: absolute and relative for dynamically adapting the population size. A brief empirical study showed that DESAP performed in a similar manner when compared with the conventional DE with a static population size.

Brest *et al.* proposed another self-adaptive version of DE that automatically adjusts its control parameters F and C_r at an individual level [Brest *et al.* (2006)]. Each individual in the population is extended with two additional components, F and C_r. Each individual chromosome is thus composed of its genotype and its control parameters as follows:

$$x_i^G = \langle x_{i,1}^G, x_{i,2}^G, \cdots, x_{i,N-1}^G, x_{i,N}^G, F_i^G, C_{r_i}^G \rangle$$

As the algorithm runs, these values of F and C_r are evolved in a way similar to evolution strategy (ES). More specifically, for each principle parent x_i^G, when an offspring is generated using differential mutation and crossover operation (see Section 3.4.4) new F and C_r values are calculated for it as follows:

$$F_i^{G+1} = \begin{cases} F_l + rand_1 * F_u, & \text{if } rand_2 < \tau_1 \\ F_i^G & \text{otherwise} \end{cases} \tag{5.9}$$

$$C_{r_i}^{G+1} = \begin{cases} rand_3 & \text{if } rand_4 < \tau_2 \\ C_{r_i}^G & \text{otherwise} \end{cases} \tag{5.10}$$

where $rand_j$, $j \in \{1, 2, 3, 4\}$, are uniform pseudo-random values $\in [0, 1]$, τ_i and τ_2 are constants that represent the probabilities to adjust F and C_r, respectively. F_l represents the minimum value that can be assigned to F_i^{G+1} and the F_u represent the maximum random variation added to F_l. The genetic operators and the selection mechanism are identical to that of a standard DE.

Qin and Suganthan [Qin and Suganthan (2005)] have taken the self-adaptability of DE one step further by choosing the learning strategy, as well as the parameter settings, adaptively, according to the learning experience. Their proposed "self-adaptive DE" (SaDE) does not use any particular learning strategy, nor any specific setting for the control parameters F and C_r. SaDE uses its previous learning experience to adaptively select the learning strategy and parameter values, which are often problem-dependent.

5.4.2 Differential evolution with adaptive XLS

Success of an MA depends on the balance between the exploration capability of its global search component (EA) and the exploitation capability of its LS component [Ishibuchi *et al.* (2003)]. The best result can be obtained if we can adjust the global search and the local search intensity adaptively with the progress of the search [Nguyen *et al.* (2009)]. In this section we present a scheme to adjust the LS intensity adaptively and thereby balance the exploration and exploitation ratio automatically [Noman and Iba (2008a)].

As mentioned in Section 5.3.2, several decisions are involved in hybridizing a crossover-based LS (XLS) in an EA, e.g. length of the XLS, selection of individuals that undergo the XLS, selection of auxiliary parents participating in the crossover operation, deterministic/stochastic application of XLS, etc. Here we are concerned in adapting the LS intensity. Depending on the way the search length (LS intensity) is selected, different XLSs can be classified into three categories:

Static Length XLS generates a predetermined number of offspring to search the neighborhood of the parent individuals. In other words, here the LS intensity is fixed beforehand and does not change during evolution. This type of search has been presented in Section 5.3.2 and also has been used in [Yang and Kao (2000); Lozano *et al.* (2004); Noman and Iba (2005a)].

Dynamic Length XLS varies the intensity of the LS according to some deterministic rule. For example, with the progress of the search the LS intensity can be gradually reduced, i.e. starting with lengthier XLS at the beginning of the search, the length can be gradually made shorter towards the end of the search.

Adaptive Length XLS determines the direction and length of the search by taking some sort of feedback from the search.

In static length XLS, the crucial challenge is to identify the most suitable length for the LS. It is important because a short length XLS may be unsuccessful in exploring the neighborhood of the solution well, and in improving the quality of the search. On the other hand, a lengthy XLS

AHCXLS(P^G, n_P)

Step 1 $Q[1] = \text{BestIndex}(P^G)$

Step 2 **for** $i = 2$ to n_P **do**

Step 3 $Q[i]=$ select random individual from
                    P^G without replacement

Step 4 **end**

Step 5 $C = \text{SPX\_Crossover}(Q)$

Step 6 **if** C is better than $Q[1]$ **then**

Step 7 $Q[1] = C$

Step 8 **else**

Step 9   **return** $(Q[1])$

Step 10 **end**

Step 11 Go to **Step 5**

Fig. 5.11   Adaptive local search scheme AHCXLS

may waste fitness evaluations and make the search costly. However, finding a single length for XLS that gives optimized results for each problem in each dimension is almost impossible [Lozano *et al.* (2004)]. The study in Section 5.3.3.1 also presented the same observation. Similarly, determining a robust adjustment rate is not easy for dynamic length XLS. Therefore, Noman and Iba proposed a local search that adaptively determines the length of the search by taking feedback from the search [Noman and Iba (2008a)]. This local search strategy was named as "adaptive hill-climbing XLS" (AHCXLS) because it uses a simple hill-climbing algorithm to determine the search length adaptively. The pseudo-code of AHCXLS is shown in Fig. 5.11.

Another issue in designing XLS is selecting the individuals that will undergo the local search process (as discussed earlier). XLS can be applied on every individual or on some deterministically/stochastically selected individuals. In principle, the XLS should be applied only to individuals that will productively take the search towards the global optimum. This is particularly important because the application of XLS on an ordinary individual may unnecessarily waste function evaluations and turn out to be expensive. Unfortunately, there is no straightforward way to select the most promising individuals for XLS. In EC, the solutions with better fitness values are generally preferred for reproduction, as they are more likely to be in the proximity of a basin of attraction. Therefore, the best individual of the population was deterministically selected for exploring its neighborhood using the XLS and thereby it is expected to end with a nearby better solution [Noman and Iba (2005a, 2008a)]. The other individuals that participate in the crossover operation of XLS are chosen randomly to keep the implementation simple and to promote population diversity. So for both AHCXLS and FIR schemes, the parent individuals are chosen in a similar fashion. The last decision is about which crossover operation could be used in the XLS scheme. It was shown in Section 5.3.3 that SPX was a promising operation for local tuning, and therefore SPX was used as the crossover operation in AHCXLS. The AHCXLS with SPX was named AHCSPX and the new version of DE with the AHCSPX operation is titled as DEahcSPX [Noman and Iba (2008a)]. The DEahcSPX algorithm is same as the DEFIR algorithm shown in Fig. 5.7 except the FIR strategy is replaced with the AHCXLS strategy.

The primary difference between the DEahcSPX algorithm and the DEfirSPX algorithm is that we are no more required to look for a good search length for the XLS operation. The simple rule of hill-climbing adaptively determines the best length by taking feedback from the search. Hence, using the best length (according to the heuristics) for the local search adaptively, the DEahcSPX algorithm makes best use of the function evaluations and thereby identifies the optimum at a higher velocity compared to DEfirSPX. Furthermore, the DEfirSPX is only suitable for high-dimensional optimization problems because of its fixed-length XLS strategy that consumes a fixed number of function evaluations in each call. On the other hand, because of the adaptive XLS length adjustment capability of AHCXLS, the DEahcSPX algorithm is applicable to optimization problems of any dimension [Noman and Iba (2008a)]. Finally, because of the simple hill-climbing mechanism, the adaptive local search does not add any additional complexity or any additional parameter to the original algorithm.

5.4.3 *Experimental study using DEahcSPX*

In this section, we present a brief study comparing the performance of DE, DEfirSPX and DEahcSPX using the test suite described in Section 3.4.7. Here, we just show that the adaptive LS (e.g. AHCSPX) can make DE more efficient compared to the fixed length LS (e.g. FIR). Since in Section 5.3.3 the FIR strategy was incorporated with the DE/rand/1/exp variant, here we also experiment by hybridizing the AHCSPX with the same DE scheme. A more detailed study on DEahcSPX using the DE/rand/1/bin variant can be found in [Noman and Iba (2008a)].

Table 5.6   Comparison among DE, DEfirSPX and DEahcSPX (N=50)

	DE	DEfirSPX	DEahcSPX
f_{Sph}	0 [145703.7 ± 22113.7]	0[101649.4 ± 14842.6]	0 [57023.4 ± 976.8]
f_{Ros}	7.99E+01 ± 1.03E+02	6.81E+01 ± 4.23E+01	4.28E+01 ± 1.66E+01
f_{Ack}	0 [161401.9 ± 17471.5]	0[138447.6 ± 9712.1]	0 [82720.9 ± 1044.3]
f_{Grw}	0 [129545 ± 28418.3]	0[114993.8 ± 17656.1]	0 [58867.1 ± 1918.5]
f_{Ras}	0 [98840 ± 26608.2]	0[79041.6 ± 14065.3]	0[78057.2 ± 15032.8]

Table 5.7   Comparison among DE, DEfirSPX and DEahcSPX (N=100)

	DE	DEfirSPX	DEahcSPX
f_{Sph}	1.75E-05 ± 8.95E-05 (93.3%)	0[345124.5 ± 22515.7]	0 [238693.4 ± 1809.8]
f_{Ros}	1.30E+02 ± 4.78E+01	1.08E+02 ± 2.69E+01	9.08E+01 ± 5.62E-01
f_{Ack}	1.08E-06 ± 4.87E-07 (90%)	0[404276.2 ± 10553.6]	0 [337571.9 ± 2746.1]
f_{Grw}	0 [340765.7 ± 35477.28]	0[297807.5 ± 50001.4]	0 [235056.6 ± 2531.1]
f_{Ras}	0 [261150.7 ± 17976.1]	0[204120.8 ± 19879.2]	0[197792.1 ± 23598.4]

For evaluating the performance of the algorithms, the same criteria given in Section 5.3.3.1 was used. Here, the results of the experiments performed in N=50 and N=100 dimensions are presented. The parameter setting was also the same as in Section 5.3.3.1, i.e. $F = 0.5$, $C_r = 0.8$ and $P = N$. For SPX $p = 3$, and in FIR $L = 10$ was used.

The results presented here are intended to show that the adaptive LS, such as the AHCXLS strategy, can improve the performance of DE. Additionally, when compared to the FIR strategy AHCXLS can outperform it under the same experimental conditions. The results presented in Table 5.6 and Table 5.7 clearly show that in every case DEahcSPX took fewer fitness evaluations compared to DEfirSPX (and compared to DE as well) in locating the global optimum. And for cases in which these algorithms failed to reach the global optimum, DEachSPX achieved better fitness values. In Section 5.3.3 we have already established the competitiveness of DEfirSXP with other MAs, and here we showed that DEahcSPX outperformed DEfirSPX. Therefore, it is obvious that DEahcSPX will outperform those MAs.

The success of a memetic algorithm considerably depends on balancing the local search and global search capabilities [Ishibuchi *et al.* (2003)]. Though a fixed-length LS can improve the convergence velocity of an EA, finding a robust intensity for the LS is not easy. Generally, the intensity of the local search, best suited for the exploration of an individual's neighborhood, is essentially problem-dependent, and even varies with the problem dimension or with the progress of the global search. Therefore, it is very difficult to find a single length for the LS that performs best for all sort of problems in all dimensions. And such problem-specific tuning of the local search intensity is not easy and makes the local search problem-dependent.

To address this problem, we need to design an LS that can adjust its intensity according to requirements. Here, we studied a scheme for LS length adaptation, hybridizing it with DE. Using empirical study, it was shown that an LS that can adapt the intensity of the search (by taking feedback from the search) can be useful in designing effective MAs. Finally, the design of AHCSPX is so simple and generalized that it can be hybridized with any of the DE variants or even with other EAs for designing self-adaptive MAs.

Chapter 6

Real-world Applications of Evolutionary Algorithms

6.1 EAs for solving real-world problems

In this last chapter of the book, we present some applications of EAs for solving real-world problems. Many of the real-world problems arising in different fields of engineering, science and industry require finding optimal parameters. Optimization using traditional methods is too slow in finding a solution in complex search spaces. Moreover, many of these methods demand additional requirements such as differentiability, continuity of objective function, etc., which may not be possible to satisfy for many real-world problems.

On the contrary, searching with EAs needs almost no information about the search space. Hence, for complex and poorly understood search spaces, which is the case in most real-world problems, EAs are the most attractive choice. Besides, the robust and reliable performance, global search capability and inherent parallelism make EAs an appealing choice for solving real-world problems. Hence, EAs have found applications in almost all fields from engineering to finance and from robotics to biotechnology.

Here, we carefully select a few significant real-world problems from a wide range of subject areas to show why evolutionary algorithms are a better choice over traditional methods in solving those problems. The problem suite ranges from financial data analysis to electrical power engineering and architectural optimization to bioinformatics. This problem set was deliberately chosen to show the vast applicability and appeal of EA/MA to real-world problems. Then we experimentally show that EA and/or MA can generate better solutions to these problems in reasonable computational budget.

Our first application is the optimization of profitable trading rules for financial data, e.g. foreign exchange (FX) or stock prices. The stock market data should be handled quite differently from other time series data, because they are given in an event-driven manner and because they are highly influenced by indeterminate dealing. We use a GA-based system to automatically generate trading rules based on Technical Indexes. Using historical exchange rate data with extremely short intervals and applying a variety of Technical Indexes, the most profitable trading rule for the period is evolutionarily optimized by GA. This rule is applied for the time period immediately after the training set, without being re-trained beforehand. Here we demonstrate the effectiveness of the GA-based method and a performance comparison is carried out vis-à-vis traditional methods, e.g. neural networks.

Then we present how an adaptive EA can be used in finding the most economical solution (minimizing the operating cost) to meet the load demand in a power system. It is one of the most important problems in power system planning and operation, commonly known as "economic load dispatch" (ELD). Though the core objective of the problem is to minimize the operating cost fulfilling the load demands, various types of physical and operational constraints make ELD a highly nonlinear constrained optimization problem, particularly for large systems. Through this study it was shown that careful and intelligent scheduling of the electrical power system units using proper algorithms can not only significantly reduce the operating cost, but also assure higher reliability and improved security. In addition, the derived solutions by EAs are the best known solutions so far for those problems.

The next application deals with the optimal door/exit placement for evacuation planning. An optimal placement of doors when designing a building can effectively decrease the time for evacuation and thus can be a life saver. The task of finding the best locations for exits is made more difficult by additional constraints like existence of other obstacles (e.g. beams) in the room layout. The existing method tries to choose the best set of doors from a fixed set of possible door positions. In this section, we present a more flexible door/exit placement method that searches from all possible door positions to choose the best one. This is formulated as an optimization problem for which EA is applied to find the optimal number of doors with their optimal positions in a given room layout. Each candidate solution is evaluated by using a computer simulation of the evacuation.

Finally, we apply an EA to extract regulatory relationships among genes by analyzing microarray data. The highly nonlinear and dynamic nature of the "gene regulatory network" (GRN) makes this problem challenging. Due to the limited amount of gene expression data and a significant level of noise present in the data, inferring the regulatory relationships among genes becomes quite difficult. We select a model-based reconstruction of GRN and then use an EA to optimize the model parameters to capture the dynamics in the time series data.

6.2 Generating trading rules for foreign exchange (FX)

6.2.1 *Foreign exchange market and GA search*

Nowadays, we see a growing trend to solve problems in the financial field by mathematical methods, [Lipton-Lifschitz (1999); Hellström and Holmström (2000)] particularly, in the sub-discipline of active decision-making for stock markets, foreign exchange and investment credit. The foreign exchange (FX) market is the largest financial market in the world. At its core are exchange rates and market timing. Based on these two elements, a large variety of financial instruments have been created. Exchange rates are under the influence of myriad factors. It is very complicated to predict exchange rates based on fundamental analysis, which studies all relevant economic and financial indicators.

Therefore, technical analysis is a sound alternative to forecasting short-term FX market movements [Yao *et al.* (2007)]. Its advocates do not concern themselves with fundamental values such as account balance or economic conditions, they rather base their ideas on the hypothesis that any factor that truly influences the market will immediately show up in the FX rate. Therefore, this technique only studies indices and the charts that describe their movements.

To avoid the difficult problem of forecasting the precise exchange rate, we can use an alternative way to optimize FX trading based on the timing of an investment decision [Hirabayashi *et al.* (2009)]. The aim is to raise the profit taken from an investment (assume that we start off with a certain amount of Japanese yen) by buying and selling foreign exchange in very short periods. Here a GA-based system searches for the optimal combination of Technical Indexes that will allow us to accurately judge the timing of rise or fall in exchange rate [Hirabayashi *et al.* (2009)]. Furthermore, by actually introducing the concept of leverage in accordance with the settings employed by FX companies in Japan, we also consider the profit generated through application of the above method. The goal here is to design and implement an evolutionary system which is able to learn the nuances of trading rules in FX markets, and to adapt to its changing conditions.

In this problem, we need to find the preferable trading strategies from the past time series data of FX rate (Data for Learning). But searching all the patterns requires a considerably large amount of time. Therefore, the application of GA may bring about a huge reduction in computing time. We know that GA is a search technique used to find exact or approximate solutions to optimization and search problems. In addition, the evolutionary operators of GA allow the successful rules for past problems to adapt to changes in the market conditions.

6.2.2 *Background: FX and technical analysis*

The FX market is different from the stock market in several ways. First, individual FX traders can deal 24 hours a day, due to time differences around the world. Because of this, FX traders have many more chances to deal compared to stock traders who can only deal during local business hours.

Second, FX trading does not require an agreement time. This means that traders can buy or sell foreign currencies at the current rate almost immediately for all major currencies.

Finally, the commission fee in FX is relatively cheap. The asking price is set a little higher than the bidding price by most FX brokerage firms. So, trading fees have less influence in FX trading than in stock markets. Technical Indexes are tools to forecast and analyze the change of price in the future, from the change of price observed in the past. Here, three typical Technical Indexes used to forecast and analyze the stock or FX prices are described [Achelis (2000)]:

(1) Relative Strength Index (RSI)

$$\text{RSI}[\%] = \frac{|U|}{|U| + |D|} \times 100 \tag{6.1}$$

$|U|$: Sum of the absolute value of rising width in the past n days
$|D|$: Sum of the absolute value of falling width in the past n days

RSI is one of the "contrary" type indices that aims to buy when the currency is sold too much (the price is low), and to sell when it is bought too much (the price is high). It is normal to use 9 or 14 as n. As a general guideline, an RSI value below 30 indicates that the currency has been sold too much, while an RSI higher than 70 indicates that the currency has been bought too much.

(2) Moving Average (MA)

The moving average is a technique for smoothing the short-term variation of price (longitudinal data), and it can be obtained by calculating the mean value of prices in the past n days. The moving average is used to understand the present trend, and as such, it is called a "trend following" type of index, opposite to the contrary type. There are several types of MAs, depending on how past prices are weighed.

First, the "simple moving average" (SMA) indicates a simple mean value with identical weights assigned to past prices. Second, the "weighted moving average" (WMA) is a kind of index that puts higher weights on more recent prices. An example of weight assignment would be to give weight n to the price at the current time (time t), weight $n-1$ to the price at time $t-1$, $n-2$ to $t-2$ and so on.

Finally, we refer to the "exponentially weighted moving average" (EWMA) which is applied in this study. Contrary to the linear weights used in WMA, EWMA assigns weights exponentially. One example of weight assignment is shown in Eq. (6.2), α is an arbitrary coefficient with a range of $0 < \alpha < 1$ [Fernández-Blanco *et al.* (2008)].

$$\text{EWMA}_M = \frac{p_M + \alpha p_{M-1} + \alpha^2 p_{M-2} + \cdots}{1 + \alpha + \alpha^2 + \cdots} \qquad (6.2)$$

(3) Percent Difference from Moving Average

$$\text{Difference}[\%] = \frac{(CurrentPrice) - (MovingAverage)}{(MovingAverage)} \times 100 \qquad (6.3)$$

This index indicates how much the current rate differs from the moving average described in 2). Like RSI, percent difference is a "contrary" type index. And it is normal to use either 5 days or 25 days or 13 weeks or 26 weeks as the period n. According to experts, the currency is sold too much when this index is lower than -10%, while it is bought too much when this index is higher than +10%.

6.2.3 Related work

Although many attempts are being made to apply AI techniques to solve problems in finance, most of those are related to stock prediction and very few studies have considered the FX market [Chen (2002)], [Schwaerzel and Bylander (2006)].

However, a few works which attempt to analyze the movements in the FX market using the approach of the "Artificial Market" can be seen [Izumi and Ueda (2000)]. The Artificial Market is a virtual market created in a computer that makes use of the concept of complex systems. The Artificial Market enables the analysis of economic phenomenon in the real world and can also be used to verify economic theories.

Fuente *et al.* [de la Fuente *et al.* (2006)] attempted to optimize the timing of an automated trader using GA to generate trading rules for short time periods. Technical Indexes, such as RSI, were used as the chromosome for GA. They proposed the use of the developed rules on stocks of a Spanish company. The description in that work was too preliminary to allow for a comparison with the current system to be made.

Schoreels *et al.* [Schoreels *et al.* (2004)] tried to generate the buying and selling signals against the stocks of 30 companies in Germany (DAX30). They used a combination of Technical Indexes applied to GA as in the work of [de la Fuente *et al.* (2006)], and then ranked the stocks according to the strength of signals to restructure the portfolio. However, they did not devise any criterion for profit cashing and loss cutting.

6.2.4 GA-based method

The overall flow of the GA-based technique presented here is shown in Fig. 6.1. Basically, using historical exchange data for learning, the system searches for buying and selling rules that return the highest profit. These rules are composed of a combination of Technical Indexes and their parameters, and are used as the GA's genotype. Once training is completed, the acquired rule is applied to a test data set (historical data that immediately follows the training data) to validate the efficiency of the method.

6.2.4.1 Training data set

The training data used here consists of historical rates of the U.S. dollar against the Japanese yen (USD/JPY) and euro against the yen (EUR/JPY).

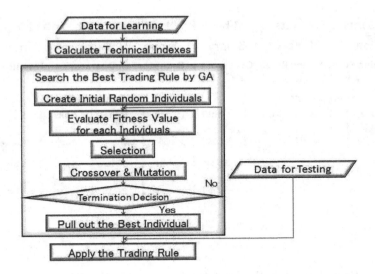

Fig. 6.1 Flow of the GA-based method

For each data set, we use the hourly closing price, and the developed system analyzes the trading signals every hour. The same setting applies for the testing data sets, which are the historical rates immediately following the training data set.

6.2.4.2 *Calculation of technical indices*

For each of the foreign exchange data sets previously mentioned, the following Technical Indexes were calculated to use with the trading rules:

(1) RSI of the original data [RSI1]
(2) Percent difference from moving average of the original data [PD]
(3) Rising (falling) rate since one hour ago for the original data [RR]
(4) RSI of exponentially weighted moving average [RSI2]

Generally, indices 1, 2, 3 are considered to be of contrary type. On the other hand, index 4 is a trend-following type, because it is the RSI calculated on current trend. By using both types of indexes, a wider variety of trading patterns can be covered.

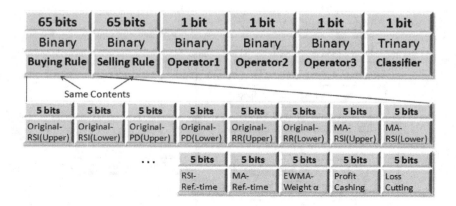

Fig. 6.2   Chromosome design

6.2.5   *Searching for the best trading rule with GA*

The GA chromosome contains the information needed to build buy and sell rules. It has a binary representation that can be divided into three main parts (as shown in Fig. 6.2).

The first 65 bits represent the buying rule. The bits are grouped in fives, each grouping representing one of 32 values between the maximum and minimum possible values for the indices represented by the grouping. For instance, in the case of the RSI, for which values range from 0 to 100, each bit pattern in the grouping represents an increment of 3.125.

The first 8 groupings (40 bits), represent lower and higher limits for the above-mentioned 4 indices. If the current value for the indices is between these limits, a buying signal is indicated. The next 3 groupings (15 bits) represent parameters for calculating the indices (described in the previous section). The final 2 groupings (10 bits) determine the profit cashing and loss cutting values which are used to end transactions.

The next 65 bits represent the selling rule. These bits follow the exact same rules as used for the buying rule bits.

The final 4 bits indicate the rule that will be used to determine the timing for trading. The fourth bit determines which of rules A, B or C (in Table 6.1) will be used. The first 3 bits determine whether operators 1–3 are AND operators, or OR operators. If the rule is evaluated to a TRUE value, the system starts the trading, else, it does not trade in this time period.

Table 6.1   Conditional equation

[A]	$\{ (c_1 < \text{RSI1} < c_2)$ |Op.1| $(c_3 < \text{PD} < c_4) \}$ |Op.2| $\{ (c_5 < \text{RR} < c_6)$ |Op.3| $(c_7 < \text{RSI2} < C_8) \}$
[B]	$\{ (c_1 < \text{RSI1} < c_2)$ |Op.1| $(c_5 < \text{RR} < c_6) \}$ |Op.2| $\{ (c_3 < \text{PD} < c_4)$ |Op.3| $(c_7 < \text{RSI2} < C_8) \}$
[C]	$\{ (c_1 < \text{RSI1} < c_2)$ |Op.1| $(c_7 < \text{RSI2} < c_8) \}$ |Op.2| $\{ (c_3 < \text{PD} < c_4)$ |Op.3| $(c_5 < \text{RR} < C_6) \}$

Step 1. Generation of Initial Individuals

In this GA the population size is set to 1500. The individuals are initialized with random chromosomes following the structure in Fig. 6.2 and Table 6.1.

Figures $c_1 - c_8$ in Table 6.1 correspond to the ranges of Technical Indexes shown in the second-line bits in Fig. 6.2. And third-line bits are parameters to calculate the Technical Indexes.

Step 2. Calculation of Fitness

For each individual generated in Step 1, the fitness value is given as the profit gained by trading during the period of the training data set. The flow of investment management is shown in Fig. 6.3.

Every hour, the system checks the current value of the indices against the conditional equations shown in Table 6.1. If the ranges of the Technical Indexes calculated at time i satisfy either the buying equation or the selling equation, the trading system buys or sells the currency.

If both equations are satisfied at the same time, the chromosome is invalid, and the individual receives zero fitness (the lowest value) automatically.

After successfully realizing a buy or sell operation, the system stays in that state until the profit cash or loss cut conditions are met. These conditions are defined in the chromosome (see Fig. 6.2).

Step 3. Selection

Tournament selection is used as the selection method for the GA in this system. This method selects a number of individuals from the population, and holds a "tournament" among them, and the winner is selected to perform the crossover. Selection pressure can be easily adjusted by changing the tournament size. If the tournament size is larger, weak individuals have a smaller chance for getting selected. Tournament size is set at 50 in this experiment. Besides, in order to retain highly fit individuals, the elite 1%

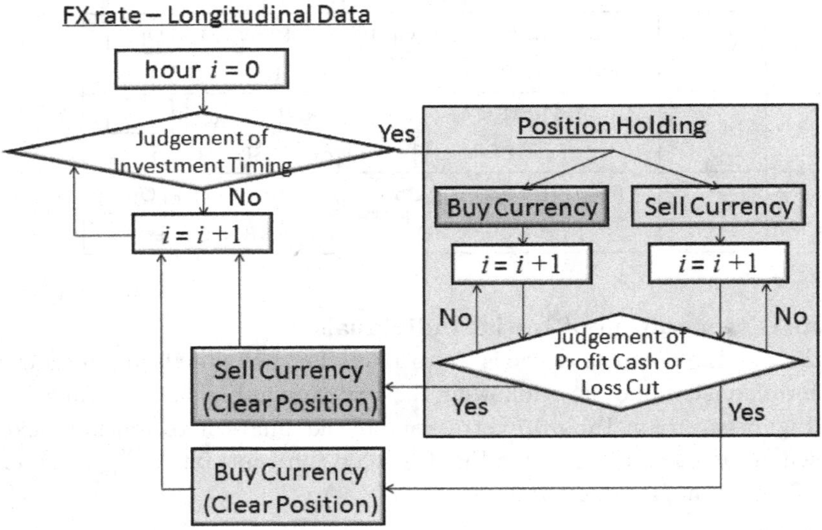

FX rate – Longitudinal Data

Fig. 6.3   Flow of investment management

(the top 1% individuals in terms of fitness value) are preserved in every generation [Branke (1999)].

Step 4. Crossover and Mutation
Two-point crossover is used in this GA. This method chooses two points at random in each parent individual. All bits between these two points are swapped between the parents, generating two child individuals. Mutation is a genetic operator used to maintain genetic diversity from one generation of a population of chromosomes to the next. Concretely, mutation is done by flipping bits with very low probability. The last trinary part of the genome is not altered by mutation. The probability of crossover and mutation are 60% and 1%, respectively.

After repeating Steps 2 to 4 for 100 generations, or if the fitness of the best individual does not improve for 10 successive generations, the optimization is terminated. The best individual of the final generation is chosen as the optimized trading rule.

Table 6.2   An example of optimized trading rule

Range of Technical Indexes to Invest (Buying Rule)	
{(75% < RSI1 < 87.5%) ‖ (0.1% < RR < 0.25%) } && {(−0.35% < PD < −0.05%) ‖ (62.5% < RSI2 < 97.5%)}	
RSI-Reference Time Length	24 hours
EWMA-Reference Time Length	13 hours
EWMA-Weight α	0.65
Profit Cashing	+0.8 JPY/1 USD
Loss Cutting	−1.5 JPY/1 USD

6.2.6   *Testing data set*

As described in Section 6.2.4, the data immediately following the training data set is used for testing, and the individual with the best fitness found in the learning phase is used as the trading rule.

6.2.7   *Application of investment rules*

An example of the optimized trading rule (buying rule only) is shown in Table 6.2.

As with the training data, the four Technical Indexes indicated in Section 6.2.4.2 were calculated in accordance with the optimized trading rule for the testing data. Then the foreign exchange trades were executed for a time period that is consistent with the conditional equation for the range of indices shown in Table 6.2.

Now we can conduct an experiment using leverage. We decided to permit an investment with ten times maximum leverage.

1. Application of Leverage

In order to determine when leverage should be applied, r, the correlation coefficient of the 24-hour period immediately preceding the execution of foreign exchange trading and the subsequent 24-hour period both coming within the period of the training data, is calculated for all time periods:

$$r = \frac{\sum_{i=1}^{24}(x_i - \bar{x})(y_i - \bar{y})}{\sqrt{\sum_{i=1}^{24}(x_i - \bar{x})^2}\sqrt{\sum_{i=1}^{24}(y_i - \bar{y})^2}} \tag{6.4}$$

Next, for the periods in the training data for which $r > 0.75$, the tendency of the foreign exchange rate to either increase or decrease immediately after a trade is judged based on the following equation:

$$F = \sum_{i=1}^{24}(x(t + i) - x(t)) \times (24 - i) \tag{6.5}$$

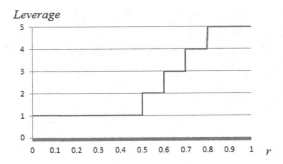

Fig. 6.4   Determination of leverage

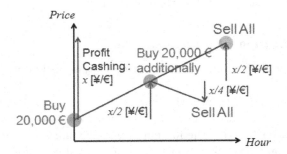

Fig. 6.5   Example of additional buying

where $F > 0$ in the case of buying, and $F < 0$ in the case of selling. The relative proportions of buying and selling trades are calculated and leverage is determined based on the calculated proportion, r. Fig. 6.4 shows the correspondence between r and leverage, where the example leverage is a maximum of five times.

2. Additional Buying and Selling

In addition to leverage, when a profit was made for a given traded position, a further position is added in the same direction. Fig. 6.5 shows a specific example of such additional buying.

Normally, when 20,000 EUR are bought at a certain price, profits are taken when the EUR increases by x above that purchase price [JPY/EUR]. However, under the additional buying rules used here, it is decided to buy an additional 20,000 EUR at the point where the EUR increased by x/2 [JPY/EUR]. Subsequently, if the EUR increases further by x/2 [JPY/EUR], reaching the original profit-taking position, then it is possible to obtain 1.5 times the ordinary profit by selling the entire holding at that time. On the contrary, if the EUR falls by x/4 [JPY/EUR] after additional buying, then selling the entire holding at that time would result in zero profit or loss. When coupled with the application of leverage, the net leverage of additional buying and selling reaches a maximum of ten times.

A similar rule can also be applied in the case of further selling. By applying the further buying and further selling method, we have adopted a strategy aimed at increasing profit while managing risk.

6.2.8 *Experiment conditions & data used*

1. Trading Fees

The trading simulation is done in conjunction with a Japanese FX brokerage firm in conducting the experiment. Spread (the difference between asking price and bidding price) is 0.03 JPY per 1 USD trading, 0.04 JPY per 1 EUR trading, and 0.06 JPY per 1 AUD trading.

2. Initial Capital and Investment Amount

The experiments on USD/JPY, EUR/JPY, and AUD/JPY investment are held independently. The initial capital is 1,250,000 JPY for the USD investment, 1,600,000 JPY for the EUR investment, and 1,000,000 JPY for the AUD investment. In all the cases, the investment amount is $n \times 10,000$ (USD or EUR or AUD) per trade operation (either buying or selling), while n is equal to "leverage" defined in Section 6.2.7.

3. Data Used

The following historical FX rate data sets are used for testing. Each data set contains the hourly closing values for the FX rates:

(1) USD/JPY (2005–2008, 4 years)
(2) EUR/JPY (2005–2008, 4 years)
(3) AUD/JPY (2005–2008, 4 years)

To separate the training and test data, a rolling window method is used. The training was for a six-month period, and the testing was for a three-month period. Then for each subsequent experiment, both the training and the testing periods were moved three months forward (see Fig. 6.6).

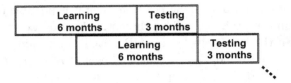

Fig. 6.6   Method of learning & testing

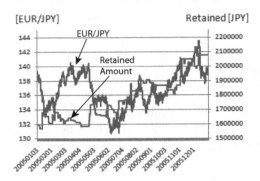

Fig. 6.7   EUR/JPY chart in 2005 & operating result

6.2.9   *Dealing results*

First, as examples, results of investment management for EUR in 2005 and USD in 2006 are shown (Fig. 6.7, Fig. 6.8). The "Retained Amount" line shows how the trading rule grows the asset. For reference, the chart of rate (EUR/JPY or USD/JPY or AUD/JPY) is also shown.

In a similar way, the results of EUR and AUD in 2008 are shown in Fig. 6.9 and Fig. 6.10, respectively. Finally, the example of optimized trading rule (buying rule only, for EUR, period: 2006, 4–9) is shown in Table 6.3.

First, as notably observed in Fig. 6.7 and Fig. 6.8, the movement of the retained amount has a strong tendency to behave similarly to that of the real FX rate. However, although the price at the beginning of the year is almost the same as that at the end of the year, this GA-based method could gain a certain amount of profit, in both cases, demonstrating its effectiveness to some extent.

Next, as we can see in Fig. 6.9 and Fig. 6.10, the method gained a quite large profit in the sharp falling period of exchange ratio (caused by the

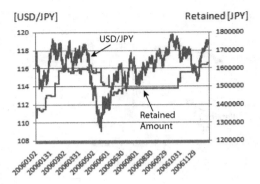

Fig. 6.8   USD/JPY chart in 2006 & operating result

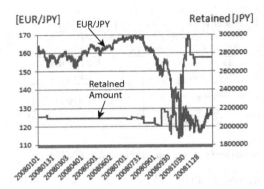

Fig. 6.9   EUR/JPY chart in 2008 & operating result

financial crisis triggered by the collapse of Lehman Brothers). Especially note the case of the EUR (Fig. 6.9), in which once having made a loss, it gained twice as much profit as the loss.

Through these results, we can see that a market with a rapidly falling price is easily understandable to the Machine Learning method, allowing it to extract large profits from it.

Besides, considering the profitable buying rule shown in Table 6.3, both RSI of original data and RSI of EWMA have a tendency to take high values. It implies that when the market price is rising, following that trend may bring profits with higher probability, especially in short-period trading.

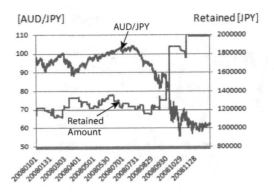

Fig. 6.10   AUD/JPY chart in 2008 & operating result

Table 6.3   An example of optimized trading rule

Range of Technical Indexes to Invest (Buying Rule)	
{(81.25% < RSI1 < 93.75%) && (−0.3% < RR < 0.1%) } ‖ {(−0.15% < PD < 0.7%) && (75% < RSI2 < 97.5%)}	
RSI-Reference Time Length	31 hours
EWMA-Reference Time Length	23 hours
EWMA-Weight α	0.7
Profit Cashing	+2.3 JPY/1 USD
Loss Cutting	−1.7 JPY/1 USD

6.2.10 *Comparison with neural networks (NN)*

To confirm the effectiveness of the GA-based method, its results were compared with that of a neural network-based method (NN) proposed by [Wong and Selvi (1998)].

To be consistent with the GA-based method, the same four technical indices were used as input signals in NN-based method. For the signals, the binary numerals 0 and 1 rounded to 32 values were used. For teaching signals, the values calculated using the following equation were used:

$$Out = \sum_{i=1}^{23}(x(t + i) - x(t)) \times (24 - i) \tag{6.6}$$

where $x(t)$ indicates the exchange rate on day t. As output signals, we used the values obtained by summing the product of a coefficient and the increase in the exchange rate i days later, with the increase in the rate in the 24-hour period immediately following i. In other words, the higher the best-fit value, the greater the tendency for the exchange rate to increase

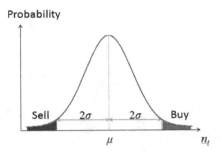

Fig. 6.11 Buy & Sell timing

within a 24-hour period. As with the input signals, we used the binary numerals 0 and 1 rounded to 32 values for the output signals.

The NN weights were optimized by back-propagation (BP) for pairs of a fixed period spanning several minutes of input signals and teaching signals. In addition, we set the intermediate layer unit number to 8, the learning rate to 0.5, and the coefficient of inertia to 0.03.

In the testing period, we performed an investment simulation similar to that of the GA-based method using the weights optimized during the learning period.

On the basis of the technical indices calculated for each period, t, we took the output calculated using the NN weights as n_t.

We then determined buying and selling times for n_t using the following relations:

$$\text{Buying time:} \quad n_t > \mu + 2\sigma \tag{6.7}$$

$$\text{Selling time:} \quad n_t < \mu - 2\sigma \tag{6.8}$$

where μ and σ are the mean values for exchange rates derived from the learning period and the standard deviation, respectively.

Normally, financial price fluctuations are considered to conform to a normal distribution, with the timing for buying and selling considered to fall within the upper (Eq. (6.7)) and lower (Eq. (6.8)) 2.28% bounds of this distribution, respectively.

The results of an investment simulation using the loss cutting and profit cashing settings of the GA-based method are given below.

We show the profit margin on the initial retention of USD and EUR in Fig. 6.12 and Fig. 6.13, respectively. We also compare the GA-based method with the methods based on NN and buy & hold strategies. The

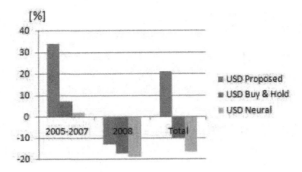

Fig. 6.12   Comparison of percentage profit (USD)

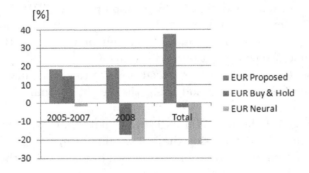

Fig. 6.13   Comparison of percentage profit (EUR)

presented results for GA are the average of five experimental runs. "2005–2007" means the total results for three years.

For all situations, NN's performance was inferior to GA. NNs performance was even lower than that of the buy & hold strategy. In fact, a comparison of the three-year totals for each method reveals that the performance of GA was consistently better than NN.

If we compare the Fig. 6.12 with Fig. 6.9 and Fig. 6.10, we observe that the fall of the USD in 2008 was not as fast as the EUR or AUD, hence it was rather difficult to understand the market and achieve profit.

6.3   Economic load dispatch for least cost power generation

"Economic load dispatch" (ELD) is essential for real-time control of power systems. It is one of the most important problems to be solved in the operation and planning of a power system. The ELD problem can be defined as determining the least cost power generation schedule from a set of online generating units to meet the total power demand at a given point in time [Wood and Wollenberg (1996)]. Though the core objective of the problem is to minimize the operating cost while fulfilling the load demand, various types of physical and operational constraints make ELD a highly nonlinear constrained optimization problem, particularly for large systems [Victoire and Jeyakumar (2004)]. However, careful and intelligent scheduling of the units can not only significantly reduce the operating cost, but also assure higher reliability, improved security and less environmental impact [Abido (2006)].

Traditionally, in ELD, the input-output characteristics (or cost function) of a generator is approximately represented by a single quadratic function. Practically, operating conditions of many generating units require the cost function to be represented as a piecewise quadratic function [Lee *et al.* (1998)]. However, higher-order nonlinearities and discontinuities are observed in real input-output characteristics due to valve-point loading in fossil fuel-burning plants [Lin *et al.* (2002)]. Moreover, the units may have prohibited operating zones due to machine faults or faults in associated auxiliaries, such as boilers, feed pumps, etc., leading to instabilities in certain ranges of the unit loading [Orero and Irving (1996)]. Furthermore, the operating range for online units is actually restricted by their ramp-rate limits [Pereira-Neto *et al.* (2005)]. These and many other constraints transform an ELD problem into a hard non-convex optimization problem.

Because of the highly nonlinear characteristics of the problem with many local optimum solutions and a large number of constraints, the classical calculus-based method and the Newton-based algorithms cannot perform well in solving ELD problems. Though dynamic programming is not affected by the nonlinearity and discontinuity of the cost curves, it suffers from the "curse of dimensionality" and local optimality [Sinha *et al.* (2003)]. Among the other artificial intelligence approaches, neural networks have been successful in solving the ELD problems with different constraints [Lee *et al.* (1998); Park *et al.* (1993)]. However, some of these neural network-based approaches may suffer from excessive numerical iterations, resulting in huge calculations. Evolutionary algorithms (EAs), such as genetic algorithms (GA), evolution strategy (ES) and evolutionary programming (EP), are faster than simulated annealing (SA) because of their inherent parallel search mechanism. Consequently, many researchers have found EAs effective in solving ELD problems. Among different variants of EA, particle swarm optimization (PSO) [Gaing (2003); Victoire and Jeyakumar (2004, 2005); Park *et al.* (2005)] and differential evolution (DE) [Perez-Guerrero and Cedenio-Maldonado (2005); dos S. Coelho and Mariani (2006); Chiou (2007); Noman and Iba (2008b)] have received much attention in solving ELD.

6.3.1   *ELD problem formulation*

The primary objective of the ELD problem is to determine the most economic loading of the generating units such that the load demand in the power system can be met successfully [Swarup and Kumar (2006)]. Additionally, ELD planning must satisfy different equality and inequality constraints. In general, the problem is formulated as follows.

Consider a power system having N generating units, each loaded to P_i MW. The generating units should be loaded in such a way that minimizes the total fuel cost, F_T, while satisfying the power balance and other constraints. Therefore, the classic ELD problem can be formulated as an optimization process with the following objective:

$$\min F_T = \min \sum_{i=1}^{N} F_i(P_i) \tag{6.9}$$

where the fuel input-power output cost function of the i-th unit is represented by the function F_i. The fuel cost function $F_i(P_i)$ for generator i loaded with P_i MW is approximated by the following quadratic function:

$$F_i(P_i) = a_i P_i^2 + b_i P_i + c_i + \alpha |d_i \sin(f_i(P_i^{min} - P_i))| \tag{6.10}$$

where, if the valve point loading is taken into account then $\alpha = 1$ otherwise $\alpha = 0$. a_i, b_i, c_i are cost coefficients of generator i and d_i, f_i are constants from the valve point effect of the i-th generating unit. In reality, the generating units with multi-valve steam turbines have very different input-output curves compared to the smooth cost function. Therefore, the inclusion of the valve-point loading effects makes the representation of the incremental fuel cost function of the generating units more practical.

Another case of using the non-smooth cost function for a more realistic representation of generating units is the multiple fuel problems, where the fuel cost function is expressed as a piecewise quadratic function as follows:

$$F_i(P_i) = \begin{cases} a_{i_1} P_i^2 + b_{i_1} P_i + c_{i_1} & \text{if } P_i^{min} \le P_i \le P_{i_1} \\ a_{i_2} P_i^2 + b_{i_2} P_i + c_{i_2} & \text{if } P_{i_1} \le P_i \le P_{i_2} \\ \vdots & \vdots \\ a_{i_k} P_i^2 + b_{i_k} P_i + c_{i_k} & \text{if } P_{i_{k-1}} \le P_i \le P_i^{max} \end{cases} \tag{6.11}$$

where, a_{i_f}, b_{i_f} and c_{i_f} are the cost coefficients of the generating unit i for fuel type f, where $f = 1, 2, \cdots, k$.

In order to achieve truly economical operations for the given load demand, some of the generator constraints must be taken into account. Among these constraints, the following are the most prominent:

A. Power balance constraint

The following equality constraint must be satisfied for power balance, i.e. the generated power should be equal to the total load demand plus the total line loss:

$$\sum_{i=1}^{N} P_i = (P_L + P_D) \tag{6.12}$$

P_i is the power generation output of generator i (in MW), P_D is the system's total demand (in MW); P_L represents the total line losses (in MW). Calculation of P_L using the B-matrix loss coefficients is expressed as a quadratic function of the following form.

$$P_L = \sum_{i=1}^{N} \sum_{j=1}^{N} P_i B_{ij} P_j + \sum_{i=1}^{N} B_{0i} P_i + B_{00} \tag{6.13}$$

B. Capacity constraint

The generating capacity constraint is given by

$$P_i^{min} \le P_i \le P_i^{max} \tag{6.14}$$

where P_i^{min} and P_i^{max} are the minimum and maximum power outputs of the generating unit, i (in MW), respectively.

C. Ramp-rate limit constraint

The ramp-rate limit constraints of generator-i can be described as

$$\max(P_i^{min}, P_i^0 - DR_i) \le P_i \le \min(P_i^{max}, P_i^0 + UR_i) \tag{6.15}$$

where, P_i presents output power and P_i^0 is the previous output power. UR_i and DR_i are the up-ramp and down-ramp limits of the i-th generator, respectively.

D. Prohibited operating zones constraint

The prohibited operating zones constraint of generator-i can be described as

$$P_i \in \begin{cases} P_i^{min} \leq P_i \leq P_{i,1}^l \\ P_{i,k-1}^u \leq P_i \leq P_{i,k}^l & k = 2, \cdots, n_i \\ P_{i,n_i}^u \leq P_i \leq P_i^{max} \end{cases} \tag{6.16}$$

where $P_{i,k}^l$ and $P_{i,k}^u$ are the lower and upper bounds of the k-th prohibited zone of generator-i; n_i is the number of prohibited zones for generator-i.

E. Line flow constraints

The real power flow of a line is less than or equal to the maximum power flow of that line. All the transmission lines follow this rule. If $P_{f,k}$ is the real power flow of line k and L is the number of transmission lines, then the constraints can be described as

$$|P_{f,k}| \leq P_{f,k}^{max} \qquad k = 1, 2, \cdots, L \tag{6.17}$$

The inclusion of additional constraints, such as the environmental effect etc., can result in a more accurate modeling of the ELD problem.

6.3.2   *Self-adaptive DE for ELD problems*

From the description in the previous section, it is clear that ELD is a constrained optimization problem. Here, we applied "DE with self-adaptive control parameters" (DE with SACP) proposed by Brest *et al.* [Brest *et al.* (2006)] to minimize the total generation cost of the power system within a defined interval, while satisfying the load demand and other specified constraints. The details of DE with SACP were presented in Section 5.4.1. Therefore, here we present only how DE with SACP can be used for solving ELD problems.

6.3.2.1   *Representation*

As introduced in earlier chapters, DE is a population-based algorithm where each individual represents a solution to the problem. Before using the DE algorithm for ELD, the solution must be represented in a suitable format that facilitates the application of the DE operators.

Here, the generated power output of each unit is represented as a gene, and the collection of all genes (i.e. output of all generating units) comprise an individual. Each individual within the population represents a candidate solution for solving the ELD problem. Additionally, DE with SACP has two control parameters, namely F and C_r, to be evolved. Therefore, the dimension of each individual will be $(N + 2)$, where N is the number of units to be operated to provide power to the loads. Consequently, the i-th individual x_i^G of generation G can be represented as follows:

$$x_i^G = \{x_{i,1}^G, x_{i,2}^G, \cdots, x_{i,N-1}^G, x_{i,N}^G, F_i^G, C_{r_i}^G\} \qquad (6.18)$$

where, $i = 1, 2, \cdots, P$ and P is the population size, $x_{i,t}^G$ $(t = 1, 2, ..., N)$ is the power output of the t-th unit, F_i^G and $C_{r_i}^G$ are the amplification factor and the crossover rate, respectively.

6.3.2.2 *Fitness function*

The challenges of ELD problems have attracted the attention of many researchers and a variety of EA-based solutions have been proposed. Different fitness functions coupled with suitable algorithms have also been proposed for evaluating the candidate solution. Here a fitness function is presented that was found to work better with DE with SACP. Like many other previous works, the penalty method was chosen to handle problem constraints. The fitness function is

$$f = \frac{\sum_{i=1}^{N} F_i(P_i) - F_{min}}{F_{max} - F_{min}} + \left(\sum_{i=1}^{N} P_i - P_D - P_L\right)^2 + \sum_{i=1}^{N} V_i \qquad (6.19)$$

$$\text{where} \quad V_i = \begin{cases} 1, & \text{if } P_i \text{ violates the prohibited zones,} \\ 0, & \text{otherwise} \end{cases} \qquad (6.20)$$

F_{min} is the minimum generation cost among all individuals in the initial population and F_{max} is the maximum generation cost among all individuals in the initial population. This fitness function is designed to convert the multi-objective ELD problem into a single objective problem whose goal is to keep the fitness score as low as possible.

There are three parts in this fitness function: the normalized cost function, the penalty for power balance constraints and the penalty for prohibited zone constraints. Please note that if a solution (individual) satisfies all the constraints, then it will have a lower fitness value, otherwise it will be penalized and its fitness value will grow larger.

In most of the existing fitness criteria, a penalty factor or a penalty constant is associated with the penalty term(s) and the values of these factors are determined by empirical tuning or by using some heuristic rule. Fixing the values of these factors is time-consuming and problem specific.

Table 6.4   Characteristic data of 6-unit system

Unit	P_i^{min} (MW)	P_i^{max} (MW)	a_i ($/MW)	b_i ($/MW)	c_i ($)	P_i^0	UR_i (MW/h)	DR_i (MW/h)	Prohibited zones Zone1	Zone 2
1	100	500	0.0070	7.0	240	440	80	120	[210 240]	[350 380]
2	50	200	0.0095	10.0	200	170	50	90	[90 110]	[140 160]
3	80	300	0.0090	8.5	220	200	65	100	[150 170]	[210 240]
4	50	150	0.0090	11.0	200	150	50	90	[80 90]	[110 120]
5	50	200	0.0080	10.5	220	190	50	90	[90 110]	[140 150]
6	50	120	0.0075	12.0	190	110	50	90	[75 85]	[100 105]

In the fitness function used here, the default value of the penalty factors is 1 and no such tuning is necessary. And with that setting competitive solutions for different problem instances were found. Further tuning might improve the result but it is not considered here.

6.3.3   *Simulation results*

Two different instances of the ELD problem with different power demand, dimension and complexity are taken into consideration as case studies. The systems consist of 6 and 15 thermal units, respectively. Non-smooth characteristics of generators like the capacity constraints, ramp-rate limit, prohibited operating zone, power balance constraints and transmission loss are considered for both systems.

Tables 6.4 and 6.5 represent the capacity constraints, cost coefficient, ramp-rate limit and prohibited zones of 6-unit and 15-unit systems, respectively. The B coefficients for 6- and 15-unit systems, are given below. For the power system consisting of 6 thermal units, the load demand is 1263 MW, where the load demand for the power system with 15 thermal units is 2630 MW.

$$\mathbf{B1} = \begin{pmatrix} 0.0017 & 0.0012 & 0.0007 & -0.0001 & -0.0005 & -0.0002 \\ 0.0012 & 0.0014 & 0.0009 & 0.0001 & -0.0006 & -0.0001 \\ 0.0007 & 0.0009 & 0.0031 & 0.0000 & -0.0010 & -0.0006 \\ -0.0001 & 0.0001 & 0.0000 & 0.0024 & -0.0006 & -0.0008 \\ -0.0005 & -0.0006 & -0.0010 & -0.0006 & 0.0129 & -0.0002 \\ -0.0002 & -0.0001 & -0.0006 & -0.0008 & -0.0002 & 0.0150 \end{pmatrix}$$

$$\mathbf{B1_0} = 10^{-3} \times [-0.3908, -0.1297, 0.7047, 0.0591, 0.2161, -0.6635]$$

$$\mathbf{B1_{00}} = 0.056$$

Table 6.5 Characteristic data of 15-unit system

Unit	P_i^{min} (MW)	P_i^{max} (MW)	a_i ($/MW^2)	b_i ($/MW)	c_i ($)	P_i^0	UR_i (MW/h)	DR_i (MW/h)	Zone1	Zone 2	Zone 3
1	150	455	0.000299	10.1	671	400	80	120	-	-	-
2	150	455	0.000183	10.2	574	300	80	120	[185 255]	[305 335]	[420 450]
3	20	130	0.001126	8.8	374	105	130	130	-	-	-
4	20	130	0.001126	8.8	374	100	130	130	-	-	-
5	150	470	0.000205	10.4	461	90	80	120	[180 200]	[305 335]	[390 420]
6	135	460	0.000301	10.1	630	400	80	120	[230 255]	[365 395]	[430 455]
7	135	465	0.000364	9.8	548	350	80	120	-	-	-
8	60	300	0.000338	11.2	227	95	65	100	-	-	-
9	25	162	0.000807	11.2	173	105	60	100	-	-	-
10	25	160	0.001203	10.7	175	110	60	100	-	-	-
11	20	80	0.003586	12.2	186	60	80	80	-	-	-
12	20	80	0.005513	9.9	230	40	80	80	[30 40]	[55 65]	-
13	25	85	0.000371	13.1	225	30	80	80	-	-	-
14	15	55	0.001929	12.1	309	20	55	55	-	-	-
15	15	55	0.004447	12.4	323	20	55	55	-	-	-

$$\mathbf{B2_{i,j}} = 10^{-3} \times$$

$$\begin{pmatrix}
1.4 & 1.2 & 0.7 & -0.1 & -0.3 & -0.1 & -0.1 & -0.1 & -0.3 & -0.5 & -0.3 & -0.2 & 0.4 & 0.3 & -0.1 \\
1.2 & 1.5 & 0.3 & 0.0 & -0.5 & -0.2 & 0.0 & 0.1 & -0.2 & -0.4 & -0.4 & 0.0 & 0.4 & 1.0 & -0.2 \\
0.7 & 1.3 & 7.6 & -0.1 & -1.3 & -0.9 & -0.1 & 0.0 & -0.8 & -1.2 & -1.7 & 0.0 & -2.6 & 11.1 & -2.8 \\
-0.1 & 0.0 & -0.1 & 3.4 & -0.7 & -0.4 & 1.1 & 5.0 & 2.9 & 3.2 & -1.1 & 0.0 & 0.1 & 0.1 & -2.6 \\
-0.3 & -0.5 & -1.3 & -0.7 & 9.0 & 1.4 & -0.3 & -1.2 & -1.0 & -1.3 & 0.7 & -0.2 & -0.2 & -2.4 & -0.3 \\
-0.1 & -0.2 & -0.9 & -0.4 & 1.4 & 1.6 & 0.0 & -0.6 & -0.5 & -0.8 & 1.1 & -0.1 & -0.2 & -1.7 & 0.3 \\
-0.1 & 0.0 & -0.1 & 1.1 & -0.3 & 0.0 & 1.5 & 1.7 & 1.5 & 0.9 & -0.5 & 0.7 & 0.0 & -0.2 & -0.8 \\
-0.1 & 0.1 & 0.0 & 5.0 & -1.2 & -0.6 & 1.7 & 16.8 & 8.2 & 7.9 & -2.3 & -3.6 & 0.1 & 0.5 & -7.8 \\
-0.3 & -0.2 & -0.8 & 2.9 & -1.0 & -0.5 & 1.5 & 8.2 & 12.9 & 11.6 & -2.1 & -2.5 & 0.7 & -1.2 & -7.2 \\
-0.5 & -0.4 & -1.2 & 3.2 & -1.3 & -0.8 & 0.9 & 7.9 & 11.6 & 20.0 & -2.7 & -3.4 & 0.9 & -1.1 & -8.8 \\
-0.3 & -0.4 & -1.7 & -1.1 & 0.7 & 1.1 & -0.5 & -2.3 & -2.1 & -2.7 & 14.0 & 0.1 & 0.4 & -3.8 & 16.8 \\
-0.2 & 0.0 & 0.0 & 0.0 & -0.2 & -0.1 & 0.7 & -3.6 & -2.5 & -3.4 & 0.1 & 5.4 & -0.1 & -0.4 & 2.8 \\
0.4 & 0.4 & -2.6 & 0.1 & -0.2 & -0.2 & 0.0 & 0.1 & 0.7 & 0.9 & 0.4 & -0.1 & 10.3 & -10.1 & 2.8 \\
0.3 & 1.0 & 11.1 & 0.1 & -2.4 & -1.7 & -0.2 & 0.5 & -1.2 & -1.1 & -3.8 & -0.4 & -10.1 & 57.8 & -9.4 \\
-0.1 & -0.2 & -2.8 & -2.6 & -0.3 & 0.3 & -0.8 & -7.8 & -7.2 & -8.8 & 16.8 & 2.8 & 2.8 & -9.4 & 128.3
\end{pmatrix}$$

$$\mathbf{B2_0} = 10^{-3} \times [-0.1, -0.2, 2.8, -0.1, 0.1, -0.3, -0.2, -0.2, 0.6,$$
$$3.9, -1.7, -0.0, -3.2, 6.7, -6.4]$$

$$\mathbf{B2_{00}} = 0.055$$

6.3.3.1 *Experimental setup*

In order to verify the suitability of the DE with SACP algorithm with the above given fitness function, 50 independent runs of the algorithm were performed. The variation during the evolutionary processes was observed and

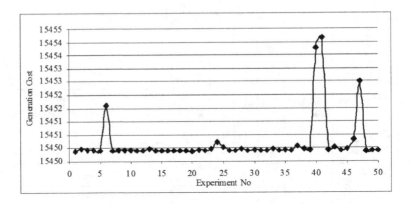

Fig. 6.14   Generation cost based on different runs (6 units) using DE with SACP

Table 6.6   Best solution for the 6-unit system

	ESO †	GA ‡	PSO §	Classic DE	DE with SACP
P1	446.87	474.8066	447.497	447.49352	447.47699
P2	173.62	178.6363	173.3221	173.25269	173.87321
P3	263.78	262.2089	263.4745	263.50978	262.38885
P4	139.09	134.2826	139.0594	139.00131	139.03089
P5	165.47	151.9039	165.4761	165.55416	165.18408
P6	87.13	74.1812	87.128	87.14724	87.9915
Total Production	1275.96	1276.03	1276.01	1275.95873	1275.94553
Total loss	12.95	13.0217	12.9584	12.96025	12.95063
Generation Cost	15449.83	15459.23942	15449.8822	15449.879	15449.852178

† ESO [Orero and Irving (1996)]; ‡ GA [Gaing (2003)]; § PSO [Gaing (2003)].

solutions were compared by quality, convergence characteristics and computational efficiency. The initial values of F_i and C_{r_i} were taken randomly from the range [0.1, 1.0].

6.3.3.2   Results

The generation costs of the best solutions for the 6-unit system in 50 different runs (generation number 540, population size 60) are plotted in Fig. 6.14. According to Fig. 6.14, DE with SACP is robust in generating solutions almost identical to the best known solutions so far.

The best solution found using classic DE and DE with SACP is compared with many other existing methods in Table 6.6 and Table 6.7, respectively. From the results presented in Table 6.6 and Table 6.7, it is obvious that the best results were obtained using DE with SACP with minimum

Table 6.7 Performance comparison for the 6-unit system in 50 trial tests

Algorithm Name	Generation Cost			Avg CPU time
	Max	Min	Avg	
PSO [Gaing (2003)]	15492	15450	15454	14.89
GA [Gaing (2003)]	15524	15459	15469	41.58
ESO [Orero and Irving (1996)]	15449	15449	15449	1.23
DE with SACP	15454	15449	15450	0.14

Table 6.8 Performance comparison for the 15-unit system in 50 trial tests

Algorithm Name	Generation Cost			Avg CPU time
	Max	Min	Avg	
PSO [Gaing (2003)]	33331.0000	32858.0000	33039.0000	26.59
GA [Gaing (2003)]	33337.0000	33113.0000	33228.0000	49.31
ESO § [Orero and Irving (1996)]	32734.0000	32694.0000	32710.0000	1.31
DE with SACP (1500 Generation)	32945.9776	32787.6743	32874.3648	2.12
DE with SACP (2000 Generation)	32885.3154	32747.6448	32827.9133	2.76

§ ESO did not satisfy the power balance constraints

time requirements. The results generated by classic DE is very close to DE with SACP, but needed extra fine-tuning of control parameters. In these experiments the parameter settings for classic DE was $P = 600$, $F = 0.8$ and $C_r = 0.9$.

In the second case study, the best solution generated by DE with SACP is compared with other methods and the results are presented in Table 6.8 and Table 6.9.

It is evident from Table 6.8 that ESO produced the minimum generation cost for the 15-unit system. But in reality ESO did not satisfy the power balance constraints. There is a power shortage of 15.85935 MW that cannot be ignored as shown in Table 6.9. Moreover, the transmission loss for ESO is larger. DE with SACP gives better results than PSO and GA methods. In another experiment, it was found that the solution quality could be improved by increasing the generation number in the DE with SACP method. If we compare the solution of classic DE, then it is found that DE with SACP gives better results for 2,000 iterations.

Both the classic DE and DE with SACP algorithms have been implemented and tested on the economic dispatch problem. The results show that DE with SACP is better or at least comparable to the classic DE algorithm. In addition, the use of DE with SACP does not incur the extra burden of tuning the values of F and C_r. In the work of Noman and Iba 36 different experiments were conducted to get the best value for F and C_r

Table 6.9   Best solution of the 15-unit system

Unit power output	PSO	GA	ESO	classic DE	DE with SACP (2000 Generation)	DE with SACP (1500 Generation)
P1	439.1162	415.3108	455.0000	454.5663	454.5392	453.6924
P2	407.9727	359.7206	380.0000	379.4427	375.4466	367.9508
P3	119.6324	104.4250	130.0000	129.9701	127.7094	123.0455
P4	129.9925	74.9853	130.0000	129.9485	129.0959	127.6591
P5	151.0681	380.2844	170.0000	169.7703	165.1859	168.1529
P6	459.9978	426.7902	460.0000	429.9338	458.6522	457.4539
P7	425.5601	341.3164	430.0000	429.5488	429.1617	424.8942
P8	98.5699	124.7867	69.2100	62.0332	79.0996	87.9630
P9	113.4936	133.1445	56.6000	127.3447	83.6660	81.2860
P10	101.1142	89.2567	159.1900	124.9618	138.5870	148.5653
P11	33.9116	60.0572	80.0000	79.3511	75.5338	79.0922
P12	79.9583	49.9998	80.0000	79.7344	77.8426	71.9798
P13	25.0042	38.7713	25.0000	25.3248	26.6850	29.4610
P14	41.4140	41.9425	15.0000	22.2424	18.7240	23.6737
P15	35.6140	22.6445	15.0000	17.5041	20.9591	17.0696
Total Power Output	2662.4196	2663.4359	2655.0050	2661.6777	2660.8880	2661.9393
P_L	32.4306	38.2782	40.8648	31.6892	30.8824	31.9525
$\sum_{i=1}^{N} P_i$ $-(P_L + D)$	-0.0110	-4.8423	-15.8590	-0.0114	0.0055	-0.0131
Total Generation Cost	32858.00	33113.00	32693.91	32769.29	32747.64	32787.67

[Noman and Iba (2008b)]. The best solution of classic DE with the most commonly used combination of F and C_r is compared with that of DE with SACP. From these results, it can be concluded that DE with SACP produces better results for the 6-unit system and for the 15-unit system compared to classic DE and many other algorithms.

In this section an adaptive EA, namely DE with SACP, has been successfully employed to solve the ELD problems with generator constraints. The performance of DE with SACP, with a new fitness function, stands out from other methods due to its simplicity and canonical form. Additionally, the solution found using the adaptive DE method is better or at least comparable to the existing ones. The adaptive DE approach has demonstrated its ability to provide a high-quality solution, a stable convergence feature and good computational efficiency.

6.4   Optimum door placement for evacuation planning

Emergency escape design or evacuation planning to assure safety standards, has been a major concern for fire safety engineers engaged in building design. A suitable modeling or simulation method may be required in order to analyze how the complexities of the building layout may affect potential evacuation of its occupants [Thompson and Marchant (1995)]. The draw-backs to perform a full-scale evacuation drill are the threat of injury of the participants, failure to mimic the real panic, limited confidence and high expenses.

Another potential alternative to assess evacuation planning of buildings lies in computer-based evacuation modeling and simulation. Computer-based simulation for safety assessment is more viable and advantageous than full-scale evacuation drills. Moreover, full-scale evacuation drills are impractical and expensive in an optimal exit location placement search problem due to the trial-and-error nature of the experiment. Computer-based simulation used to assess the suitability of an exit location configuration is a more viable option in such cases.

The concept of building evacuation and the factors that affect the emergency egress time are central to this particular research study. Total evacuation time can be divided into three components: the time to recognize a dangerous situation, the time to decide for evacuation and the time for movement towards safety. The last component, egress time, is studied closely in this research. The time of egress or evacuation time is affected by factors like level of emergency, human behavior in a panic situation, the number of evacuees per square meter, etc. In contrast to refining the escape behavior model for evacuees, finding an optimal placement of exits can be another research direction with a much broader scope. An optimal placement of doors at the time of designing a building can effectively decrease evacuation time and thus can be a life saver.

6.4.1 Problem description

Before we get into the method to minimize total evacuation time for a number of occupants, let us take a step back and consider the general problem of defining what a "successful evacuation" is. The effectiveness of an evacuation is based on several factors. The first goal, as indicated, is keeping evacuation time to a minimum. Second, it is imperative that the evacuation route be as safe as possible. The third factor affecting the success of an evacuation is how long, on average, it takes the occupants to get safely evacuated through the minimum number of exits [Santos and Benigno (2004)]. Summarizing all these factors, it can be said that the evacuation problem is a multi-objective optimization problem. One objective is to make the evacuation time shorter. Our second concern is safe evacuation that is, collisions and getting trampled by other evacuees should be

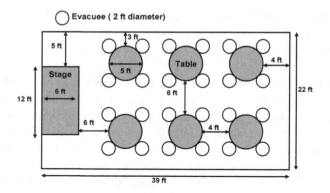

Fig. 6.15   Hall room layout for simulation

avoided, and finally, keeping the number of exits as minimum as possible. An aggregation-based fitness function [Zitzler *et al.* (2004)] is used in this work to address this multi-objective optimization problem.

This work is concerned with finding an optimal placement of exits in a specified room layout in order to evacuate people as quickly as possible. Here, a particular room layout, used by Garrett *et al.* [Garrett *et al.* (2006)], is chosen for experiments. As Fig. 6.15 shows, the layout represents a rectangular hall room with 7 obstacles and 24 evacuees.

The room consists of 6 dining tables (represented by the bigger circles) each with a 5-foot diameter and a stage of 12×6 feet, all of which act as obstacles to the evacuees at the time of evacuation. The smaller circles around the tables represent evacuees with a 2-foot diameter each. The room itself is a rectangular area of 39×22 feet.

The evacuation problem addresses the safe and swift evacuation of the occupants in an emergency, with a minimum number of doors in the room. The solution to the evacuation problem is a possible set of minimum door/ exit locations which gives the shortest evacuation time.

6.4.2   *The evacuation model*

The escape behavior of a human being in an emergency is very unpredictable, partly due to social interaction. Research on optimizing human evacuation in any emergent situation has taken two different approaches so far. For the past few decades, the evacuation problem has been studied with emphasis on the human escape behavior and how panic and other environmental factors affect the evacuation. Nevertheless, some recent research has attempted to improve evacuation time by optimizing placement of doors.

There have been many models [Pauls (1980); Ozel (1992); Graat *et al.* (1999); Pelechano and Malkawi (2008)] developed in order to enable designers for forecasting evacuation times for buildings. In spite of advanced knowledge of fire behavior, building design, specification, estimation of the number of occupants and computer applications, the subject of building evacuation in emergencies still provides a wide research scope, mainly due to the stochastic nature of the problem.

All these research studies were aimed at developing a refined human escape behavior model, so that the time for evacuation could be predicted and factors affecting human evacuation could be analyzed. Recently a new approach to solve the evacuation problem was presented by Garrett *et al.* [Garrett *et al.* (2006)]. Their research tackled the evacuation problem with a different approach that sought to minimize evacuation time by finding the optimal placement of exit locations. They used genetic algorithms (GA) and "estimated distribution algorithms" (EDA) to find the optimal door placement as a solution to the evacuation problem.

A model for evacuee escape behavior is required to evaluate a candidate design of door placements. After evaluating various models, we selected the one used in [Garrett *et al.* (2006)]. In the chosen model, both physical and behavioral aspects of human movement were considered for evacuee movement simulation [Helbing *et al.* (2000)]. Each individual evacuee is designed to mimic human intelligence, or an approximation of it, with respect to the surrounding environment. Three types of interactions affect an evacuee's movements and thereby trigger the decision-making process. These are:

- **Evacuee-evacuee interactions:** Interactions with other evacuees in the room.
- **Evacuee-structure interactions:** Interactions with the obstacles and surrounding walls of the room.
- **Evacuee-door interactions:** The interactions with the exits.

The movement of the evacuees was simulated by an artificial potential field model similar to the one used in [Garrett *et al.* (2006)] and O. Khatib's work [Khatib (1985)]. The interactions among objects in the simulation are modeled as forces. Evacuee movement at each time-step is controlled by the resultant force of attraction and repulsion. In this model, each evacuee is treated as a circular particle with a uniform body mass and radius (physical properties). The repulsion exerted by another evacuee depends on the distance between evacuees – the closer the other evacuee is, the higher the experienced repulsion force. Also, a minimum amount of proximity needs to be maintained for an evacuee to produce a repulsive force to another evacuee. It is quite natural and practical like real human movements, because humans do not start to adjust their moves to avoid collisions if the other person is very far away. This mechanism addresses the behavioral aspect of evacuee movement. Each object in the simulation can interact with all other objects. For example, there will be forces acting on each evacuee due to the walls, and separate forces acting on each evacuee due to every other evacuee in the room [Eldridge and Maciejewski (2005)]. The evacuee-evacuee force, for example, models the tendency of real people to keep a minimum amount of personal space.

In this evacuation model, the door locations produce an attractive force on each evacuee, and the obstacles and other evacuees produce repulsive forces. The evacuee should follow the gradient of this resultant force at every time-step of the simulation. The total force on an evacuee can be summed as:

Resultant force $= \sum$ Attractive force (force coming from doors)

$- \sum$ Repulsive force (force from obstacle $+$ force from other evacuees).

In this model, the forces (attractive or repulsive) working on a evacuee are assumed to be inversely proportional to the square of the distance between that evacuee and the origin of the force. Let us assume A, O, and E represent the set of all attraction, obstacle, and evacuee vectors, respectively, and the Euclidean distance between two vectors $\vec{p}$ and $\vec{q}$ is denoted by $d(\vec{p}, \vec{q})$. Then for a particular evacuee position, the resultant force acting on this evacuee, $F(\vec{p})$, is given by

$$F(\vec{p}) = \sum_{\vec{a} \in A} \frac{\alpha}{d(\vec{p}, \vec{a})^2} - \sum_{\vec{a} \in O} \frac{1}{d(\vec{p}, \vec{o})^2} - \sum_{\vec{e} \in E, \vec{e} \neq \vec{p}} \frac{1}{d(\vec{p}, \vec{e})^2} \qquad (6.21)$$

The parameter α corresponds to the aggressiveness of the evacuee and is used as a scaling factor to represent the power of the attraction to exit locations. The higher the value of α, the higher the urgency and aggressiveness of the evacuees to go towards exits. According to Eq. (6.21), when $\alpha = 0$, the evacuees will not feel any attraction toward the exits and will cease to move. Likewise, for negative values of α, the exits will act as repulsive forces and they will move away from the exits. With the increase of α, the force of attraction to the exits begins to outweigh the net repulsive force from the obstacles and other evacuees. Eventually evacuees are trampled to death or killed by attempting to run through obstacles. Therefore, we also optimize the amount of aggressiveness that the evacuees should possess, in a given configuration of exits, in order to escape safely from the room. Here, α was constrained to the interval $[0, 15]$ like in [Garrett *et al.* (2006)]. The gradient of F, that determines the direction of evacuee's move, is given by Eq. (6.22), (6.23), and (6.24).

$$\nabla F = \left\langle \frac{\partial F}{\partial x}, \frac{\partial F}{\partial y} \right\rangle \tag{6.22}$$

$$\frac{\partial F}{\partial x} = \sum_{\vec{a} \in A} \frac{-2\alpha(p_x - a_x)}{d(\vec{p}, \vec{a})^4} - \sum_{\vec{o} \in O} \frac{-2(p_x - o_x)}{d(\vec{p}, \vec{o})^4} - \sum_{\vec{e} \in E, \vec{e} \neq \vec{p}} \frac{-2(p_x - e_x)}{d(\vec{p}, \vec{e})^4} \tag{6.23}$$

$$\frac{\partial F}{\partial y} = \sum_{\vec{a} \in A} \frac{-2\alpha(p_y - a_y)}{d(\vec{p}, \vec{a})^4} - \sum_{\vec{o} \in O} \frac{-2(p_y - o_y)}{d(\vec{p}, \vec{o})^4} - \sum_{\vec{e} \in E, \vec{e} \neq \vec{p}} \frac{-2(p_y - e_y)}{d(\vec{p}, \vec{e})^4} \tag{6.24}$$

Since we consider the repulsive forces emanating from obstacles (or other evacuees) within a maximum distance from the evacuee under consideration, we first check to see if the $\vec{o}$ or $\vec{e}$ vectors are within the proximity. If they are not, then we do not include the contribution of those particular repulsive vectors in our summation.

The movement of evacuees in this model is directed by the resultant forces acting upon each individual evacuee as pointed out earlier. The evacuees will naturally proceed to the doors as doors exert attractive forces while obstacles and other evacuees exert repulsive forces. Still, the possibility of collisions can not be omitted due to the variation of aggressiveness determined by the value of α which represents the level of urgency for evacuees. If any evacuee overlaps another evacuee by an amount greater than half of his diameter (in our simulation, 1 foot) the evacuee is considered to be killed. The killed evacuees can no longer produce a repulsive force to other evacuees. The number of casualties due to trampling or crushing is taken into account when calculating fitness. As evacuees reach exits, they tend to cluster with close proximity to each other. However, this clustering cannot be taken as a collision, as they are close enough to the door and therefore considered safe. So a minimum distance from the door is reserved as a safe area for evacuees, where other evacuees do not produce repulsive forces any more.

6.4.3   *Methodology*

A new flexible door placement method for finding the optimal exit locations is presented in this study. A separate simulation environment is developed to model the evacuee movements. This simulation is also used to evaluate the effectiveness of the suggested door positions for safe evacuation. Differential evolution (DE) is used for finding optimal placement of doors in a room layout that gives a shorter evacuation time over the existing methods.

6.4.3.1   *Evaluation criteria*

In order to compare the flexible door positioning method with that proposed in [Garrett *et al.* (2006)] we used the same room layout and the same fitness function. Garrett *et al.* [Garrett *et al.* (2006)] designed the fitness function by taking into account all the issues, including evacuation time, number of killed evacuees due to trampling or crushing and the number of exits. To address this multi-objective optimization problem, an aggregation-based fitness assignment [Deb (2001)] has been used, which represents the multi-objective problem as a single objective problem. In order to keep the number of killed evacuees and the number of doors as minimum as possible, a high penalty has been used for killed evacuees and the number of doors exceeding two.

Each configuration of exit locations were used in simulation for a maximum of 20,000 milliseconds and based on the results of the simulation (i.e. how successful and safe the evacuation was) the fitness of that configuration was calculated. If all evacuees could successfully exit in some time $t < 20000$, the fitness score for the configuration in [Garrett *et al.* (2006)] was given by

$$t + 2000(\max(n, 2) - 2) \qquad (6.25)$$

where n represents the number of doors in the configuration. Note that for $(n \leq 2)$, the fitness is simply equal to the evacuation time without any penalty. Thus, the fitness gives privilege to configurations with two doors or less.

If some evacuees could not escape within the maximum time limit or were trampled to death, then the fitness score becomes

$$20000 * a + 30000 * d + 2000 * (\max(n, 2) - 2) \qquad (6.26)$$

where a represents the number of evacuees who are alive but could not escape from the room, and d represents the number of evacuees who died during evacuation.

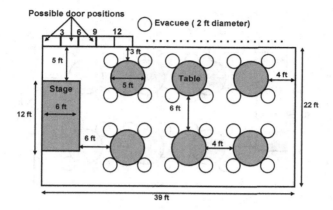

Fig. 6.16   Fixed-position door placement method proposed in [Garrett *et al.* (2006)]

6.4.4   *Flexible door positioning*

This work aims at exploring the possibility of optimal door placement searching all possible positions rather than a few fixed positions.   In the existing approach [Garrett *et al.* (2006)], the possible door locations were determined by calculating how many three-foot-wide doors could fit along each exterior wall with no separation between them (as illustrated in Fig. 6.16). As the figure shows, the starting position of a door is restricted to a multiple of three (door width) along the wall exterior. Note that such an approach will never be able to find an optimal door position at an arbitrary location (e.g. 4.57th feet position from the starting point) even though it exists.

In the quest for finding more optimal placement of doors to minimize the evacuation time, a flexible method for placing doors at arbitrary locations is presented. The starting location of a door is not restricted to multiples of door width, but allowed at any position, in this method. Fig. 6.17 illustrates the idea.

Possible optimal positions for a door could be the area marked by dashed boxes. But the arbitrary placement of doors may incur additional challenges to deal with, such as the requirement of variable length chromosomes, invalid chromosomes due to door overlapping and placement of doors at a corner.   However, a clever encoding scheme, described in the next sub-section, successfully deals with all the possible difficulties.

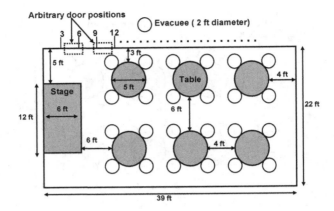

Fig. 6.17   Arbitrary door placement method

6.4.4.1   *Genotype creation*

Each chromosome in the population was encoded by an array of D floating point values, where D is the maximum possible number of doors that could be placed along the walls of a room. Each door in our evacuation model is assumed to be three feet wide. The total length of the wall, in the problem under consideration, is $2*(39+22) = 122$. So, the last location that a door could possibly be placed is at $122-3 = 119$th foot. The maximum number of doors is $119/3 = 39.6666 \approx 40$. Therefore, here a fixed chromosome size of 40 of real values is used to encode the possible door positions. This array consisting of 40 real values is taken using a random function to create the initial population. This requirement of a variable length chromosome was tactfully handled by using a fixed-length chromosome.

6.4.4.2   *Conversion to phenotype*

Although a fixed-length chromosome of a size of $D = 40$ is used in genotype, the actual number of doors in the solution would be quite fewer to make it a practical solution for evacuation planning. It is quite impractical to have 40 doors in a 39×22 foot room. So, a phenotype or mapping of doors along the walls is derived from the genotype. The first door location is taken as the first gene value, i.e. **geno[1]**. For the subsequent door locations, the mapping from genotype to phenotype is done as follows:

```
for(i = 2; i < GENE_SIZE; i++)
    phenotype[i] = phenotype[i-1] + 3 + geno[i];
```

a) A Sample Genotype

1.22, 75.90, 92.15, 32.56, 25.93, 50.50, 107.77, 114.74, 95.52, 78.18, 96.08, 69.55, 106.87, 57.87, 39.30,

108.93, 21.37, 78.80, 83.60, 12.97, 105.38, 5.02, 100.19, 85.53, 13.31, 39.96, 112.69, 112.64, 12.42,

44.72, 81.46, 51.84, 75.99, 82.01, 32.90, 42.20, 108.32, 95.55, 67.83, 58.27

Chromosome

1.22	75.90	92.15	32.56	25.93	....	58.27

b) Phenotype Conversion

1.22	80.12	-1

c) Mapping as Door Locations (represented by door centers)

Door1= (2.72, 0.0)

Door2= (20.62, 22.0)

Fig. 6.18   Encoding scheme and genotype to phenotype mapping

The upper-left corner is considered the starting position and doors will be assigned starting with the far-left door in the upper wall and continuing in the clockwise direction. The same process is followed for each of the four walls. However, once a phenotype value (**phenotype[i]**) crosses the total length of the wall (in this example, at 119 feet), the subsequent genes (**geno[i]**) are discarded. Additionally, if a door falls in the wall against the stage (between 105 feet and 117 feet) then it is discarded. The encoding scheme and mapping used in the presented method is illustrated in Fig. 6.18.

Finally, the phenotype was mapped to door coordinates. The center coordinate of each door was taken to represent the location of the door and the top-left corner of the room was considered to be (0,0) coordinate. Using this convention, the door coordinates were calculated as shown in Fig. 6.18.

One possible problem is the phenotype value suggesting the door at the point where two walls meet. For example, some portion of a door may belong to the upper wall and the rest of it to the right wall. This type of scenario may occur as the whole perimeter was considered as a continuous wall when we calculated the maximum possible number of doors for that room. The solution to this problem is addressed as follows: only if a given wall can accommodate the whole three-foot-wide door is it then assigned to that wall; otherwise the door is shifted to the next wall.

This method of placing doors at arbitrary locations rather than fixed locations, as done in [Garrett *et al.* (2006)], opens the possibility of more optimal placement of doors.

6.4.4.3   *Optimization algorithm*

In order to search the optimum door placement for evacuation, classic differential evolution (DE) with binomial crossover is employed. Since DE has been already described extensively in previous chapters, we avoid reiteration of the algorithm here.

6.4.5   *Simulation and results*

To achieve the goal of finding optimal placement of doors to make evacuation as quick as possible, the door placements are evolved by a population-based stochastic algorithm. Each configuration found by applying the DE algorithm is evaluated according to the requirement to find the best configuration of door locations.

6.4.5.1   *Judging the suitability of a solution*

To assess the fitness of a given configuration of exit locations a computer-based simulation is used to mimic the evacuees' movement. Simulation is run for a maximum of 20,000 milliseconds. It was assumed that each movement takes 100 milliseconds, so each evacuee is allowed a maximum of 200 movements for evacuation. If all evacuees escape safely before the time expires or when the simulation loop terminates, fitness of the configuration is calculated.

6.4.5.2   *Choosing the best α*

For a set of door locations, different values of α are tested while simulating the movement. As stated earlier, α, representing the aggressiveness associated with the current configuration, strengthens attractions to the exit locations. Actually, α represents how urgent the situation is. The larger the value of α, the higher the aggressiveness of the evacuees to go towards doors to escape. Therefore, for a given configuration of exits, an attempt was made to optimize the amount of aggressiveness that the evacuees need to employ in order to safely escape from the room. Here, α was constrained to the interval $[0, 15]$. In the simulation the value of α that gives the best score is chosen for each configuration of exit locations.

6.4.5.3   *Results*

For a certain setup of control parameters, 50 different runs were carried out and the average fitness score and the standard deviation were calculated.

Table 6.10   Study of best suited C_r-F for DE algorithm in evacuation problem

$C_r \backslash F$	0.1	0.2	0.3	0.4	0.5	0.6	0.7	0.8	0.9
0.1	5194±129	5259±133	5243±129	5164±126	5198±132	5240±133	5246±134	5207±129	5280±134
	4024 (13)	4024 (13)	4024 (13)	4024 (13)	4024 (13)	4024 (13)	4024 (13)	4024 (13)	4024 (13)
0.2	5122±126	5048±115	5131±125	5043±119	4910±112	5046±123	5132±127	4971±115	5035±123
	4024 (13)	4024 (13)	4024 (13)	4024 (13)	4024 (13)	4024 (13)	4024 (13)	4024 (13)	4024 (13)
0.3	5017±117	5048±121	4996±119	5056±123	5049±120	5087±125	5138±124	4973±117	5003±118
	4024 (13)	4024 (3)	4024 (13)	4024 (3)	4024 (13)	4024 (13)	4024 (13)	4024 (13)	4024 (13)
0.4	4913±109	4962±118	4943±116	4704±81	4981±120	4948±114	5005±120	4815±103	5094±124
	4024 (13)	4024 (3)	4024 (13)	4024 (3)	4024 (13)	4024 (13)	4024 (3)	4024 (13)	4024 (13)
0.5	4891±109	4925±110	4813±99	4898±103	4847±107	4788±97	5033±123	4826±104	5022±122
	4024 (13)	4024 (3)	4024 (13)	4024 (13)	4024 (13)	4024 (13)	4024 (13)	4024 (13)	4024 (13)
0.6	4794±99	4774±90	4798±102	4691±82	4858±108	4867±108	4860±104	4808±97	4748±100
	4024 (13)	4024 (13)	4024 (13)	4024 (3)	4024 (13)	4024 (13)	4024 (13)	4024 (13)	4024 (13)
0.7	4851±103	4868±105	4763±96	4983±114	4845±103	4898±112	4911±114	4967±113	4872±108
	4024 (13)	4024 (13)	4024 (13)	4024 (13)	4024 (13)	4024 (13)	4024 (13)	4024 (13)	4024 (13)
0.8	4841±108	4840±100	4885±111	4710±81	4836±108	4902±112	4844±108	4931±112	4860±109
	4024 (13)	4024 (13)	4024 (13)	4024 (13)	4024 (13)	4024 (13)	4024 (13)	4024 (13)	4024 (13)
0.9	4823±103	4857±106	4863±110	4799±94	4875±111	4977±119	4805±101	4931±110	4818±103
	4024 (13)	4024 (13)	4024 (13)	4024 (13)	4024 (13)	4024 (13)	4024 (13)	4024 (13)	4024 (13)

Interpretation of each cell: 1st Line: Avg Fitness ± SD; 2nd Line: Best fitness (α)

The average value and the standard deviation hint at the reliability of the DE algorithm for solving the evacuation problem. A fixed number of function evaluations (15,000) is used before termination. Though DE uses only three control parameters (population size P, crossover rate C_r and mutation rate or scaling factor F), the choice of these parameters is critical because the performance of DE is sensitive to these parameters and also because this sensitivity varies from problem to problem. For this reason, the best parameter values for DE are identified by grid search. The result of this grid search is given in Table 6.10.

Summarizing the table above, it is seen that $C_r = 0.6$ and $F = 0.4$ gives the best result on average for this particular problem. Therefore, in the subsequent experiments, this $C_r - F$ combination is used as a fixed parameter setting. In order to study the effect of population size, some more experiments were performed with three different C_r-F settings. The summary of the study on population size is shown in Fig. 6.19. It shows that with the increase of population size (up to a certain extent) the quality of the solution improves. The best ever fitness score inferred by DE is 4024.

Best Location of Doors
Door 1 = (2.72, 0.0)
Door 2 = (17.5, 22.0)

The figures in the parentheses correspond to the center of the doors in the x-y direction of the room layout. The optimal door placement found in the research is illustrated in Fig. 6.20.

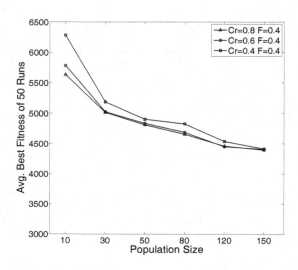

Fig. 6.19   Population study for three different $C_r - F$ combinations

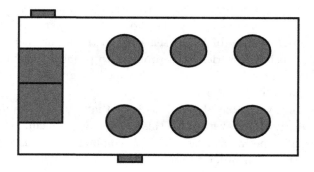

Fig. 6.20   Best door found in arbitrary door placement method (fitness = 4024)

The performance of the existing fixed position method [Garrett *et al.* (2006)] and the arbitrary door placement method is compared and tabulated in Table 6.11. The optimal placements found in these two methods are also graphically compared in Fig. 6.21.

The results from the simulation show that the arbitrary door placement method outperformed the existing fixed-door placement method in terms of best fitness and the number of exit locations. The best fitness found in the existing fixed-door placement method is 9300 with three doors whereas

Table 6.11   Comparison of best results between Garrett *et al.* (2006) method and the flexible door positioning method

	Best fitness	α	Dead	Escaped	Number of Doors
Garrett *et al.* (2006) method	9300	-	0	24	3
Flexible door positioning method	4024	13	0	24	2

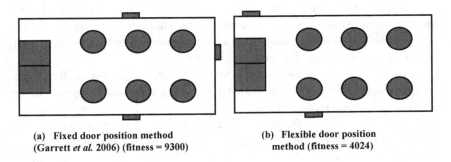

(a) **Fixed door position method (Garrett *et al.* 2006) (fitness = 9300)**   (b) **Flexible door position method (fitness = 4024)**

Fig. 6.21   Comparison of inferred door locations in fixed and flexible method

the method presented here gives a best fitness score of 4024 with only two doors and shows its efficiency in the evacuation process.

In difficult real-world problems where the behavior of the problem is not very well defined, evolutionary algorithms have proven to be very effective. The evacuation problem is such a real-world problem where human movement is stochastic and the factors influencing the evacuees in such an emergent situation are also not well defined. Noting these observations and also seeing the promising use of evolutionary algorithms in various real-world problems including engineering and medical science, a new generation evolutionary algorithm called DE was used in this study. The results support the speculations used in choosing DE. The results reveal the suitability of using DE in solving real-world evacuation planning and room layout design, which emphasizes the promise of DE as a different type of problem solver and optimizer.

6.5   Gene network reconstruction by analyzing microarray data

Gene regulation, the core of many biological processes, may be thought of as a combination of *cis*-acting regulation by the extended promoter of a gene, and of *trans*-acting regulation by the transcription factor products of other genes. If we simplify the *cis*-action using a phenomenological model that can be tuned to data, then the full *trans*-acting interaction between multiple genes can be modeled as a network which is commonly known as "gene circuits", "gene regulatory network" (GRN) or "gene network" [Mjolsness (2001)]. However, the mechanism behind such biological networks which are dynamic and highly nonlinear, is quite complicated. Because of poor understanding of the biological components, their dependencies, interaction and nature of regulation grounded on molecular level, studies of such systems have been impeded until very recently.

Several cutting-edge technologies such as DNA microarrays and oligonucleotide chips have opened the door to surveying thousands of genes under hundreds of varying conditions. Monitoring transcriptomes on a genome-wide scale, scientists are forming global views of the structural and dynamic changes in genome activity during different phases in a cell's development and following exposure to external agents. In order to draw meaningful inference, such data sets may be analyzed using a range of methods with increasing depth. Beginning with cluster analysis and the determination of mutual information content, it is possible to capture the control processes shared among genes. However, the ultimate goal of analyzing expression data is the detailed identification of the molecular mechanism of gene regulatory networks. Nevertheless, the success of such analyses largely depends on the breadth, sensitivity and precision of experimental data to accurately identify the underlying biological system.

Given a dynamic model of gene interactions, the problem of gene network inference is equivalent to learning the structural and functional parameters from the time series representing the gene expression kinetics, i.e. the network architecture is reverse engineered from its activity profiles. It is often wondered whether it is at all possible to reverse engineer a genetic network from gene expression data. Though reverse engineering is possible in principle, the success depends on the characteristics of the model, the availability of gene expression data and the level of noise present in the data.

Reverse engineering of an extremely complex system like a genetic network, needs the use of a reliable, robust and expert methodology. Moreover, the poor understanding of the molecular constituents, limited availability of the information, and poor and limited amount of dynamic responses make the reconstruction task even more difficult. Evolutionary algorithms (EAs) have established themselves as a suitable approach for working in such an environment and hence the field of genetic network inference has seen a

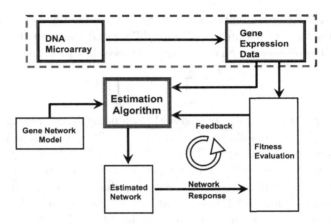

Fig. 6.22   Model-based estimation of gene regulatory networks

surge of applications of EAs. A schematic diagram of the EA-based gene network reconstruction is shown in Fig. 6.22.

As shown in Fig. 6.22, the other components involved in the process are the model of genetic regulation, the evaluation criteria for candidate networks and the gene expression data. Each of these components is of fundamental importance in this research. Therefore, each of them will be explained in this section.

6.5.1   *S-system model of GRN*

A genetic network model aims to capture the interrelated regulatory mechanisms among genes. Several genetic network models have been proposed, that integrate biochemical pathway information and expression data to trace genetic regulatory interactions. The modeling spectrum ranges from abstract Boolean descriptions to detailed differential equation based models, each having its own strengths, weaknesses and domain of applicability [Savageau (1992); Kauffman (1993); Arkin *et al.* (1998); D'haeseleer *et al.* (1999); Matsuno *et al.* (2000)]. In general, the modeling spectrum varies in terms of details of biochemical interactions incorporated, discrete or continuous gene expression level used, deterministic or stochastic approach applied, etc. [D'haeseleer *et al.* (2000)]. In general, the modeling spectrum

Among the familiar models for describing biochemical networks, a well-studied one is the S-system which is rich enough to reasonably capture the nonlinearity of genetic regulation [Savageau (1976)]. The S-system model is based on a set of nonlinear ordinary differential equations in which the component processes are characterized by power-law functions of the form

$$\frac{dX_i}{dt} = \alpha_i \prod_{j=1}^{N} X_j^{g_{ij}} - \beta_i \prod_{j=1}^{N} X_j^{h_{ij}} \tag{6.27}$$

where N is the number of network components or reactants (X_i), $i, j (1 \leq i, j \leq N)$ are suffixes of components. The terms g_{ij} and h_{ij} represent interactive affectivity of X_j to X_i. The first term represents all influences that increase X_i, whereas the second term represents all influences that decrease X_i. From the biological point of view, the two terms in the right-hand side of (6.27) represent the productive and inhibitory regulation, respectively, influencing the variable at the left-hand side of the equation. The parameters that define the S-system are: $\Omega = \{\alpha, \beta, g, h\}$. In a biochemical engineering context, the non-negative parameters α_i and β_i are called "rate constants", and the real-valued exponents g_{ij} and h_{ij} are referred to as "kinetic orders".

Since the details of the molecular mechanisms that govern interactions among system components are neither substantially known nor well understood, the description of these processes requires a representation that is general enough to capture the essence of the experimentally observed response. The S-system model is organizationally rich enough to reasonably capture various dynamics and mechanisms that could be present in a complex system of genetic regulation. The strength of the S-system model is its structure which is rich enough to satisfy these requirements and to capture all relevant dynamics; an observed response (dynamic response) may be monotonous or oscillatory, it may contain limit cycles or exhibit deterministic chaos [Tominaga *et al.* (2000)]. Furthermore, the simple homogeneous structure of the S-system has a great advantage in terms of system analysis and control design, because the structure allows analytical and computational methods to be customized specifically for this structure [Irvine and Savageau (1990)].

However, the problem of reconstructing a genetic network using the S-system has the difficulty of high dimensionality, since $2N(N + 1)$ S-system parameters must be determined in order to solve the set of differential equations (6.27). The estimation of parameters for a $2N(N + 1)$ dimensional function optimization problem often causes bottlenecks and fitting the model to experimentally observed responses (time course of relative state variables or reactants) is never straightforward and is almost always difficult. Therefore, the application of the S-system model has been limited to inference of small-scale gene networks only.

Maki *et al.* [Maki *et al.* (2002)] used a problem decomposition strategy for decoupling the canonical S-system model and facilitating its application to larger gene network inference problem. Using the suggested decomposition strategy the original optimization problem is divided into N sub-problems [Maki *et al.* (2002); Kimura *et al.* (2004)]. In each of these sub-problems, the parameter values of gene i are estimated for realizing the temporal profile of gene expression. In other words, this disassociation technique divides a $2N(N + 1)$ dimensional optimization problem into N sub-problems of $2(N + 1)$ dimension. In the i-th sub-problem, the parameter set for gene-i, $\Omega_i = \{\alpha_i, \beta_i, g_{i,j}, h_{i,j}\}$, is estimated by solving the following differential equation:

$$\frac{dX_i}{dt} = \alpha_i \prod_{j=1}^{N} Y_j^{g_{ij}} - \beta_i \prod_{j=1}^{N} Y_j^{h_{ij}} \tag{6.28}$$

For solving the differential equation (6.28) we need the concentration levels Y_j $(j = 1, \cdots, N)$. In the i-th sub-problem, corresponding to gene i, the concentration level $Y_{j=i}$ is obtained by solving the differential equation, whereas the other expression levels $Y_{j \neq i}$ are estimated directly from the observed time-series data. The optimization task for the tightly coupled S-system model is not trivial because Eq. (6.27) is nonlinear in all relevant cases, thus requiring iterative optimization in a larger parameter space, where 95% of the total optimization time is spent for numerical integration of the differential equations [Voit and Almeida (2004)]. Therefore, such disassociation could be very useful in reducing the computational burden. Moreover, the experimental results showed their usefulness in estimating the network parameters [Maki *et al.* (2002); Kimura *et al.* (2005)]. Here this decoupled form of S-system model has been used and any subsequent reference to the decoupled form will indicate this particular form of S-system. For direct estimation of expression levels $Y_{j \neq i}$ linear spline interpolation [Press *et al.* (1995); Eubank (1999)] was chosen.

6.5.2 *Model evaluation criteria*

6.5.2.1 *Generic fitness evaluation function*

We need some measure for evaluating different candidate models that are encountered while searching for the set of optimal parameters for the target network. The most commonly used evaluation criterion is the discrepancy between the numerically calculated gene expression levels and the observed system dynamics. Tominaga *et al.* used "mean squared error" (MSE) as the fitness evaluation function which was minimized by GA [Tominaga *et al.* (2000)]. Since a single set of time course can not give any general conclusion about the overall behavior of a complex dynamic system [Streichert *et al.* (2004)], the use of multiple sets of time courses was found to be more helpful. So, in the decoupled form, the MSE-based fitness evaluation function for the subproblem-*i* (corresponding to the gene-*i*), using multiple sets of time dynamics, becomes:

$$f_i^{MSE} = \sum_{k=1}^{M} \sum_{t=1}^{T} \left\{ \frac{X_{k,i}^{cal}(t) - X_{k,i}^{exp}(t)}{X_{k,i}^{exp}(t)} \right\}^2 \tag{6.29}$$

where $X_{k,i}^{exp}(t)$ and $X_{k,i}^{cal}(t)$ are the expression levels of gene-*i* in the *k*-th set of time courses at time *t* in experimental and calculated data, respectively. *M* is the set of time series used, *T* is the number of sampling points in the experimental data. And in subproblem *i* we try to estimate the parameters $\Omega_i = \{ \alpha_i, \beta_i, g_{i,j}, h_{i,j} \ (j = 1 \cdots N) \}$ for gene-*i* that minimizes f_i^{MSE}.

6.5.2.2 *Attaining skeletal network structure*

Generally, very few genes or proteins interact with a particular gene in biological networks [Arnone and Davidson (1997)]. But one major difficulty in the S-system-based network inference process is detecting the skeletal system architecture that generates the experimentally observed dynamics. Because of the high degree of freedom of the model, there exist many local minima in the search space that mimic the time courses very closely. Therefore, any method attempting to reproduce the time dynamics only, often gets stuck on some locally optimum solution and fails to obtain the skeletal structure [Kikuchi *et al.* (2003)]. Kikuchi *et al.* [Kikuchi *et al.* (2003)] suggested to penalize the fitness function by using all the "kinetic orders" of the network. Use of such a "pruning term" or "penalty term", based on Laplacian regularization term, in the basic MSE-based fitness function was useful for finding a sparse network architecture in the canonical optimization problem [Kikuchi *et al.* (2003); Noman and Iba (2005b)]. But because of high dimensionality, such fitness functions can be applied to small networks only.

Following the same notion, we used the following fitness function [Noman and Iba (2005c)] modifying the proposal of Kimura *et al.* in [Kimura *et al.* (2005, 2004)]

$$f_i = \sum_{k=1}^{M} \sum_{t=1}^{T} \left\{ \frac{X_{k,i}^{cal}(t) - X_{k,i}^{exp}(t)}{X_{k,i}^{exp}(t)} \right\}^2 + c \sum_{j=1}^{2N-I} (|K_{i,j}|) \qquad (6.30)$$

where $K_{i,j}$ are given by sorting *kinetic orders* $g_{i,j}$ and $h_{i,j}$ altogether in ascending order of their absolute values (i.e., $|K_{i,1}| \le |K_{i,2}| \le \cdots \le |K_{i,2N}|$).
I is the maximum allowed cardinality (in-degree) of the network and c is the penalty constant. This penalty term, as well as the one proposed in [Kimura *et al.* (2005)], includes the maximum allowed in-degree of the genes and will penalize only when the number of genes that directly affect the i-th gene is higher than the maximum allowed in-degree I, and thereby will cause most of the genes to disconnect when this penalty term is applied. However, the penalty term of (6.30), considering both synthetic and degradative regulations together rather than separately (as in [Kimura *et al.* (2005)]), was found to be more effective in identifying the skeletal architecture and the correct parameter values compared to the one proposed in [Kimura *et al.* (2005)].

6.5.3 *Reverse engineering algorithm*

Here we present an algorithm that was used to reconstruct GRN using S-system formalism. In order to estimate S-system model parameters, we optimized the objective function (6.30) for each subproblem i ($i = 1 \cdots N$) using the DE (DE/rand/1/exp) algorithm with a local search procedure explained later. Here we explain the optimization process for a specific subproblem. The same is applied for other subproblems to obtain a complete set of parameters for the full network.

In order to estimate the parameters more accurately and to avoid premature convergence to some local minima optimization, a two-phase method was performed. In each phase the parameter values of the gene-i, Ω_i, are represented as an individual of DE. In the first phase we perform many trials of optimization starting with different random initial individuals. In each of these trials, at the end of the optimization using DE augmented with local search procedure we obtain a solution for the subproblem i.e. a set of parameters for the target gene. However, the optimization process possibly converged to a local optimum and may have failed to attain actual parameter set. And because of local convergence it may lose some essential regulatory interaction among the genes. In other words we can say, due to convergence to local minima some parameter value could go down to zero, which is not actually zero in the target parameter set. Since trials are repeated with different initial values, candidate solutions are obtained as possible different local minima. To obtain a more robust and accurate solution we perform double optimization using elite individuals from different trials in the second phase of the algorithm. Double optimization could automatically detect the essential parameters by optimizing multiple local minima once again [Kikuchi *et al.* (2003)]. The solutions obtained in the first phase retained some essential parameters. So by applying another optimization on these solutions we can identify the correct regulations, accurate strength of the regulation and avoid deletion of any necessary parameter.

In each phase of the optimization process the overall procedure for estimating the model parameters for each sub-problem is as follows:

(1) Prepare the initial population P_G with candidate solutions.
(2) Create the new generation P_{G+1} applying recombination/selection operations of DE.
(3) Apply local search to the best individual and a randomly selected individual from P_{G+1}.
(4) Stop if the termination criteria satisfied. Otherwise Set G=G+1 and go to Step 2.

In the first phase, the initial population P_G is created randomly. And Γ trials of the first phase is repeated. In the second phase, the elite individuals from different trials of the first phase, together with some random individuals, are used for initialization.

6.5.3.1   *Local search procedure*

As discussed in Chapter 5, hybridization of local search with EAs can provide a more effective global optimization method. In order to take advantage of both the exploration abilities of EAs and the exploitation abilities of local search (LS), we introduce a local search method inside the DE algorithm for estimating S-system parameters. In the local refinement procedure a greedy search operation is performed on the best individual and on a random individual selected from each generation. The local search around the best individual and a random individual will accelerate the optimization process as well as maintain the diversity of the population. The local searching is performed as follows: All the kinetic orders are sorted in ascending order of their absolute values. Then the kinetic order of the lowest absolute value is set to zero and the fitness of this new individual

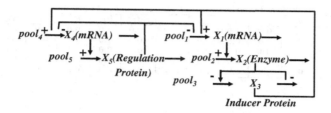

Fig. 6.23 Target gene regulatory network

is evaluated. If this modification improves the fitness of the individual, then the new solution is accepted otherwise its parent solution is restored. And this process is repeated for each kinetic order in the increasing order of their absolute values. This local search process allows us to identify the zero-valued parameters by mutating them in the increasing order of their strength and thus helps us to identify the skeletal network structure. And the restore capability of the greedy search also allows the recovery from wrong elimination of any essential regulation. By hybridizing this greedy local search procedure with the DE algorithm we can identify the sparse network structure efficiently and the strength of regulations more accurately.

6.5.4 *Reconstruction experiments and results*

In order to investigate how successfully the inference method can reconstruct the network topology and estimate the kinetic parameters we experimented using an artificial gene network. As the target network we used a small-scale S-system model which was first studied by Tominaga in [Tominaga *et al.* (2000)] and later many others have extensively experimented with it [Kikuchi *et al.* (2003); Kimura *et al.* (2004); Streichert *et al.* (2004); Kimura *et al.* (2005); Noman and Iba (2005b); Tsai and Wang (2005)]. Hence this network that represents a typical gene interaction system consisting of five genes, has become like a benchmark network for evaluating the performance of optimization algorithms for S-system models.

The system, consisting of five genes (see Fig. 6.23), adequately demonstrates different types of positive and negative modes of regulatory controls among the reactants. In this typical regulatory system the gene interaction takes place, centering two genes (genes 1 and 4). X1 is the mRNA produced from gene 1, X2 is an enzyme protein that gene 2 produces, and

Table 6.12   S-system parameters for the target network

i	α_i	g_{i1}	g_{i2}	g_{i3}	g_{i4}	g_{i5}	β_i	h_{i1}	h_{i2}	h_{i3}	h_{i4}	h_{i5}
1	5.0	0.0	0.0	1.0	0.0	-1.0	10.0	2.0	0.0	0.0	0.0	0.0
2	10.0	2.0	0.0	0.0	0.0	0.0	10.0	0.0	2.0	0.0	0.0	0.0
3	10.0	0.0	-1.0	0.0	0.0	0.0	10.0	0.0	-1.0	2.0	0.0	0.0
4	8.0	0.0	0.0	2.0	0.0	-1.0	10.0	0.0	0.0	0.0	2.0	0.0
5	10.0	0.0	0.0	0.0	2.0	0.0	10.0	0.0	0.0	0.0	0.0	2.0

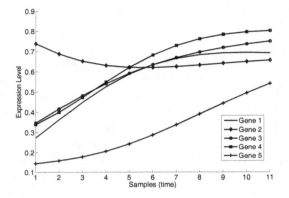

Fig. 6.24   Typical expression data for the target network

X3 is an inducer protein catalyzed by X2. X4 is an mRNA produced from gene 4 and X5 is a regulator protein produced by gene 5. Positive feedback from the inducer protein X3 and negative feedback from the regulator protein X5 are assumed in the mRNA production processes of genes 1 and 4. This model has been developed to analyze the interaction of regulator and effector genes [Kikuchi *et al.* (2003)]. S-system parameters for the target network are listed in Table 6.12.

Generally, many candidate solutions evolve if the model parameters are estimated using an insufficient amount of time series data. Therefore, $M = 10$ sets of time series data were used for ensuring a sufficient amount of observed gene expression levels. The sets of time series were obtained by solving (6.27) on the model of Table 6.12. Initial concentration level for each time series was generated randomly in $[0.0, 1.0]$. Sampling 11 points from each time course, $10 \times 11 = 110$ gene expression samples were used for each gene. A typical gene expression data set of the target network is shown in Fig. 6.24.

Table 6.13   Inferred parameters for the network from noise-free expression data

i	α_i	g_{i1}	g_{i2}	g_{i3}	g_{i4}	g_{i5}	β_i	h_{i1}	h_{i2}	h_{i3}	h_{i4}	h_{i5}
1	4.631	-0.094	0.000	1.035	0.000	-1.042	9.522	1.978	0.000	0.000	0.000	0.003
2	10.207	1.989	0.013	0.000	0.000	0.000	10.154	0.030	1.963	0.000	-0.007	0.000
3	9.685	0.000	-1.003	-0.017	0.000	0.000	9.686	0.000	-1.003	2.058	0.000	0.000
4	8.136	0.000	-0.017	1.927	0.013	-0.988	10.269	0.000	0.000	0.000	1.961	0.000
5	9.728	0.000	0.000	0.000	2.041	-0.027	9.710	-0.005	0.000	0.000	-0.021	2.029

6.5.4.1   *Experimental setup*

The experiment was carried out under the following setup. The search regions of the parameters were $[0.0, 20.0]$ for α_i and β_i, and $[-3.0, 3.0]$ for g_{ij} and h_{ij}. The maximum cardinality I was chosen 5, and the penalty coefficient c was 1.0. The parameter values for the DE algorithm were $F = 0.5$, $C_r = 0.8$ and the population size was 60. The maximum number of generations in each trial in the first phase and in the second phase was 850. In the first phase, 5 ($\Gamma = 1, \cdots, 5$) independent trial solutions were evolved from which elite individuals were selected for optimization in the second phase. The algorithm was implemented in Java language and the time required for solving each sub-problem was approximately 10 minutes using a PC equipped with a 1700 MHz Intel Pentium processor and 512 MB of RAM.

In order to reduce the computational burden, a structure skeletalizing was applied in a similar fashion used by Tominaga *et al.* in [Tominaga *et al.* (2000)]. If the absolute value of a parameter is less than a threshold value δ then structure skeletalizing resets it to zero. This process reduces the computational cost as well as helps to identify the nonexistent regulations quickly. In different experiments $\delta = 0.001$ was used. For assuring the effectiveness of the stochastic search algorithm, five repetitions for each experiment were performed.

6.5.4.2   *Reconstruction result from noise-free expression data*

The first experiment was intended to verify the effectiveness of the inference algorithm in an ideal environment, i.e. in the absence of noise in the simulated gene expression data. Table 6.13 shows the parameters estimated by the developed algorithm in a typical run. From noise-free expression data the method extracted all the correct regulations and a few false interactions. The reconstruction process inferred not only all the interactions correctly but also the type of regulation (synthesis or degradation) accurately. Estimated parameter values were also very close to target parameters. Only a few false positive regulations were predicted and the parameter values of

Table 6.14   Inferred parameters for the network from 5% noisy gene expression data

i	α_i	g_{i1}	g_{i2}	g_{i3}	g_{i4}	g_{i5}	β_i	h_{i1}	h_{i2}	h_{i3}	h_{i4}	h_{i5}
1	4.816	0.000	0.105	1.420	0.000	-1.392	9.900	2.640	0.000	0.000	0.000	-0.445
2	12.092	2.335	0.000	0.396	-0.145	0.161	12.777	0.000	2.188	0.000	0.000	0.000
3	6.418	0.000	-0.890	-0.372	0.000	-0.172	7.493	0.000	-0.840	3.000	0.000	0.000
4	7.071	0.000	0.000	2.370	-0.086	-1.027	10.209	0.743	0.000	0.000	1.987	0.000
5	14.404	0.000	0.000	0.422	1.254	0.000	12.651	0.410	-0.170	0.000	0.000	1.030

all of those false positive predictions were small enough to discard those regulations.

6.5.4.3   *Reconstruction result from noisy expression data*

Noise is inevitable in microarray data and the real challenge lies in designing inference algorithms capable of constructing the network from noisy data. Therefore, we test the performance of the inference algorithm simulating a real-world environment, i.e. conducting the experiments with a set of noisy time series data.

The same network used in the previous experiment with the same target parameter set was selected as the target model. Data points were generated using the same sets of initial expression levels. We added 5% Gaussian noise to the time series data in order to simulate the measurement error between true expression and observed expression. Eleven sample points from each time course were used for optimization. The rest of the settings were same as in the previous experiments.

The set of parameters inferred by the reconstruction method in a typical run using the noisy data is presented in Table 6.14. Even using 5% noise-corrupted data the reconstruction method was successful in extracting all the correct regulations. The number of false-negative interactions was also zero. In some cases the estimation of kinetic constants were pretty far away from the target value and some false predicted parameter values were too large to ignore. Although all the parameter values were not estimated accurately, the underlying regulations were always inferred correctly.

However, even such a clue may turn out to be very useful for biologists to design additional experiments or confirm the existence of the regulation. Moreover, the use of additional time courses can decrease the number of false predictions as well as increase the accuracy of parameter estimation. So these experiments once again conclusively show the effectiveness of EAs in solving complex problems such as inferring gene networks in bioinformatics.

Appendix A

GA Simulators

A.1 Introduction

To better understand GA and its extensions, software described in this book can be downloaded from the website of the laboratory to which one of the authors belongs (http://www.iba.t.u-tokyo.ac.jp/).

The intention of making these software packages available online is to allow users to "play" with different EAs and gain hands-on experience. The web pages contain (1) instructions for downloading the packages, (2) a user's manual, and (3) a bulletin board for posting questions. Readers are welcome to use these facilities.

Users who download and use these programs should bear the following in mind:

- We accept no responsibility for any damage that may be caused by downloading these programs.
- We accept no responsibility for any damage that may be caused by running these programs or by the results of executing such programs.
- We own the copyright to these programs.
- We reserve the right to alter, add to, or remove these programs without notice.

In order to download the software in this book, please visit the following link, and then follow the instructions:

http://www.iba.t.u-tokyo.ac.jp/english/

If inappropriate values are used for the parameters (for instance, elite size greater than population size), the programs may crash. Please report any bugs to: ibalabweb@iba.t.u-tokyo.ac.jp.

A.2   Information on GA-2D and GA-3D simulators

The following Excel simulators are available for experiencing the hill-climbing and GA-based searches:

- GA-2D simulator: For testing optimization of one-dimensional functions.
- GA-3D simulator: For testing optimization of two-dimensional functions.

The function can be specified by using the "Input" button. Functions that can be used in Excel can be written here, and the principal functions that can be used are listed in Table 2.1. If you make a mistake, press "Reset" to start over. When you have input the function, press "OK". This displays a schematic diagram of the function. To better visualize a function in a three-dimensional space, there is a button that rotates the graph from top to bottom and from left to right. Each time an arrow button is pressed, the figure is turned 45 degrees. The movement options are as follows:

Elevation (up/down): $-45°, 0°, 45°$
Rotation (left/right): $0°, 45°, 90°, 135°, 180°, 225°, 270°, 315°$

The menu options for setting search methods are as follows:

- Genetic Algorithm (GA)
- Steepest-ascent hill-climbing (SAHC)
- Next-ascent hill-climbing (NAHC)
- Random-mutation hill-climbing (RMHC)
- Iteration count (specified when using hill-climbing)

Execution will start when you press "Start" button. The "Result" window will comprise of the following items:

- Generation: Maximum number of generations
- Max Fitness: Best fitness value
- AVG Fitness: Mean fitness value
- Best Gene: The coordinate(s) of the best individual ultimately found and the function values are displayed.

The principal parameters for GA can be set in the "GA Parameter" panel. These are summarized below:

- Coding: Either "binary" or "gray" or "real" is selected as the coding method
- Generation: Maximum number of generations
- Population: Population size
- Gene length: The bit length to be coded is determined based on this length (for binary and gray coding)
- Elite: The number of individuals remaining with the elite strategy; if this is set to 0, no individuals will be carried over to the next generation
- Crossover rate: Normally, whether or not crossovers are carried out is determined randomly; the crossover rate is used to set this probability
- Mutation rate: It specifies the probability of genes in the chromosome being mutated
- Sharing: This is turned on if the niche segregation function is to be used (See Section 2.4 for details)
- Selection Method: Available selection methods include the fitness-proportionate strategy (Roulette), the tournament strategy (Tournament) and the random method (Random)

The crossover method and mutation method are specified if a real GA is being used. The above items can be specified in greater detail by pressing the "GA Setting" button. In particular, the following items can be specified in the "GA Setting" window.

- The tournament size used with the tournament strategy.
- The δ_{share} of the assignment function used in sharing method.

Pressing the "Step" button opens the "Step Command" window. Execution can be paused every few generations to view detailed information as well as change parameters. The items in this window have the following meanings:

- Step: This specifies how many generations are to be processed before execution is paused.
- Current Gen: This is the number of the current generation.
- Next Gen: This specifies the number of the next generation after which execution is to pause, and is the value of Current Gen + Step.

After setting appropriate values for these items and pressing the "Start"/"Continue" button, execution should pause, when the generation specified for "Next Gen." is reached. Holding down this button executes the

⟨Search Points⟩			⟨2D⟩			Fitness
x Axis	**y Axis**		**x**	**y**		**Fitness**
15.33984	7.716524		0	0		7.716524
14.14453	8.072184		0.17	0.089842		8.072184
14.14453	8.072184		0.34	0.207088		8.072184
11.48828	5.060213		0.51	0.371341		5.060213
11.48828	5.060213		0.68	0.588613		5.060213
10.29297	4.702008		0.85	0.849039		4.702008
13.61328	7.455837		1.02	1.128705		7.455837
11.48828	5.060213		1.19	1.395132		5.060213
14.14453	8.072184		1.36	1.615053		8.072184
11.48828	5.060213		1.53	1.762506		5.060213
13.67969	7.561985		1.7	1.825202		7.561985
12.41797	6.205752		1.87	1.807549		6.205752
16.80078	7.700337		2.04	1.729562		7.700337
11.75391	5.494321		2.21	1.621952		5.494321
13.34766	7.023029		2.38	1.518616		7.023029
16.93359	7.633508		2.55	1.448446		7.633508
11.75391	5.494321		2.72	1.428525		5.494321
13.34766	7.023029		2.89	1.460428		7.023029
14.94141	7.804467		3.06	1.530541		7.804467
16.80078	7.700337		3.23	1.614312		7.700337
9.496094	4.747685		3.4	1.683313		4.747685

Fig. A.1   Coordinate values for fitness function

simulator for the specified number of generations. Pressing the "Parameter" button when execution is paused displays the "GA Parameter Setting" window. Parameters can be confirmed and changed in this window. After execution is complete, pressing the "Report" button provides detailed information about the population. The genes of the parents and offspring generations are displayed here, along with the maximum fitness value and average fitness value. The gene information comprises the following items:

- No.: Gene number
- GTYPE: Genotype
- Raw Fitness: Fitness value calculated from $F(x)$
- GA operations: How the offspring genes were generated

  - Elite: The genes were copied exactly as they were, as elite individuals (the gene number of the parent is displayed).
  - Crossover: The genes were generated by means of one-point crossovers (the two parent individuals and crossover points are displayed).
  - Mutation: The genes were generated as a result of mutation (the

Coding	Generatio	Populatio	Length
binary	50	30	8
binary	1	1	4
gray	5	10	6
real	10	30	8
	50	50	12
	100	100	50

	1	Search M		1	Evaluation Time	
	0	GA		1	200	AVG
			1		1	
		x			Xmin	Xmax
		15.73828			0	17
		y	Function	Ymin	Ymax	
		8	sin(x)^3+0.	0	8.10976	

Function 4

Generatio	Max	AVG
50	8.072	6.696

F(x,y)	x
8.072	14.145

Elite	Crossove	Mutation	Selection
2	0.8	0.05	Roulette
1	0.65	0.01	Roulette
2	0.7	0.05	Tournament
5	0.8	0.1	Random
10	0.9	0.5	
0	0	0	

Now	Step	Next
50	1	50
14.34375	8.109434	

X_max	Y_max
14	8

Crossove	Mutation	Sharing	Trn
UNDX	ND	on	6
BLX-α	UD	on	
UNDX	ND	off	

α	size	sigma
0.5	10	2
SD	SD	
0.5	0.5	

Fig. A.2   GA parameter values

number of the parent and the mutation point are displayed).
- Survival: The genes are not elite, but were copied just as they were, applying neither crossover nor mutation (the number of the parent is displayed).

With this GA simulator, information is displayed in the cells of an Excel spreadsheet. For example, when executing the GA-3D, the following items are recorded:

- The coordinate values for the fitness value function (Fig. A.1)
- The GA parameters (Fig. A.2)
- The execution results (Fig. A.3)

These can be used to produce graphs and to carry out statistical processing.

A.3   TSP simulator

The TSP simulator is a GA-based simulator for solving TSP in Excel. When you run the TSP simulator in Excel, an execution window similar to that

Child Population	50	0								
Individual Number	Ptype(x)	Ptype(y)	y=F(x)	Gtype	Fitness	GA Operation	Parent 1	Parent 2	Crossover or Mutation point	List Expression
1	15.34		7.717	[1110011 1]	7.717	Elite	16	-	-	No.1 [11100111] 7.717 : Elite (16,-) -
2	14.145		8.072	[10101011]	8.072	Elite	1	-	-	No.2 [10101011] 8.072 : Elite (1,-) -
3	14.145		8.072	[10101011]	8.072	Crossover	29	1	2	No.3 [10101011] 8.072 : Crossover (29,1) 2
4	11.488		5.06	[10110101]	5.06	Crossover	29	1	2	No.4 [10110101] 5.06 : Crossover (29,1) 2
5	11.488		5.06	[10110101]	5.06	Survival	14	-	-	No.5 [10110101] 5.06 : Survival (14,-) -
6	10.283		4.702	[11011001]	4.702	Mutation	28	-	6	No.6 [11011001] 4.702 : Mutation (28,-) 6
7	13.613		7.456	[10110011]	7.456	Survival	26	-	-	No.7 [10110011] 7.456 : Survival (26,-) -
8	11.488		5.06	[10110101]	5.06	Survival	9	-	-	No.8 [10110101] 5.06 : Survival (9,-) -
9	14.145		8.072	[10101011]	8.072	Survival	1	-	-	No.9 [10101011] 8.072 : Survival (1,-) -
10	11.488		5.06	[10110101]	5.06	Survival	23	-	-	No.10 [10110101] 5.06 : Survival (23,-) -
11	13.68		7.562	[01110011]	7.562	Crossover	20	13	7	No.11 [01110011] 7.562 : Crossover (20,13) 7
12	12.418		6.206	[11011101]	6.206	Crossover	20	13	7	No.12 [11011101] 6.206 : Crossover (20,13) 7
13	16.801		7.7	[10111111]	7.7	Survival	21	-	-	No.13 [10111111] 7.7 : Survival (21,-) -
14	11.754		5.494	[10001101]	5.494	Survival	6	-	-	No.14 [10001101] 5.494 : Survival (6,-) -
15	13.348		7.023	[10010011]	7.023	Crossover	15	5	7	No.15 [10010011] 7.023 : Crossover (15,5) 7
16	16.934		7.634	[11111111]	7.634	Crossover	15	5	7	No.16 [11111111] 7.634 : Crossover (15,5) 7
17	11.754		5.494	[10001101]	5.494	Crossover	15	6	1	No.17 [10001101] 5.494 : Crossover (15,6) 1
18	13.348		7.023	[10010011]	7.023	Crossover	15	6	1	No.18 [10010011] 7.023 : Crossover (15,6) 1
19	14.941		7.804	[10000111]	7.804	Crossover	2	21	5	No.19 [10000111] 7.804 : Crossover (2,21) 5
20	16.801		7.7	[10111111]	7.7	Crossover	2	21	5	No.20 [10111111] 7.7 : Crossover (2,21) 5
21	9.496		4.748	[11110001]	4.748	Crossover	21	17	1	No.21 [11110001] 4.748 : Crossover (21,17) 1
22	16.801		7.7	[10111111]	7.7	Crossover	21	17	1	No.22 [10111111] 7.7 : Crossover (21,17) 1
23	13.613		7.456	[10110011]	7.456	Crossover	29	15	3	No.23 [10110011] 7.456 : Crossover (29,15) 3
24	11.223		4.686	[10010011]	4.686	Crossover	29	15	3	No.24 [10010011] 4.686 : Crossover (29,15) 3
25	14.145		8.072	[10101011]	8.072	Survival	1	-	-	No.25 [10101011] 8.072 : Survival (1,-) -
26	13.348		7.023	[10010011]	7.023	Survival	15	-	-	No.26 [10010011] 7.023 : Survival (15,-) -
27	12.418		6.206	[11011101]	6.206	Crossover	28	19	5	No.27 [11011101] 6.206 : Crossover (28,19) 5
28	11.488		5.06	[10110101]	5.06	Crossover	28	19	5	No.28 [10110101] 5.06 : Crossover (28,19) 5
29	14.145		8.072	[10101011]	8.072	Crossover	19	1	9	No.29 [10101011] 8.072 : Crossover (19,1) 9

Fig. A.3   Results of search execution

shown in Fig. A.4 is displayed. Here, the layout of the cities is shown in the upper left of the screen. Our problem is to determine the shortest route that will allow us to pass through all cities exactly once, and come back to the starting point. To change the layout, first press the "Reset" button, and then press "Random City". The number of cities can also be changed (modify the value in the "Number of cities" field). The coordinates of the cities are displayed on an Excel spreadsheet (Fig. A.5). Changing these values allows the user to freely define the layout of the cities.

The following GA parameters can be set, among others:

- Interval of Generations: The number of generations processed from the time the "Search" button was pressed to the time the search stops
- Population Size: The size of the population
- Crossover Rate: The crossover rate
- Mutation Rate: The rate of mutation

The following elements can be specified in the lower-right section of the screen:

- Selection Method: Specifies the selection method
  - Roulette: The fitness-proportionate strategy
  - Tournament: The fitness independent tournament strategy where we can specify the tournament size
  - Random: Specifies random selection
- Elite: The elite strategy, used to specify the percentage of genes that are carried over as elite

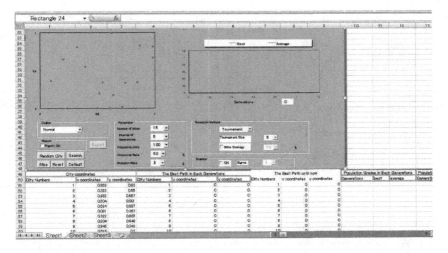

Fig. A.4   TSP simulator

City coordinates		
City number	x coordinate	y coordinate
1	0.706	0.533
2	0.58	0.29
3	0.302	0.775
4	0.014	0.761
5	0.814	0.709
6	0.045	0.414
7	0.863	0.79
8	0.374	0.962
9	0.871	0.056
10	0.95	0.364
11	0.525	0.767
12	0.054	0.592
13	0.469	0.298
14	0.623	0.648
15	0.264	0.279

Fig. A.5   City coordinate values

- Sharing: This is set to switch "ON" the niche segregation function; in this case, δ_{share} is to be specified

The parameters are displayed on an Excel spreadsheet (Fig. A.6).

When the appropriate parameters have been set, press the "Search" button. The GA search will be carried out until the generation number specified by the "Interval of Generations" parameter. Pressing the "Search" button again, executes the search repeatedly for the number of generations specified by the "Interval of Generations" parameter. Pressing the "Step"

			5 Number of cities	Interval of Generations	Population Size	Crossover Rate	Mutation Rate
Parameters			3	1	100	1	0
Number of cities	15		5	5	200	5	1
Population size	100		10	10	500	10	5
Mutation rate(%)	5		15	20	1000	50	10
Interval of Generations	5		20	50		100	50
Selection Method		2	30	100			100
Elite strategy	FALSE		50				
Sharing	FALSE		100				
Elite rate(%)	10						
Sigma	1		Elite rate	Sigma	Tournament Size		
Tournament Size	5		1	1	2		
Crossover Rate	50		5	5	3		
Coding		1	10	10	5		
Output of Genes	FALSE		20		10		
step	TRUE						
Report Mode	FALSE						
Current Generation		1					
The Best Grade Until Now	0.201016422						
Selection Method	Coding						
Roulette	Normal						
Tournament	Ordinal Representaion						
Random	Normal						
Tournament							

Fig. A.6   GA parameters for TSP

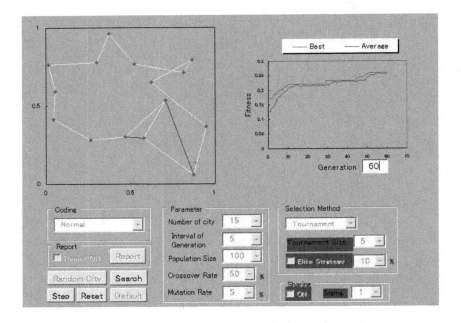

Fig. A.7   TSP search result

button executes GA one generation at a time (Fig. A.7). The best fitness
value (red) and average fitness value (green) for each generation are displayed on the graph in the upper right of the screen. The phenotypes of
each of these are indicated on the drawing of the cities at the left. The yellow path is the best solution found up to the current generation, while the

City coordinates			The best path in each generation			The best path until now			Population grades in each generation			Fitness values	
City number	x coordinate	y coordinate	City number	x coordinate	y coordinate	City number	x coordinate	y coordinate	Generation	best	average	Generation	best
1	0.706	0.533	3	0.302	0.775	3	0.302	0.775	1	0.17074451	0.1290303		
2	0.58	0.29	8	0.374	0.962	8	0.374	0.962	2	0.17833855	0.1422461		
3	0.302	0.775	7	0.863	0.79	7	0.863	0.79	3	0.17503709	0.1504081		
4	0.014	0.761	5	0.814	0.709	5	0.814	0.709	4	0.18711416	0.1593235		
5	0.814	0.709	4	0.014	0.761	4	0.014	0.761	5	0.18711416	0.1672439		
6	0.045	0.414	12	0.054	0.592	12	0.054	0.592	6	0.18641831	0.1730462		
7	0.863	0.79	2	0.58	0.29	2	0.58	0.29	7	0.18641831	0.1774707		
8	0.374	0.962	10	0.95	0.364	10	0.95	0.364	8	0.18641831	0.183913		
9	0.871	0.056	9	0.871	0.056	9	0.871	0.056	9	0.18641831	0.1865322		
10	0.85	0.364	13	0.469	0.298	13	0.469	0.298	10	0.18641831	0.188066		
11	0.525	0.767	15	0.264	0.279	15	0.264	0.279	11	0.18641831	0.1870777		
12	0.054	0.592	6	0.045	0.414	6	0.045	0.414	12	0.18641831	0.1870045		
13	0.469	0.298	14	0.623	0.648	14	0.623	0.648	13	0.18641831	0.1871572		
14	0.623	0.648	1	0.706	0.533	1	0.706	0.533	14	0.18641831	0.1870869		
15	0.264	0.279	11	0.525	0.767	11	0.525	0.767	15	0.18641831	0.1886066		

Fig. A.8   Detailed information of the TSP result

blue path is the best solution for each generation. In some cases, however, the paths overlap and only one color is visible. Detailed information about the search results can be found on the Excel spreadsheet (Fig. A.8).

After the execution, pressing the "Report" button opens the "Population Report" window, showing detailed information about the populations (see Fig. 2.75). The genes of the parent and offspring generations are displayed, along with the maximum fitness values and average fitness values. The genetic information is as follows:

- No.: Gene number
- GTYPE: Genotype
- Fitness: Fitness value
- GA operations: How the offspring genes were generated (for offspring genes)
    - Elite: The genes were copied exactly as they were, as elite individuals (the number of the parent is displayed).
    - X (Crossover): The genes were generated by means of crossover (the two parent individuals involved in crossover are displayed).
    - Mu (Mutation): The genes were generated as a result of mutation (the individual number of the parent and the mutation point are displayed).
    - Sur (Survival): The genes are not elite, but were copied just as they were, without applying either crossovers or mutations (the number of the parent is displayed).

Clicking on a gene of the offspring under "Population Report" displays a window showing detailed information about the relationship between GTYPE and PTYPE, as well as the behavior of the GA operators. The window can be opened at this point to see the PTYPEs of the parent and offspring on the map.

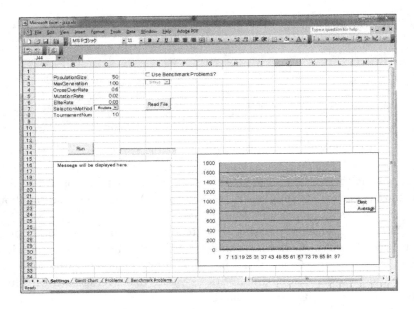

Fig. A.9   JSSP simulator

A.4   JSSP simulator

The JSSP simulator is a GA-based simulator for solving the job shop scheduling problem (JSSP) in Excel. When you run this simulator, you will see an execution window similar to that shown in Fig. A.9.

Pressing the "Run" button starts the simulator using the preset GA parameters. The parameters can be found on the spreadsheet in the upper left of the screen, and can be changed by the user. The GA parameters are those that were described in Section 2.2.4. The fitness value in GA is the total time required to finish all jobs. Consequently, the smaller the fitness value, the better.

When execution begins, the average fitness values and best fitness values for each generation are displayed on a graph at the lower right of the screen. When execution ends, the results are indicated at the lower left of the screen. The results include the following information:

- Execution result: Whether execution was completed through the last generation, and whether an optimum value was obtained.
- The genotype of the best individual acquired.
- The number of the generation in which that genotype was first obtained.

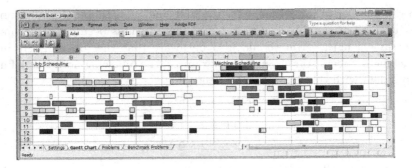

Fig. A.10   Gantt chart display

Fig. A.11   Problem definition

- The time at which the job was completed (total required time = fitness value).
- The parameter values that were used.

The schedule based on the best individual is displayed on the Gantt chart spreadsheet (Fig. A.10). The colors under "Job Scheduling" and those under "Machine Scheduling" are correlated, so that you can tell which processing is being done at what time.

The definition of the problem is noted on the "Problem" spreadsheet (Fig. A.11). The first line is the definition of the problem (file name, number of jobs and number of machines). The second and subsequent lines are a description of the problem. Each line indicates one job. The machine number and processing time are described using two cells each, in the order in which the jobs are being processed. The number of lines corresponds to the number of jobs (except for the first line). The number of machines used for all of the jobs has to be consistent. This is because all lines are the same length. You should also be aware that the job numbers and machine numbers start from 0. For example, the following notation defines a problem with three jobs and four machines:

$$0\ 5\ 1\ 7\ 2\ 3\ 3\ 9$$
$$3\ 9\ 0\ 4\ 2\ 6\ 1\ 5$$
$$1\ 3\ 3\ 2\ 2\ 5\ 0\ 1$$

Job $J0$, which is noted on the first line, is done on machine $M0$ and is carried out for a time 5, and it then moves to $M1$, $M2$, and then $M3$. The same applies to $J1$ on the second line and $J2$ on the third line.

Checking the "Use Benchmark Problem" button makes it possible to use the $MT6 \times 6$, $MT10 \times 10$ and $MT20 \times 5$ problems.

Appendix B

PSO and BUGS Simulators

B.1 PSO simulator

The PSO search process could be observed using this simulator (see Fig. B.1). This uses PSO to search for the same region as in the GA-3D simulator described in Section 2.3. For convenience, the Z axis was greatly compressed in the view of $F5$ in the PSO simulation, so it looks somewhat different from the previous figure.

Download and unzip the file "Particle Swarm Optimization ver1.0" (402 kB). It contains 3 files: EquToDbl.dll, EquToDbl.txt, and PSO.exe. Click PSO.exe to start the simulator.

The following commands allow the user to make basic use of the simulator:

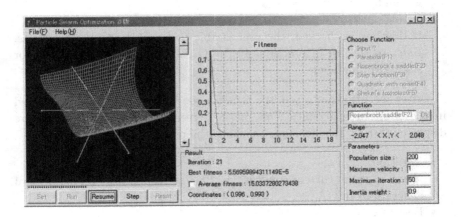

Fig. B.1   PSO simulator

- Set button
  When pressed, an initial population is generated.
- Run button
  When pressed, execution is initiated.
- Stop button
  Pressing this button halts calculations. It is used when the user wants to observe the movement of individuals during the simulation.
- Step button
  This button can be used after pressing the Stop button to sequentially observe motions at every generation.
- Reset button
  After a simulation has been completed, pressing this will re-start execution.

The following parameters can be set by the user.

- Population size
  Number of individuals in the population.
- Maximum velocity
  The maximum velocity of any individual in motion. All individuals are prevented from moving any faster.
- Maximum iteration
  Maximum number of replications of the simulation.
- Inertia weight
  Attenuation coefficient. The default value is 0.9, causing the speed to gradually decrease with time.
- Input?
  If this box is checked, the user is able to freely define the functions. Refer to the list of functions in the GA-3D Simulator (Table 2.1) for standard functions.

After execution is started, the fitness value for each replication is plotted in the chart area at the center of the screen. The following items are displayed in the "Result" panel beneath the plot:

- Iteration
  Number of the current replication. This corresponds to the number of generations in GA.
- Best fitness
  Best (minimum) fitness value among all individuals.

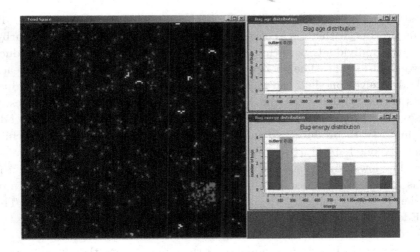

Fig. B.2   BUGS simulator

- Average fitness
  Average fitness value of all individuals. If this box is checked, the average fitness is plotted in the above graph.
- Coordinates
  This shows the coordinates of the best fitness.

B.2   BUGS simulator

This program simulates the evolution of predatory activity of insects. Fig. B.2 is a screenshot of the program.

The insects are colored green (young) or yellow (adults). The insects survive by consuming bacteria (the red dots), which are randomly generated throughout the space. An insect obtains 40 units of energy for each bacterium it consumes. An insect uses up one unit of energy for each step it moves, and dies if its energy reserve reaches zero. It must optimize its method of motion in order to live a long life. Its motion is determined by genetic codes; these consist of the six integer values expressing the directions {Forward, Right, Hard Right, Reverse, Hard Left, Left} (see Fig. 3.25). The greater the value of any one integer, the higher the probability that the individual will move in that direction. For example, an individual with the gene 1,9,1,1,1,1 tends to take the Right direction and ends up running in clockwise circles. An individual reaches maturity after 800 steps, and after its energy exceeds 1,000, it engages in sexual reproduction. In this process, if there is another equally mature and strong insect nearby, the two individuals perform genetic crossover and mutation, and produce two child insects. The energy of each parent is then cut in half and each child receives one-half the mean energies of the parents. If an individual has traveled 1,000 steps and has over 1,300 units of energy, it engages in asexual reproduction. In asexual reproduction, the parent's genetic code is mutated to produce two child insects, and the parent dies. Each child receives one-half the parent's energy.

The lower right region of the figure is called the "Garden of Eden"; it has a higher generation rate of bacteria. The insects near the Garden of Eden evolve a tendency to move so as to remain within this area. The "Eden" parameter in the "ModelSwarm" probe activates or deactivates the Garden of Eden.

The age of insects in a population (how many steps they have moved) and the distribution of energy are shown on a bar graph. The horizontal axis represents age (energy) and the vertical axis represents the number of insects.

The following buttons are used to operate BUGS:

- Start button: This initiates the simulation
- Stop button: This temporarily stops the simulation
- Next button: This advances the stimulation to the next time-step
- Save button: This cannot be used in this simulation
- Quit button: This stops the simulation

The following relationships are included in the "ModelSwarm" parameter probes:

- worldXSize: Extent of space (horizontal axis)
- worldYSize: Extent of space (vertical axis)
- seedProb: Growth rate of bacteria under initial conditions
- bugDensity: Growth rate of insects under initial conditions
- Eden: Application of the Garden of Eden, i.e. 1 (Yes) or 0 (No)

This system is designed to run on Swarm, developed by the Santa Fe institute. The following are necessary in order to use Swarm:

- JAVA SDK
- Swarm software package

- Script revision

Please read the most recent information on installing Swarm on our homepage.

Appendix C

Mathematical Model of NFL

C.1 Definitions

Take X and Y as finite sets. Let k be a natural number that satisfies $k < |X|$.

Definition 1. Assume that a set of the whole mapping from X to Y is F as follows:

$$F = \{f : X \to Y\} \tag{C.1}$$

Definition 2.

$$D_k^X = \{(x_1, x_2, \cdots, x_k) \in X^k \mid \forall i \, \forall j \, [i \neq j \to x_i \neq x_j]\} \tag{C.2}$$

$$D_k^Y = Y^k \tag{C.3}$$

$$D_k = D_k^X \times D_k^Y \tag{C.4}$$

Definition 3. Define $\|_k^x : D_k^X \times X \to X^{k+1}$ as

$$(x_1, x_2, \cdots, x_k)\|_k^x x = (x_1, x_2, \cdots, x_k, x) \tag{C.5}$$

Similarly define C $\|_k^y : D_k^Y \times Y \to D_{k+1}^Y$ as

$$(y_1, y_2, \cdots, y_k)\|_k^y y = (y_1, y_2, \cdots, y_k, y) \tag{C.6}$$

Also define $\|_k : D_k \times (X \times Y) \to X^{k+1} \times D_{k+1}^Y$ as

$$(d_k^x, d_k^y)\|_k(x, y) = (d_k^x\|_k^x x, d_k^y\|_k^y y) \tag{C.7}$$

These are operators which simply add a trace. Hereafter, for simplicity, a subscript will be omitted and written simply as $\|$.

Definition 4.

$$A_k = \{a_k : D_k \to X \mid \forall d_k \, \forall i \, [a_k(d_k) \neq x_i]\} \tag{C.8}$$

$$A = X \times A_1 \times A_2 \times \cdots \times A_{m-1} \tag{C.9}$$

where $d_k = (d_k^x, d_k^y) \in D_k^Y$, $d_k^x = (x_1, x_2, \cdots, x_k)$. The first X in A represents the first candidate solution.

Lemma 1. *If $a_k \in A_k$, $d_k = (d_k^x, d_k^y) \in D_k$ is assumed,*

$$\forall a_k \forall d_k \ [d_k^x || a_k(d_k) \in D_{k+1}^X] \tag{C.10}$$

Proof. If $d_k^x = (x_1, x_2, \cdots, x_k)$ is assumed,

$$d_k^x || a_k(d_k) = (x_1, x_2, \cdots, x_k, a_k(d_k)) \tag{C.11}$$

where $d_k^x \in D_k^X$. Therefore, $\forall i \ \forall j \ [i \neq j \rightarrow x_i \neq x_j]$. From the definition of A_k, $\forall i \ [a_k(d_k) \neq x_i]$. Thus there is no duplication and we have $d_k^x || a_k(d_k) \in D_{k+1}^X$. $\qquad \square$

Definition 5.

$$F(d_k) = \{ f \in F \mid \forall i \ [f(x_i) = y_i] \ \} \tag{C.12}$$

where $d_k = ((x_1, x_2, \cdots, x_k), (y_1, y_2, \cdots, y_k))$.

Definition 6. For $a = (a_0, a_1, \cdots, a_{m-1}) \in A$, $f \in F$, recursively define $S_k : A \times F \rightarrow D_k$ from

$$S_1(a, f) = (a_0, f(a_0)) \tag{C.13}$$

$$x = a_i(S_i(a, f)) \tag{C.14}$$

$$S_{i+1}(a, f) = S_i(a, f) || (x, f(x)) \tag{C.15}$$

This is obviously well defined. Assuming $S_k(a, f) = (d_k^x, d_k^y)$, define

$$S_k^x(a, f) = d_k^x \tag{C.16}$$

$$S_k^y(a, f) = d_k^y. \tag{C.17}$$

Definition 7. For $a = (a_0, a_1, \cdots, a_{m-1}) \in A$, $t = (y_1, y_2, \cdots, y_k) \in D_k$, recursively calculate

$$c_1 = (a_0, y_1) \tag{C.18}$$

$$c_{i+1} = c_i || (a_i(c_i), y_{i+1}) \tag{C.19}$$

Define $R_k : A \times D_k^y \rightarrow D_k$ from

$$R_k(a, t) = c_k \tag{C.20}$$

This is obviously well defined. Assuming $R_k(a, t) = (d_k^x, t)$, define

$$R_k^x(a, t) = d_k^x \tag{C.21}$$

$$R_k^y(a, t) = t. \tag{C.22}$$

Note that R_k^y provides identity mapping for $t \in D_k^y$.

C.2 Lemma

Lemma 2. *If $a \in A$, $t \in D_k^Y$ is assumed,*

$$\forall a \; \forall t \; \forall f \in F(R_k(a,t)) \; [S_k(a,f) = R_k(a,t)] \tag{C.23}$$

Proof.

$$a = (a_0, a_1, \cdots, a_{m-1}) \tag{C.24}$$

$$t = (\eta_1, \eta_2, \cdots, \eta_k) \tag{C.25}$$

$$S_k(a,f) = ((x_1, x_2, \cdots, x_k), (y_1, y_2, \cdots, y_k)) \tag{C.26}$$

$$R_k(a,t) = ((\xi_1, \xi_2, \cdots, \xi_k), t) \tag{C.27}$$

With the above assumption, we have $\forall i \; [f(\xi_i) = \eta_i]$ from $f \in F(R_k(a,t))$. Then,

$$(\xi_1, \eta_1) = (\xi_1, f(\xi_1)) = (a_0, f(a_0)) = (x_1, y_1) \tag{C.28}$$

holds. Thus the first part of the trace is consistent. Assume that trace $d_i \in D_i$ up to the ith is consistent, $\xi_{i+1} = a(d_i) = x_{i+1}$ holds since the same search algorithm is used. Hence

$$\eta_{i+1} = f(\xi_{i+1}) = f(x_{i+1}) = y_{i+1} \tag{C.29}$$

Therefore, a newly added trace is consistent. Hence all the search traces are consistent by mathematical induction. $\quad\square$

Lemma 3. *If $a \in A$, $t \in D_k^Y$ is assumed,*

$$\forall a \; \forall t \; \forall f \in F(R_k(a,t)) \; [P(\mathcal{D}_k^y = t \,|\, \mathcal{A} = a, \mathcal{F} = f) = 1] \tag{C.30}$$

Proof. From Lemma 2, the following equation holds:

$$S_k^y(a,f) = R_k^y(a,t) = t \tag{C.31}$$

Hence when $f \in F(R_k(a,t))$ is used, $\mathcal{D}_k^y = t$ always holds. Now the proposition has been proved. $\quad\square$

Bibliography

Aarts, E. and Verhoeven, G. (1997). *Handbook of Evolutionary Computation*, chap. Genetic Local Search for the Traveling Salesman Problem (Bristol and Oxford University Press, New York), pp. G9.5:1–G9.5:7.

Abido, M. A. (2006). Multiobjective evolutionary algorithms for electric power dispatch problem, *IEEE Trans. on Evolutionary Computations* **10**, 3, pp. 315–329.

Abraham, A., Jain, L. C. and Goldberg, R. (eds.) (2005). *Evolutionary Multiobjective Optimization: Theoretical Advances and Applications* (Springer-Verlag, New York).

Achelis, S. B. (2000). *Technical Analysis from A to Z* (McGraw-Hill, New York).

Adams, J., Balas, E. and Zawack, D. (1988). The shifting bottleneck procedure for job shop scheduling, *Management Science* **34**, 3, pp. 391–401.

Angeline, P. J. (1998). Evolutionary optimization versus particle swarm optimization: Philosophy and performance differences, in *Proceedings of the 7th International Conference on Evolutionary Programming*, pp. 601–610.

Arkin, A., Rossb, J. and McAdamsa, H. H. (1998). Stochastic kinetic analysis of developmental pathway bifurcation in phage λ-infected *Escherichia coli* cells, *Genetics* **149**, pp. 1633–1648.

Arnone, M. and Davidson, E. (1997). The hardwiring of development: Organization and function of genomic regulatory systems, *Development* **124**, 10, pp. 1851–1864.

Arthur, W. B. (1994). *Increasing Returns and Path Dependence in the Economy* (University of Michigan Press, Ann Arbor, Michigan).

Atkeson, C. G., Moore, A. W. and Schaal, S. (1997). Locally weighted learning, *Artificial Intelligence Review* **11**, pp. 11–73.

Bäck, T. (1996). *Evolutionary Algorithms in Theory and Practice* (Oxford University Press, New York).

Bäck, T., Fogel, D. B. and Michalewicz, Z. (eds.) (2000). *Evolutionary Computation 1: Basic Algorithms and Operators* (Institute of Physics Publishing, Bristol).

Bambha, N. K., Bhattacharyya, S. S., Teich, J. and Zitzler, E. (2004). Systematic integration of parameterized local search into evolutionary algorithms,

IEEE Transactions on Evolutionary Computation **8**, 2, pp. 137–155.

Banzhaf, W., Nordin, P., Keller, R. E. and Francone, F. D. (1998). *Genetic Programming – An Introduction; On the Automatic Evolution of Computer Programs and its Applications* (Morgan Kaufmann, San Francisco, California).

Bellman, R. (1961). *Adaptive Control Processes: A Guided Tour* (Princeton University Press, Princeton, New Jersey).

Bentley, J. L. (1992). Fast algorithms for geometric traveling salesman problems, *ORSA Journal on Computing* **4**, pp. 387–411.

Beyer, H. G. and Deb, K. (2001). On self-adaptive features in real-parameter evolutionary algorithms, *IEEE Transactions on Evolutionary Computation* **5**, 3, pp. 250–270.

Branke, J. (1999). Evolutionary approaches to dynamic optimization problems – a survey, in *GECCO Workshop on Evolutionary Algorithms for Dynamic Optimization Problems*, pp. 134–137.

Brest, J., Greiner, S., Bošković, B., Mernik, M. and Žumer, V. (2006). Self-adapting control parameters in differential evolution: A comparative study on numerical benchmark problems, *IEEE Transactions on Evolutionary Computation* **10**, 6, pp. 646–657.

Carlier, J. and Pinson, E. (1989). An algorithm for solving the job-shop problem, *Management Science* **35**, 2, pp. 164–176.

Chakraborti, N., Misra, K., Bhatt, P., Barman, N. and Prasad, R. (2001). Tight-binding calculations of Si-H clusters using genetic algorithms and related techniques: Studies using differential evolution, *Journal of Phase Equilibria* **22**, 5, pp. 525–530.

Chen, S.-H. (2002). *Genetic Algorithms and Genetic Programming in Computational Finance* (Kluwer Academic Publishers, Boston).

Chiou, J.-P. (2007). Variable scaling hybrid differential evolution for large-scale economic dispatch problems, *Electric Power Systems Research* **77**, 3-4, pp. 212–218.

Chvatal, V. (1983). *Linear Programming* (W. H. Freeman and Company, New York).

Clerc, M. and Kennedy, J. (2002). The particle swarm – explosion, stability, and convergence in a multidimensional complex space, *IEEE Transactions on Evolutionary Computation* **6**, pp. 58–73.

Coello, C. A. C., Lamont, G. B. and Veldhuizen, D. A. (2007). *Evolutionary Algorithms for Solving Multi-Objective Problems* (Springer, New York).

Davis, L. D. (1991). *Handbook of Genetic Algorithms* (Van Nostrand Reinhold Company, New York).

Dawkins, R. (1976). *The Selfish Gene* (Clarendon Press, Oxford).

De Jong, K. A. (1992). Are genetic algorithms function optimizers? in *Proceedings 2nd Parallel Problem Solving from Nature*, pp. 3–14.

de la Fuente, D., Garrido, A., Laviada, J. and Gomez, A. (2006). Genetic algorithms to optimize the time to make stock market investment, in *Proceedings of Genetic and Evolutionary Computation Conference*, pp. 1857–1858.

Deb, K. (2001). *Multi-Objective Optimization Using Evolutionary Algorithms*

(John Wiley & Sons, New York).

Deb, K. and Agrawal, R. B. (1995). Simulated binary crossover for continuous search space, *Complex Systems* **9**, 2, pp. 115–148.

Deb, K., Anand, A., and Joshi, D. (2002). A computationally efficient evolutionary algorithm for real-parameter optimization, *Evolutionary Computation* **10**, 4, pp. 371–395.

Dewdney, A. K. (1989). Simulated evolution: Wherein bugs learn to hunt bacteria, *Scientific American*, pp. 138–141.

D'haeseleer, P., Liang, S. and Somogyi, R. (2000). Genetic network inference: from co-expression clustering to reverse engineering, *Bioinformatics* **16**, 8, pp. 707–726.

D'haeseleer, P., Wen, X., Fuhrman, S. and Somogyi, R. (1999). Linear modeling of mRNA expression levels during CNS development and injury, in *Proceedings of Pacific Symposium on Biocomputing 4*, pp. 41–52.

dos S. Coelho, L. and Mariani, V. C. (2006). Combining of chaotic differential evolution and quadratic programming for economic dispatch optimization with valve-point effect, *IEEE Transactions on Power Systems* **21**, 2, pp. 989–996.

Eberhart, R. C. and Hu, X. (1999). Human tremor analysis using particle swarm optimization, in *Proceedings of the Congress on Evolutionary Computation*, pp. 1927–1930.

Eberhart, R. C. and Shi, Y. (1998). Comparison between genetic algorithms and particle swarm optimization, in *Proceedings of the 7th International Conference on Evolutionary Programming*, pp. 611–616.

Eiben, A. E. and Smith, J. E. (2003). *Introduction to Evolutionary Computing* (Springer, New York).

Eldridge, B. and Maciejewski, A. (2005). Using genetic algorithms to optimize social robot behavior for improved pedestrian flow, in *Proceedings of IEEE International Conference on Systems, Man and Cybernetics*, pp. 524–529.

Eshelman, L. J. and Schaffer, J. D. (1993). *Foundations of Genetic Algorithms 2*, chap. Real-Coded Genetic Algorithms and Interval Schemata (Morgan Kaufmann, San Mateo, California), pp. 187–202.

Eubank, R. L. (1999). *Nonparametric Regression and Spline Smoothing* (Marcel Dekker, New York).

Fan, H. Y. and Lampinen, J. (2003). A trigonometric mutation operation to differential evolution, *Journal of Global Optimization* **27**, 1, pp. 105–129.

Fernández-Blanco, P., Bodas-Sagi, D. J., Soltero, F. J. and Hidalgo, J. I. (2008). Technical market indicators optimization using evolutionary algorithms, in *Proceedings of Genetic and Evolutionary Computation Conference*, pp. 1851–1857.

Fitzpatrick, J. M. and Grefenstette, J. J. (1998). Genetic algorithms in noisy environments, *Journal Machine Learning* **3**, 2–3, pp. 101–120.

Fletcher, R. (2000). *Practical Methods of Optimization* (John Wiley & Sons, New York).

Fogel, D. B. (1999). *Evolutionary Computation: Toward a New Philosophy of Machine Intelligence* (IEEE Press, New York).

Fogel, L. J., Owens, A. J. and Walsh, M. J. (1966). *Artificial Intelligence through Simulated Evolution* (John Wiley & Sons, New York).

Forrest, S. and Mitchell, M. (1993). What makes a problem hard for a genetic algorithm? Some anomalous results and their explanation, *Machine Learning* **13**, 2–3, pp. 285–319.

Freisleben, B. and Merz, P. (1996a). A genetic local search algorithm for solving symmetric and asymmetric traveling salesman problems, in *Proceedings of the IEEE International Conference on Evolutionary Computation*, pp. 616–621.

Freisleben, B. and Merz, P. (1996b). New genetic local search operators for the traveling salesman problem, in *Proceedings of Parallel Problem Solving From Nature-PPSN*, pp. 890–900.

Gaing, Z.-L. (2003). Particle swarm optimization to solving the economic dispatch considering the generator constraints, *IEEE Transactions on Power Systems* **18**, 3, pp. 1187–1195.

Gämperle, R., Müller, S. D. and Koumoutsakos, P. (2002). A parameter study for differential evolution, in *Proceedings of Int. Conf. on Advances in Intelligent Systems, Fuzzy Systems, Evolutionary Computation*, pp. 293–298.

Garrett, A., Carnahan, B., Muhdi, R., Davis, J., Dozier, G., SanSoucie, M. P., Hull, P. V. and Tinker, M. L. (2006). Evacuation planning via evolutionary computation, in *Proceedings of the IEEE Congress on Evolutionary Computation*, pp. 157–164.

Glover, F. (1989). Tabu search part I, *ORSA Journal on Computing* **1**, 3, pp. 190–206.

Glover, F. and Kochenberger, G. A. (2003). *Handbook of Metaheuristics* (Kluwer Academic Publishers, Boston).

Goldberg, D. E. (1987). *Genetic Algorithms and Simulated Annealing*, chap. Simple Genetic Algorithms and the Minimal Deceptive Problem (Morgan Kaufmann, London, Pitman; Los Altos, California), pp. 74–88.

Goldberg, D. E. (1989). *Genetic Algorithms in Search, Optimization and Machine Learning* (Addison-Wesley, Reading, Massachusetts).

Goldberg, D. E. and Voessner, S. (1999). Optimizing global-local search hybrids, in *Proceedings of Genetic and Evolutionary Computation Conference*, pp. 220–228.

Graat, E., Midden, C. and Bockholts, P. (1999). Complex evacuation: Effects of motivation level and slope of stairs on emergency egress time in a sports stadium, *Safety Science* **31**, 2, pp. 127–141.

Grefenstette, J. J. and Baker, J. E. (1989). How genetic algorithms work: A critical look at implicit parallelism, in *Proceedings of the 3rd International Conference on Genetic Algorithms*, pp. 20–27.

Hart, W. E. (1994). *Adaptive Global Optimization with Local Search*, Ph.D. thesis, University of California, California.

Helbing, D., Farkas, I. and Vicsek, T. (2000). Simulating dynamical features of escape panic, *Nature* **407**, 2, pp. 487–490.

Hellström, T. and Holmström, K. (2000). The relevance of trends for predictions of stock returns, *International Journal of Intelligent Systems in Accounting,*

Finance & Management **9**, 1, pp. 23–34.

Heppner, F. and Grenander, U. (1990). *The Ubiquity of Chaos*, chap. A Stochastic Nonlinear Model for Coordinated Bird Flocks (American Association for the Advancement of Science, Washington D.C.), pp. 233–238.

Hestenes, M. R. and Stiefel, E. (1952). Methods of conjugate gradients for solving linear systems, *Journal of Research of the National Bureau of Standards* **49**, 6, pp. 409–436.

Higashi, N. and Iba, H. (2003). Particle swarm optimization with gaussian mutation, in *Proceedings of the IEEE Swarm Intelligence Symposium*, pp. 72–79.

Hinterding, R., Michalewicz, Z. and Eiben, A. E. (1997). Adaptation in evolutionary computation: a survey, in *Proceedings of the Fourth IEEE Conference on Evolutionary Computation*, pp. 65–69.

Hirabayashi, A., Aranha, C. and Iba, H. (2009). Optimization of the trading rule in foreign exchange using genetic algorithm, in *Proceedings of the 2009 Genetic and Evolutionary Computation Conference (GECCO 2009)*, pp. 1529–1536.

Holland, J. H. (1975). *Adaptation in Natural and Artificial Systems* (University of Michigan Press, Ann Arbor, Michigan).

Holstein, D. and Moscato, P. (1999). *New Ideas in Optimization*, chap. Memetic Algorithms using Guided Local Search: A Case Study (McGraw-Hill, Maidenhead, England), pp. 235–244.

Iba, H., Akiba, S., Higuchi, T. and Sato, T. (1992). Bugs: A bug-based search strategy using genetic algorithms, in *Proceedings of Parallel Problem Solving from Nature,*, pp. 165–174.

Iba, H., Higuchi, T., de Garis, H. and Sato, T. (1993). Evolutionary learning strategy using bug-based search, in *Proceedings of the 13th International Joint Conference on Artifical Intelligence*, pp. 960–966.

Iba, H., Paul, T. K. and Hasegawa, Y. (2009). *Applied Genetic Programming and Machine Learning* (CRC Press, Florida).

Imanishi, K. and Asquith, P. J. (2002). *A Japanese View of Nature: The World of Living Things* (RoutledgeCurzon, London, New York).

Irvine, D. H. and Savageau, M. A. (1990). Efficient solution of nonlinear ordinary differential equations expressed in S-system canonical form, *SIAM Journal on Numerical Analysis* **27**, 3, pp. 704–735.

Ishibuchi, H., Yoshida, T. and Murata, T. (2003). Balance between genetic search and local search in memetic algorithms for multiobjective permutation flowshop scheduling, *IEEE Transaction on Evolutionary Computation* **7**, 2, pp. 204–223.

Izumi, K. and Ueda, K. (2000). Analysis of exchange rate scenarios using an artificial market approach, *IPSJ SIG Notes ICS* **99**, pp. 1–8.

Kauffman, S. A. (1993). *The Origins of Order, Self-Organization and Selection in Evolution* (Oxford University Press, New York).

Kennedy, J. and Eberhart, R. C. (1995). Particle swarm optimization, in *Proceedings of the IEEE International Conference on Neural Networks*, pp. 1942–1948.

Kennedy, J., Eberhart, R. C. and Shi, Y. (2001). *Swarm Intelligence* (Morgan

Kaufmann, San Francisco, California).

Kennedy, J. and Spears, W. M. (1998a). Matching algorithms to problems: An experimental test of the particle swarm and some genetic algorithms on the multimodal problem generator, in *Proceedings of the IEEE Congress on Evolutionary Computation*, pp. 78–83.

Kennedy, J. and Spears, W. M. (1998b). Matching algorithms to problems: An experimental test of the particle swarm and some genetic algorithms on the multimodal problem generator, in *Proceedings International Conference on Evolutionary Computation (ICEC 1998)* (IEEE), pp. 78–83.

Khatib, O. (1985). Real-time obstacle avoidance for manipulators and mobile robots, in *Proceedings of the IEEE International Conference on Robotics and Automation*, pp. 500–505.

Kikuchi, S., Tominaga, D., Arita, M., Takahashi, K. and Tomita, M. (2003). Dynamic modeling of genetic networks using genetic algorithm and S-sytem, *Bioinformatics* **19**, 5, pp. 643–650.

Kimura, S., Hatakeyama, M. and Konagaya, A. (2004). Inference of S-system models of genetic networks from noisy time-series data, *Chem-Bio Informatics Journal* **4**, 1, pp. 1–14.

Kimura, S., Ide, K., Kashihara, A., Kano, M., Hatakeyama, M., Masui, R., Nakagawa, N., Yokoyama, S., Kuramitsu, S. and Konagaya, A. (2005). Inference of S-system models of genetic networks using cooperative coevolutionary algorithm, *Bioinformatics* **21**, 7, pp. 1154–1163.

Kirkpatrick, S., Gelatt, C. D. and Vecchi, M. P. (1983). Optimization by simulated annealing, *Science* **220**, 4598, pp. 671–680.

Koza, J. R. (1992). *Genetic Programming, On the Programming of Computers by means of Natural Selection* (MIT Press, Cambridge, Massachusetts).

Koza, J. R. (1994). *Genetic Programming II: Automatic Discovery of Reusable Programs* (MIT Press, Cambridge, Massachusetts).

Koza, J. R., Bennett, F. H., Andre, D. and Keane, M. A. (1999). *Genetic Programming III: Darwinian Invention and Problem Solving* (Morgan Kaufmann, San Francisco, California).

Koza, J. R., Keane, M. A., Streeter, M. J., Mydlowec, W., Yu, J. and Lanza, G. (2003). *Genetic Programming IV: Routine Human-Competitive Machine Intelligence* (Kluwer Academic Publishers, Norwell, Massachusetts).

Krasnogor, N. and Smith, J. (2000). A memetic algorithm with self-adaptive local search: Tsp as a case study. in *Proceedings of Genetic and Evolutionary Computation Conference*, pp. 987–994.

Krasnogor, N. and Smith, J. (2005). A tutorial for competent memetic algorithms: Model, taxonomy, and design issues, *IEEE Transactions on Evolutionary Computation* **9**, 5, 474–488.

Krink, T., Filipič, B., Fogel, G. and Thomsen, R. (2004). Noisy optimization problems – a particular challenge for differential evolution? in *Proceedings of Congress on Evolutionary Computation*, pp. 332–339.

Langdon, W. B. and Poli, R. (2002). *Foundations of Genetic Programming* (Springer, Berlin, New York).

Lee, K. Y., Sode-Yome, A. and Park, J. H. (1998). Adaptive hopfield neural networks for economic load dispatch, *IEEE Transactions on Power Systems* **13**, 2, pp. 519–526.

Levenick, J. R. (1990). Holland's schema theorem disproved? *Journal of Theoretical Artificial Intelligence* **2**, 2, pp. 179–183.

Lin, S. and Kernighan, B. (1973). An effective heuristic algorithm for the travelling salesman problem, *Operations Research* **21**, pp. 498–516.

Lin, W.-M., Cheng, F.-S. and Tsay, M.-T. (2002). An improved tabu search for economic dispatch with multiple minima, *IEEE Transactions on Power Systems* **17**, 1, pp. 108–112.

Lipton-Lifschitz, A. (1999). Predictability and unpredictability in financial markets, *Physica D* **133**, 1–4, pp. 321–347.

Liu, J. and Lampinen, J. (2005). A fuzzy adaptive differential evolution algorithm, *Soft Computing – A Fusion of Foundations, Methodologies and Applications* **9**, 6, pp. 448–642.

Lozano, M., Herrera, F., Krasnogor, N. and Molina, D. (2004). Real-coded memetic algorithms with crossover hill-climbing, *Evolutionary Computation* **12**, 3, pp. 273–302.

Maki, Y., Ueda, T., Okamoto, M., Uematsu, N., Inamura, K., Uchida, K., Takahashi, Y. and Eguchi, Y. (2002). Inference of genetic network using the expression profile time course data of mouse P19 cells, in *Genome Informatics 13*, pp. 382–383.

Matsuno, H., Doi, A. and Nagasaki, M. (2000). Hybrid petri net representation of genetic regulatory network, in *Proceedings of Pacific Symposium on Biocomputing 5*, pp. 338–349.

Mattfeld, D. C. (1996). *Evolutionary Search and the Job Shop: Investigations on Genetic Algorithms for Production Scheduling* (Springer, Berlin).

Merz, P. and Freisleben, B. (1997). Genetic local search for the tsp: New results, in *Proceedings of the IEEE International Conference on Evolutionary Computation*, pp. 159–164.

Miranda, V. and Fonseca, N. (2002). Epso - best-of-two-worlds meta-heuristic applied to power system problems, in *Proceedings of Congress on Evolutionary Computation*, pp. 1080–1085.

Mitchell, M. (1998). *An Introduction to Genetic Algorithms* (MIT Press, Cambridge, Massachusetts).

Mitchell, T. M. (1997). *Machine Learning* (McGraw-Hill, New York).

Mjolsness, E. (2001). *Computational Modeling of Genetic and Biochemical Networks*, chap. Trainable Gene Regulation Networks with Application to *Drosophila* Pattern Formation (MIT Press, Cambridge, Massachusetts, England), pp. 101–117.

Moscato, P. (1989). On evolution, search, optimization, genetic algorithms and martial arts: Towards memetic algorithms, in *Technical Report 826, Caltech Concurrent Computation Program. California Institute of Technology, Pasadena, California*.

Moscato, P. and Cotta, C. (2003). *Handbook of Metaheuristics*, chap. A Gentle Introduction to Memetic Algorithms (Kluwer Academic Publishers, Boston), pp. 105–144.

Moscato, P., Cotta, C. and Mendes, A. (2004). *New Optimization Techniques in Engineering*, chap. Memetic Algorithms (Springer, Berlin, New York), pp. 53–85.

Moscato, P. and Norman, M. G. (1992). A "memetic" approach for the traveling salesman problem implementation of a computational ecology for combinatorial optimization on message-passing systems, in M. Valero, E. Onate, M. Jane, J. Larriba and B. Suarez (eds.), *Proceedings of Parallel Computing and Transputer Applications* (IOS Press, Amsterdam), pp. 177–186.

Muth, J. F. and Thompson, G. L. (1963). *Industrial Scheduling* (Prentice-Hall, Englewood Cliffs, New Jersey).

Neri, F. and Tirronen, V. (2009). Scale factor local search in differential evolution, *Memetic Computing* **1**, 2, pp. 153–171.

Nevatia, R. (1982). *Machine Perception* (Prentice-Hall, Englewood Cliffs, New Jersey).

Nguyen, Q. H., Ong, Y. S. and Krasnogor, N. (2007). A study on the design issues of memetic algorithm, in *Proceedings of the IEEE Congress on Evolutionary Computation*, pp. 2390–2397.

Nguyen, Q. H., Ong, Y.-S. and Lim, M. H. (2009). A probabilistic memetic framework, *IEEE Transaction on Evolutionary Computation* **13**, 3, pp. 604–623.

Nikolaev, N. Y. and Iba, H. (2006). *Adaptive Learning of Polynomial Networks Genetic Programming, Backpropagation and Bayesian Methods* (Springer, New York).

Nilsson, N. J. (1980). *Principles of Artificial Intelligence* (Morgan Kaufmann, Los Altos, California).

Nilsson, N. J. (1998). *Artificial Intelligence: A New Synthesis* (Morgan Kaufmann, Los Altos, California).

Noman, N. and Iba, H. (2005a). Enhancing differential evolution performance with local search for high dimensional function optimization, in *Proceedings of Genetic and Evolutionary Computation Conference (GECCO2005)*, pp. 967–974.

Noman, N. and Iba, H. (2005b). Inference of gene regulatory networks using S-system and differential evolution, in *Proceedings of Genetic and Evolutionary Computation Conference (GECCO)*, pp. 439–446.

Noman, N. and Iba, H. (2005c). Reverse engineering genetic networks using evolutionary computation, in *Genome Informatics 16(2)*, pp. 205–214.

Noman, N. and Iba, H. (2006). A new generation alternation model for differential evolution, in *Proceedings of Genetic and Evolutionary Computation Conference (GECCO 2006)*, pp. 1265–1272.

Noman, N. and Iba, H. (2008a). Accelerating differential evolution using an adaptive local search, *IEEE Transaction on Evolutionary Computation* **12**, 1, pp. 107–125.

Noman, N. and Iba, H. (2008b). Differential evolution for economic load dispatch problems, *Elsevier Electric Power Systems Research* **78**, 8, pp. 1322–1331.

Ong, Y.-S. and Keane, A. J. (2004). Meta-lamarckian learning in memetic algorithms, *IEEE Transactions on Evolutionary Computation* **8**, 2, pp. 99–110.

Ong, Y.-S., Lim, M.-H., Zhu, N. and Wong, K.-W. (2006). Classification of adaptive memetic algorithms: A comparative study, *IEEE Transactions On Systems, Man and Cybernetics – Part B* **36**, 1, pp. 141–152.

Ono, I. and Kobayashi, S. (1997). A real-coded genetic algorithm for function optimization using unimodal normal distribution crossover, in *Proceedings of the Seventh International Conference on Genetic Algorithm*, pp. 246–253.

O'Reilly, U.-M., Yu, T., Riolo, R. and Worzel, B. (eds.) (2005). *Genetic Programming Theory and Practice II* (Springer, New York).

Orero, S. O. and Irving, M. R. (1996). Economic dispatch of generators with prohibited operating zones: a genetic algorithm approach, *IEE Proceedings of Generation, Transmission and Distribution* **143**, 6, pp. 529–534.

Ozel, F. (1992). Simulation modeling of human behavior in buildings, *Simulation* **58**, 6, pp. 377–384.

Park, J.-B., Lee, K.-S., Shin, J.-R. and Lee, K. Y. (2005). A particle swarm optimization for economic dispatch with nonsmooth cost functions, *IEEE Transactions on Power Systems* **20**, 1, pp. 34–42.

Park, J. H., Kim, Y. S., Eom, I. K. and Lee, K. Y. (1993). Economic load dispatch for piecewise quadratic cost function using Hopfield neural network, *IEEE Transactions on Power Systems* **8**, 3, pp. 1030–1038.

Pauls, J. (1980). *Fires and Human Behavior*, chap. Building Evacuation: Research Methods and Case Studies (John Wiley & Sons, New York), pp. 251–275.

Pelechano, N. and Malkawi, A. (2008). Evacuation simulation models: Challenges in modeling high rise building evacuation with cellular automata approaches, *Automation in Construction* **17**, 4, pp. 377–385.

Pereira-Neto, A., Unsihuay, C. and Saavedra, O. R. (2005). Efficient evolutionary strategy optimisation procedure to solve the nonconvex economic dispatch problem with generator constraints, *IEE Proceedings of Generation, Transmission and Distribution* **152**, 5, pp. 653–660.

Perez-Guerrero, R. E. and Cedenio-Maldonado, R. J. (2005). Economic power dispatch with non-smooth cost functions using differential evolution, in *Proceedings of the 37th Annual North American Power Symposium*, pp. 183–190.

Press, W., Teukolsky, S., Vetterling, W. and Flannery, B. (1995). *Numerical Recipes in C*, 2nd edn. (Cambridge University Press, Cambridge).

Price, K. V., Storn, R. M. and Lampinen, J. A. (2005). *Differential Evolution: A Practical Approach to Global Optimization* (Springer, Berlin, Heidelberg).

Qin, A. K. and Suganthan, P. N. (2005). Self-adaptive differential evolution algorithm for numerical optimization, in *Proceedings of IEEE Congress on Evolutionary Computation*, pp. 1785–1791.

Rahnamayan, S., Tizhoosh, H. R. and Salama, M. M. A. (2008). Opposition-based differential evolution, *IEEE Transactions on Evolutionary Computation* **12**, 1, pp. 64–79.

Rawlins, G. J. (ed.) (1991). *Foundations of Genetic Algorithms (FOGA 1)* (Morgan Kaufmann, San Mateo, California).

Rechenberg, I. (1986). *Human decision making and manual control*, chap. Evolution strategy and human decision making, pp. 349–359.

Reynolds, C. W. (1987). Flocks, herds and schools: A distributed behavioral model, *Computer Graphics* **21**, 4, pp. 25–34.

Riolo, R. and Worzel, B. (eds.) (2003). *Genetic Programming Theory and Practice* (Kluwer Academic Publishers, Boston).

Russell, S. J. and Norvig, P. (1995). *Artificial Intelligence – A Modern Approach* (Prentice-Hall, Englewood Cliffs, New Jersey).

Salmon, R. (1996). Re-evaluating genetic algorithm performance under coordinate rotation of benchmark functions. a survey of some theoretical and practical aspects of genetic algorithms, *Biosystems* **39**, 3, 263–278.

Santos, G. and Benigno, E. A. (2004). A critical review of emergency evacuation simulation models, in *NIST Workshop on Building Occupant Movement during Fire Emergencies, Disaster Research Center, University of Delaware*, pp. 27–52.

Satoh, H., Yamamura, M. and Kobayashi, S. (1996). Minimal generation gap model for GAs considering both exploration and exploitation, in *Proceedings of IIZUKA '96*, pp. 494–497.

Savageau, M. A. (1976). *Biochemical Systems Analysis. A Study of Function and Design in Molecular Biology* (Addison-Wesley, Reading, Massachusetts).

Savageau, M. A. (1992). Power-law formalism: A canonical nonlinear approach to modeling and analysis, in *Proceedings of World Congress of Nonlinear Analysts*, pp. 3323–3334.

Schoreels, C., Logan, B. and Garibaldi, J. M. (2004). Agent based genetic algorithm employing financial technical analysis for making trading decisions using historical equity market data, in *Proceedings of IEEE/WIC/ACM International Conference on Intelligent Agent Technology*, pp. 421–424.

Schwaerzel, R. and Bylander, T. (2006). Predicting currency exchange rates by genetic programming with trigonometric functions and high-order statistics, in *Proceedings of Genetic and Evolutionary Computation Conference*, pp. 955–956.

Schwefel, H.-P. (1995). *Evolution and Optimum Seeking* (John Wiley & Sons, New York).

Sharpe, O. J. (2000). *Towards a Rational Methodology for Using Evolutionary Search Algorithms*, Ph.D. thesis, University of Sussex, Sussex.

Sinha, N., Chakrabarti, R. and Chattopadhyay, P. K. (2003). Evolutionary programming techniques for economic load dispatch, *IEEE Transactions on Evolutionary Computation* **7**, 1, pp. 83–94.

Smirnov, E. N. (2001). *Conjunctive and Disjunctive Version Spaces with Instance-based Boundary Sets*, Ph.D. thesis, Department of Computer Science, Maastricht University, Maastricht.

Storn, R. (1999). System design by constraint adaptation and differential evolution, *IEEE Transactions on Evolutionary Computation* **3**, 1, pp. 22–34.

Storn, R. and Price, K. V. (1995). Differential evolution – a simple and efficient adaptive scheme for global optimization over continuous spaces, Technical Report TR-95-012, ICSI.

Storn, R. and Price, K. V. (1997). Differential evolution a simple and efficient heuristic for global optimization over continuous spaces, *Journal of Global*

   Optimization **11**, 4, pp. 341–359.

Streichert, F., Planatscher, H., Spieth, C., Ulmer, H. and Zell, A. (2004). Comparing genetic programming and evolution strategies on inferring gene regulatory networks, in *Proceedings of Genetic and Evolutionary Computation Conference (GECCO)*, pp. 471–480.

Swann, W. H. (1964). A report on the development of a new direct searching method of optimization, Tech. rep., Middlesborough, UK: ICI CENTER Instrument Laboratory.

Swarup, K. S. and Kumar, P. R. (2006). A new evolutionary computation technique for economic dispatch with security constraints, *International Journal of Electrical Power & Energy Systems* **28**, 4, pp. 273–283.

Tamarin, R. H. (2002). *Principles of Genetics* (McGraw-Hill, Boston).

Teo, J. (2006). Exploring dynamic self-adaptive populations in differential evolution, *Soft Computing – A Fusion of Foundations, Methodologies and Applications* **10**, 8, pp. 637–686.

Thompson, P. A. and Marchant, E. W. (1995). A computer model for the evacuation of large building populations, *Fire Safety Journal* **24**, 2, pp. 131–148.

Tominaga, D., Koga, N. and Okamoto, M. (2000). Efficient numerical optimization algorithm based on genetic algorithm for inverse problem, in *Proceedings of Genetic and Evolutionary Computation Conference*, pp. 251–258.

Tsai, K.-Y. and Wang, F.-S. (2005). Evolutionary optimization with data collocation for reverse engineering of biological networks, *Bioinformatics* **21**, 7, pp. 1180–1188.

Tsutsui, S., Yamamura, M. and Higuchi, T. (1999). Multi-parent recombination with simplex crossover in real coded genetic algorithms, in *Proceedings Genetic and Evolutionary Computation Conference (GECCO'99)*, pp. 657–664.

Victoire, T. A. A. and Jeyakumar, A. E. (2004). Hybrid PSO-SQP for economic dispatch with valve-point effect, *Electric Power Systems Research* **71**, 1, pp. 51–59.

Victoire, T. A. A. and Jeyakumar, A. E. (2005). Deterministically guided PSO for dynamic dispatch considering valve-point effect, *Electric Power Systems Research* **73**, 3, pp. 313–322.

Voit, E. O. and Almeida, J. S. (2004). Decoupling dynamical systems for pathway identification from metabolic profiles, *Bioinformatics* **20**, 11, pp. 1670–1681.

Whitley, L. D. (ed.) (1993). *Foundations of Genetic Algorithms (FOGA 2)* (Morgan Kaufmann, San Mateo, California).

Wilson, E. O. (1975). *Sociobiology: The New Synthesis* (Belknap Press, Cambridge, MA).

Wilson, S. W. (1987). Classifier systems and the animat problem, *Machine Learning* **2**, pp. 199–228.

Wolpert, D. H. and Macready, W. G. (1995). *No Free Lunch Theorems for Search*, Tech. Rep. SFI-TR-95-02-010, Santa Fe Institute, New Mexico.

Wolpert, D. H. and Macready, W. G. (1997). No free lunch theorems for optimization, *IEEE Transactions on Evolutionary Computation* **1**, 1, 67–82.

Wong, B. K. and Selvi, Y. (1998). Neural network applications in finance: A review and analysis of literatures (1990-1996), *Information & Management* **34**, pp. 129–139.

Wood, A. J. and Wollenberg, B. F. (1996). *Power Generation, Operation and Control* (John Wiley & Sons, New York).

Yang, J.-M. and Kao, C.-Y. (2000). Integrating adaptive mutations and family competition into genetic algorithms as function optimizer, *Soft Computing* **4**, pp. 89–102.

Yao, S., Pasquier, M. and Quek, C. (2007). A foreign exchange portfolio management mechanism based on fuzzy neural networks, in *Proceedings IEEE Congress on Evolutionary Computation*, pp. 2576–2583.

Yokoya, N., Kaneta, M. and Yamamotot, K. (1992). Recovery of superquadric primitives from a range image using simulated annealing, in *Proceedings of 11th IAPR International Conference on Pattern Recognition*, pp. 168–172.

Yu, T., Riolo, R., and Worzel, B. (eds.) (2006). *Genetic Programming Theory and Practice III* (Springer, New York).

Yuan, B. and Gallagher, M. (2003). On building a principled framework for evaluating and testing evolutionary algorithms: A continuous landscape generator, in *Proceedings of Congress on Evolutionary Computation (CEC2003)*, pp. 451–458.

Zaharie, D. (2002). Critical values for the control parameters of differential evolution algorithms, in *Proceedings of MENDEL 2002, 8th International Conference on Soft Computing*, pp. 62–67.

Zaharie, D. (2003). Control of population diversity and adaptation in differential evolution algorithms, in *Proceedings of MENDEL 2003, 9th International Conference on Soft Computing*, pp. 41–46.

Zitzler, E., Laumanns, M. and Bleuler, S. (2004). A Tutorial on Evolutionary Multiobjective Optimization, in *Metaheuristics for Multiobjective Optimisation*, pp. 3–37.

Index